AT WORK AS IN HEAVEN

AT WORK AS IN HEAVEN

Scott Ryser

AT WORK AS IN HEAVEN

© 2021 Scott Ryser

Cover Design and Interior Layout by Uberwriters Christian Ghostwriters www.uberwriters.com

Unless otherwise indicated, scripture quotations are from the ESV® Bible (The Holy Bible, English Standard Version®), copyright © 2001 by Crossway, a publishing ministry of Good News Publishers. Used by permission. All rights reserved.

Scripture quotations marked (NLT) are taken from the Holy Bible, New Living Translation, copyright © 1996, 2004, 2015 by Tyndale House Foundation. Used by permission of Tyndale House Publishers, Inc., Carol Stream, Illinois 60188. All rights reserved.

Hardback ISBN 978-1-950948-50-5
Papeback ISBN 978-1-950948-49-9
eBook ISBN 978-1-950948-51-2

Contents

Dedication

To my wife Kathleen, whom I love, and whose many sacrifices have provided me (and our boys) a loving and stable home, without which I'd have never survived two decades of entrepreneurial turbulence.

And to my Lord Jesus Christ, without Whom I have literally nothing of any value to write.

Introduction

For nearly three decades I have been on a quest to answer a simple but extraordinarily profound question: **how does my faith—specifically my Christian faith—work on any random Tuesday?** Of course, that question has led to many more questions, each more complicated and profound still. I believe my journey of deliberating on these questions is relevant to many of you. Providing insight into these questions is the purpose of this book.

Like most of you reading this, I'm at the office on any random Tuesday, so I've wrestled with these questions in the context of the workplace and my career. If you're not interested in matters of faith—or not specifically a Jesus follower—don't quit reading just yet. This is primarily a business book after all, not a "spiritual" one. It's just that those two topics go together far more than you might imagine. Please at least indulge me a reading of the Overview section before determining this book isn't for you.

A Series of Questions

I grew up in small-town Middle America, attended church every Sunday, sang in the choir, and hung out with church kids all weekend... yet I never knew Jesus. I never consciously opposed God. I had no doubt He existed. He simply wasn't part of my life. In my late twenties, when desperate circumstances forced me to confront my standing with God, I knew I was not making a decision about going to church. I'd done that. If choosing faith did not work on Tuesday, I had no reason to bother with acting the part on Sunday. There were plenty of other things to do with my time. So when I made the decision to give my life to Jesus, I knew I was deciding to live life—my whole life—from an entirely different perspective.

This meant in my faith journey I was almost immediately confronted with the question of how my faith impacted the way I approached my work and my career. If you love God, you want to honor Him, so, my main question in prayer soon transformed into, **"How can I glorify God at work?"** There really wasn't a wealth of material available on the topic back then and much of it seemed more "churchy" than business oriented, but I set about trying to figure it out.

Given my entrepreneurial bent, the Lord eventually provided an opportunity to start my own company. The key question then morphed into, **"Can I build a company that glorifies God?"** Not a "Christian company." Not a church group masquerading as a company, but a company doing business in a way that glorifies God, that causes people who are otherwise uninterested in Him, to say "Wow, God is good." Can this be done?

It turns out it can.

My quest started during the dot-com domain-name land grab days, when everyone was creating unusual company names. I followed suit, diving deep into a concordance, and emerged with what was the core concept I wanted my company to be built upon: the company name Yakabod—an Old Testament Hebrew transliteration meaning "God's glory." I wanted a constant reminder that the purpose of the company wasn't about me, but about Him.

After a few years of wrestling with this, the Lord brought me a business partner. We merged our companies into the new Yakabod, and together wrestled with this question some more, trying to work out how exactly a company can glorify God. We had some successes, some failures, some pivots, and many revelations. In the early days, when we only had our words with which to honor Him, God honored our words and those were our "witness" to Him. In time, we built a solid base of actions with which to honor Him. God honored our actions in turn, and those became our "witness" to Him. I'll certainly share these successes and hard lessons from these early days throughout the book, but this book is ultimately about something bigger, something more. After many years, right about the time we felt we had a handle on how to do this "faith at work" thing, God proceeded to give us *much* bigger questions to answer.

Our Heavenly Father made it very clear the time had come to progress from our words and actions being our testimony, to *His very presence* being our testimony. In other words, it was time to move beyond doing things *for* Him, and time to start doing things *with* Him. This in turn raised a completely new set of questions, starting with: **"Can we *partner* with God at work?"** I don't mean just churchy stuff like holding a Bible study at lunchtime; I mean actually partnering with God in real nuts-and-bolts business activities like marketing and engineering. Sounds crazy, right? Is this even possible?

It turns out it is.

As we pushed into this concept over the course of a few years, we came to understand that partnering with God changes the game, because He's playing by a *completely* different set of rules. Things just work differently in His Kingdom, the Kingdom of Heaven, than they do in the kingdom of this world. This realization led to an even bigger and more astounding question: **"Can a company look more like the Kingdom of Heaven than the kingdom of this world?"** How does that work? For example, cash is king to a startup because cash is finite in the worldly system, but God's resources are unlimited. Ancient King David noted that God owns the cattle on a thousand hills. Obviously, God can also speak the word to make a thousand more hills. Contemplate a few examples like that and it will mess you

> *This book is not about the "why." It's about the "how."*

up. Is it possible for a company to operate more like the Kingdom of Heaven, where resources for God's purposes are unlimited? Does that even work in real, everyday, corporate life on any random Tuesday?

It turns out it does.

Of course, as we pushed into that, He broadened our perspective again: "If a company can look more like His Kingdom, **can an entire ecosystem of such companies help a whole community look more like His Kingdom?**" Is this even possible? We're still exploring that question, but we think we know the answer! Before we unpack all these questions, it's probably best to provide a roadmap to help us navigate the journey.

A Roadmap for Our Journey

Perhaps by now you've figured out this is not a book about the "why" you'd want to live out your faith at your workplace. This is a book about the "how." If you've read any of the material in this "faith at work" genre, you can probably tell by the questions we'll be exploring this book is likely going to take you on a different journey than much of what you've read before.

Accordingly, the book is organized into a short Overview section, followed by three distinct main sections. The main premise of this book is that things work differently in God's Kingdom—the Kingdom of Heaven—than they do in this world. Jesus' entire ministry was premised on bringing God's Kingdom to us here and now. Not just in a church somewhere. No, Jesus made it entirely possible to live God's Kingdom in your workplace as it is in Heaven. I understand this may be a radically new or even audacious concept to many readers as it surely was to me early in my journey.

Section 1: *Overview* provides the necessary background so we're "speaking the same language."

Section 2: *Adventure By God* is a "how we got here" narrative, capturing the process of building the company, Yakabod, starting with the foundations laid from my own spiritual journey. As you will see, it was and continues to be very much a process, an adventure even, rather than an overnight transformation. If you are a Jesus follower, you might understand it is far more like sanctification than salvation.

Section 3: *Lessons from Two Decades of Tuesdays* will then provide some everyday practical examples from our journey. For some time now, we've been asking "Is this the way things work in God's Kingdom?", followed by refining our practices and observing the results in response. I'm not suggesting we have it all figured out. Rather, I hope our experiments will give you plenty of food for thought as you consider your own workplace and areas of influence. I think you'll discover, as we have, that many accepted practices or even "best practices" embedded in the way you approach your business actually run counter to the superior ways of the Kingdom of Heaven.

Likewise, I'm not suggesting this is where we started our journey. Accordingly, I'll also share our progression from the realm of more principle-based "for Him" decisions to higher level "with Him" actions. Of course, we aren't the only ones wrestling with living out our faith on Tuesday, so I'll also share some examples from friends where appropriate. All of this is intended to challenge you to approach you own workplace with the same questioning mindset, and then partner with God to uncover unique solutions that work for you.

Section 4: *Your Workplace as in Heaven* explores the practical implications of partnering with God at work; that is, not just doing things *for* God, but rather doing things *with* Him. If, after reading all the examples in the previous sections, you're not sure how these may apply in your own setting, then this section should help you get started. Many of you may already be stewing on the obvious question: "How do I do this stuff without my boss thinking I'm some crazy religious nut?" We'll explore this question through the nuance of different corporate roles, like employee, manager, and business owner in this section as well.

For The Non-believers: No Preaching. I Promise.

If you're a follower of Jesus, the "Kingdom of Heaven" should sound like a great place to you. I recognize, however, some of you reading this may have a more fundamental issue with that concept. You don't follow Jesus, you may not even believe in God, or you're just not into this "religious stuff." I assure you, I don't spend any time or effort in this book trying to convert you. Honestly, I don't need to—Heaven's ways are so radically superior to this imperfect Earth's ways that the desirability of the former will become self-evident. It is truly about the Kingdom of Heaven, after all, not about some church or religious institution.

For example, I gave the kingdom versus Kingdom contrast related to cash above, but consider also that the Kingdom of Heaven is marked by peace and joy. I'd suggest that many or most companies you regularly interact with—whether as customer, employee, or partner—are marked by things like stress, anxiety, drudgery, manipulation, hostility, shame, bitterness, and probably worse. What if your workplace was instead marked by peace and joy? Would anybody really prefer the former list over peace and joy? These are the kinds of contrasts we'll be exploring in pursuit of "at work as in Heaven."

To be very open, I struggled through many early drafts of this book, trying to explain things in sufficient detail for Jesus followers, while trying to maintain some practical value to those many others in my business network who are not spiritually inclined. Eventually, I realized the folly of my efforts. It doesn't take a Jesus follower to work in a Kingdom-minded company—it will be a far more attractive and desirable workplace to just about anyone, regardless of their spiritual inclinations or particular faith tradition. Likewise, it doesn't take a Jesus follower to implement some of the underlying principles that ultimately come from the Bible, but are just common sense—like treating a co-worker or employee with dignity and kindness.

It does, however, take a Jesus follower to put the concepts I describe fully into practice—you have to know and actively engage with the King to fully emulate His Kingdom. Accordingly, I'm writing this primarily to encourage Jesus followers to put this fully into practice—to make their areas of influence look more like the desirable and superior Kingdom of Heaven, than the inferior, fallen kingdom of this world.

As a result, and as you've already experienced, the content unavoidably contains some language of those who follow Jesus. If that's not you, but you can work through the occasional "inside" language, I believe you'll still find many practical ideas and insights in the book that you can apply to your own business and career. Don't be intimidated, because it's no different than any new domain you might engage with. For example, if you became interested in rock climbing, cycling, pottery—anything really—there would be a whole set of unfamiliar terms and phrases serious practitioners throw around. Phrases that mean plenty to them, and mean very little to you. At least at first.

I have tried to minimize such expressions. As an example, a Jesus follower would likely know that the Kingdom of Heaven is marked more precisely, by "peace, righteousness, and joy," and may even know the Bible verse in which this is declared. I understand, though, that while peace and joy are relatively universal terms, "righteousness" sounds like church-speak to a non-practitioner. For the sake of communicating the contrast between Heaven's ways and a typical business in the example above, the more relatable terms, "peace" and "joy" should be compelling enough, with little risk of diluting the concept.

That being said, while I'll do my best to keep the language user-friendly, I can't apologize for Jesus being the central part of the story, or edit Him out. Truly, without Him, I have no meaningful story to tell. If, having read the Overview section, you found it too "spiritual"—you could always read Sections 2 and 3 to gain some insight from the stories of navigating "real world" business situations, and then just skip the final section. I personally think, however, you might forego a good amount of value if you choose this route.

If faith isn't your thing, be encouraged, the language I'll use isn't difficult to translate, and the overarching concept is fairly straightforward. For example, if "transforming our company to look like the Kingdom" is too abstract for you, just substitute with, "helping our company to prosper." That's what we're talking about. We're not talking about some corporate theocracy, or your-company-acting-like-a-megachurch, or the no-infidels-allowed club. We're simply talking about your area of influence looking like it should, the way it was meant to be, in God's beautiful design and purpose. That it would be "at work as in Heaven."

> *I'll try to keep the language user-friendly, but I can't edit out Jesus. I have no story without Him.*

When in doubt about a particular phrase, just err on the side of goodness. Ask yourself, "What does goodness look like in this given situation?" Not just goodness for you, but for the broadest collection of parties. That's probably a viable translation. No matter what you may have heard, I can assure you God is a great Father, and He wants nothing more than for His children—even the ones who don't yet know Him—to experience His goodness. He knows once you do—when you see Him for who He really is instead of who He's been portrayed to be—you will very likely want to know Him more.

But Does It Really Work?

By now, you're likely wondering, "Is this guy just another consultant spouting off some theories, or does this stuff really work?" Can you do this Kingdom of Heaven stuff—with a normal group of employees, not just a bunch of "Christians"—and actually have a career or build a business?

Well, consider that recently our company Yakabod was growing rapidly when suddenly every one of our long-term contracts blew up. Instead of worrying about how we were going to find another six people to hire, I was left wondering if we'd already hired six too many. None of it was performance-related. If it were, we could try to fix that. No, unfortunately big chunks of our revenue were evaporating, contract by contract, due to circumstances entirely beyond our control. Clearly we'd have some very tough decisions to make. The way ahead would seem obvious to any business advisor type. Most companies would follow the same "best practices": furlough staff, cut other expenses, do whatever necessary to preserve as much cash as possible.

Fortunately, after the initial shock we regained our senses enough to prayerfully ask "Is this the way things work in the Kingdom?" and "What are *You* saying about this, Lord?" In time, it became clear we should take the exact opposite approach. In the midst of this blatant attack from our spiritual enemy we explained to our diverse team, comprising largely of non-believers, how we were in a spiritual battle, rather than a tangible business battle. We explained it was not a time to "hunker down," but instead we would return the attack with spiritual weapons—namely the weapons of gratitude and generosity.

Specific initiatives were launched during this time, and months later, we discovered the values of gratitude and generosity had been naturally emanating from our collective culture and from individual members of our team. The best part, though, was that we had not even discussed those values in the most recent corporate meetings. These values were naturally present, "leaking out" unprovoked from what a churchgoing believer would call a "secular" team. Did you catch that? Our "secular" team understood they were in a spiritual battle, and the team responded by living out, even prioritizing, gratitude and generosity in their daily work life, and continued to do so even when we weren't constantly talking about it. Perhaps more openly and fully than many church congregations I have visited. It's actually a key part of why they love working at Yakabod!

As beautiful as that is from the standpoint of making things "at work as in Heaven," the question remains, did the approach actually produce business results? After all, it doesn't really matter how much the team loves their workplace or how great the culture is if the doors are closed. So did the risk of taking the counter-intuitive Kingdom approach allow the company to survive long enough to recover? I suspect you've probably guessed the answer. I'll share more details of the surprising and fascinating outcome of this episode in Chapter 22.

First, though, let me share some of the foundational insights for this crazy adventure the Lord has us on...

SECTION 1: OVERVIEW

THE CALL TO THE KINGDOM

W e're going to be talking a lot about the Kingdom of Heaven in this book. I've already stated one of the core questions of my journey has been, "Can a company look more like the Kingdom of Heaven than the kingdom of this world?" Maybe that begs a few more questions for you, though. Like, would you even want it to? Or, is that even part of your call as a Jesus follower? If you're not convinced it is, there are plenty of great books out there on why this is both advisable and desirable.

> *Can a company look more like the Kingdom of Heaven than the kingdom of this world?*

Meaning why you'd want your faith to be part of your workday, and why your call as a believer is almost certainly to make your workplace look more like God's Kingdom.

Some examples are authors and speakers like Ed Silvoso, Hugh

Whelchel, Os Hillman, Andy Mason, Lance Wallnau, Kris Vallotton, Steve Thompson, Johnny Enlow, John Eldredge, Tim Keller and many others who have written and spoken extensively on this topic over the last decade or more. As I've noted, this book is not about the *why* but rather an exploration of the *what* or the *how.*

If you're not a follower of Jesus, it's still pretty easy to see the desirability of "at work as in Heaven" once we get past the religious language. To that end, it's probably a good time to explain the difference between the kingdom of this world (kingdom) and the Kingdom of Heaven (Kingdom).

Kingdom versus kingdom

The capital "K" in "Kingdom," referencing the "Kingdom of Heaven" (or the Kingdom of God, if you prefer), is the realm where God dwells and where things work His way. It's the realm Adam experienced in the Garden of Eden before the fall, and the realm Jesus said He was restoring. It's the realm His followers pray for when they pray the Lord's Prayer: "Your Kingdom come, Your will be done, on Earth as it is in Heaven."

In contrast, the lower case "k" in "kingdom," or "kingdom of this world," is the way things work here on Earth right now. I'm sure you would agree that things don't work the way God originally designed them. If this was a theology book, that statement would be worth quite a few chapters. Since this is a business book, just suffice it to say the kingdom, where we live here and now, is not Kingdom, due to:

a) Hindrances like sin (for example, people making selfish choices; it's good for me, but bad for you), and

b) The active efforts of an enemy (Satan) to spread evil through the realm.

In fact, these reasons are why it's called a kingdom (as opposed to a system); because it has a ruler. From the "fall of man" until the earthly arrival of Jesus, that ruler was Satan. He was, of course, totally defeated and thus deposed by Jesus through the resurrection, but he is still attempting to lead a resistance. So kingdom is more than just a worldview, though it does encompass that. It's the less-than-perfect world we experience every day.

On Earth as It Is in Heaven

I understand this might feel too abstract—like it's great to want Heaven, but what good does that do now? We will certainly make inroads on finding answers to this question by the end of this book. We'll unpack this more in successive chapters, but look carefully at that line in the Lord's Prayer I referenced above. Jesus says we should pray things would be "on Earth as they are in Heaven." Do you think Jesus would give us a prayer that won't or can't work? Likewise, Jesus declared during His time on Earth that the Kingdom of Heaven was at hand (meaning, it has arrived!).

Let's look at one more clue to help us understand what Jesus was saying about the Kingdom of Heaven and our interaction with it. That clue is found in the word Jesus used to describe His core team—His "apostles." It appears He chose this word rather deliberately. You may have heard that context is a key to understanding meaning in scripture, and the Greek word *apostolos* is an excellent example of such a case. In the early first century, the *apostolos* (or *apostolo* in Latin) was a Roman general who had a very specific goal— once Rome had captured a new city or territory, this ambassadorial general would oversee the infusion of Roman civilization and culture into the region. The *apostolo* would ensure the importation of Rome's language, education, government, legal, and financial systems—in effect, the entire Roman culture and system of governance—to the conquered land. The idea was for the *apostolo* to introduce Roman culture to the extent that when Caesar visited the territory, he would feel at home in the newly acquired province.

Thus, our English word "apostle" means "one sent forth." The Roman apostle's role, as one sent forth, was to bring the culture of his own kingdom—the Roman kingdom—to the conquered land. Likewise, Jesus commissioned His apostles, in the same manner, to bring His Kingdom— the Kingdom of Heaven—to this world.

Apostle is a transformational word, suggesting an apostle would have a transformational influence on those societies with whom they came into contact. In light of this, consider again that Jesus taught His to apostles to pray to the Father that, "Your Kingdom come, Your will be done, on Earth as it is in Heaven.[1]" The prayer was not, "Take us to Heaven," but rather that Heaven comes to Earth. It was a transformational prayer Jesus not only made possible, but as noted above, also made manifest. After He taught the disciples the prayer—He began demonstrating the answer to the prayer Himself!

Before Jesus arrived at a village there was deafness, blindness, lameness, and sickness. We'll look at this more in Chapter 5, but suffice it to say when Jesus showed up, the village quickly began to look different—the lame walked, the deaf could hear, the sick were healed... even the dead were raised. There was less brokenness and more wholeness. Things worked more the way God designed them to work. In other words, when Jesus showed up, the village began to look more like the Kingdom of Heaven, where no blindness, sickness, disease, or death exist.

When Jesus then sent out twelve apostles, followed by seventy disciples, he didn't tell them to go preach sermons, He instead gave them instructions to do the same stuff they'd been watching Him do (heal the sick, open the eyes of the blind, cast out demons, etc.). He also instructed them to declare the Kingdom of Heaven is at hand when people asked, "What's going on?" That is, tell them the superior Kingdom has arrived. That's literally the good news, the gospel of the Kingdom. Satan (evil) may still have partial access to this realm we live in because humans (whether knowingly or unknowingly) enable him, but Jesus has all the authority, power, and desire required to invade the fallen Earthly kingdom, squash the evil resistance, and replace it with His superior Kingdom. In fact, Jesus explicitly said He came to destroy the works of the devil, and He subsequently delegated that authority to his followers (Luke 10:19).

Jesus brought His Kingdom to Earth over two thousand years ago, charged us with continuing that work as *apostolos*, and never rescinded that call. Even there His methods are different than the kingdom's methods. Invasions in the kingdom often come through violent destruction. Invasions from the Kingdom usually come through radical love. (Of course, if you're an agent of evil this surely means violent destruction for you and your plans!)

The point is, an experience of this amazing Kingdom—the Kingdom of Heaven—is available now. Even in your workplace. It starts with a shift in mindset. A willingness to look at something and ask, "Is that the way it should be? How would that look in the Kingdom of Heaven?"

As Jesus followers, I think we have lost that call. We have been so busy trying to pull people into our churches that we haven't gone out into the world to share His beautiful Kingdom. We exhaust ourselves designing "relevant" programs to remove people from what we perceive as a dark, worldly culture, and bring them into our church where we can "save" them. Then get them so busy doing church stuff they have no impact on the culture. What if we instead spent our energy equipping people to go out? Equipping believers to bring God's goodness into their everyday

> *Jesus brought His Kingdom to earth two thousand years ago. We're still charged with expanding it.*

spheres of influence? I believe we are in a season now where God is saying, "It is time to carry the Kingdom into everyday life."

An Eternity of Purpose—Doing Things That Matter

On a personal level, this paradigm helps solve the problem of meaning and purpose in life. I understand this is an audacious statement, but it is true, and I believe by the end of this book you will agree with me. This paradigm demonstrates that you don't have to be doing traditional "church ministry" to make a difference in the world. Many people have a "ministry inferiority complex," believing that unless they are a pastor, or going to Africa or Asia to feed orphans, they are not doing real ministry. The truth is, you can have significant influence in your own sphere, where you are, right now. You never know how rapidly it may accelerate—Jesus changed the entire world with a startup of just twelve core team members!

Whatever people may say about the millennial generation, one thing is undeniable: they understand purpose is primary. I'll share more about some of the practical ways we embrace purpose in the workplace as we progress through this book, so if you are a millennial, I encourage you to read every chapter—you will likely appreciate what I share on culture and purpose.

After purpose, another spiritual problem is solved at a corporate level—the impotence of the church in societal issues. We have more churches than ever before, yet many would say our world seems darker than ever. Why isn't the Church making a difference? I believe it's because too many of us have segmented our lives into two compartments: our "spiritual life" on Sundays and our "secular life" the rest of the week. We may occasionally attend a Bible study in between, yet this merely reinforces the rigid divide between our spiritual and secular lives. We simply don't know how to apply a Kingdom vision to the forty hours (or more) of our work week. This is why so many people outside the Church don't "believe" in churches—they see the disconnect between Sunday and Tuesday. The practice of "Churchianity" is so far removed from the bulk of our daily life it often bears little relevance. The purpose of this book is to reveal that relevance.

Things Are Different in God's Kingdom

I have already pointed to the Kingdom of Heaven being marked by peace, whereas the worldly kingdom—and thus, the typical workplace—has things like stress, anxiety, chaos, manipulation, shame, and guilt, in abundance. None of these latter things exists in God's Kingdom. They only exist in this earthly, secular kingdom. They're the result of separation from God, and the active work of an inferior enemy (Satan) opposed to God. Clearly, spending your workday in an environment of peace rather than one of chaos, manipulation, or stress is far more desirable, no matter your religious or spiritual posture.

Let me give another example to illustrate the difference between Kingdom and kingdom. In the Kingdom, there's a progression to the provision you need to live; as a servant of the King, you reap what you sow (meaning your work bears results). Further, as a child of God, you receive an abundant inheritance (you are blessed with things you didn't work for). Most of us have experienced a very different system in operation during our normal, everyday work life in the worldly kingdom; sometimes you sow, but you don't reap (your work doesn't produce the desired results); sometimes you reap what you sow, and that's not good (you bear the consequences of some poor decisions and lose what you thought you had); sometimes you reap, but it's stolen, or broken, etc. (you worked, but your boss cheated you out of the overtime payment or promotion you were expecting).

Once you start looking at workplace activities through this Kingdom lens, you'll observe that many accepted business practices are actually more kingdom than Kingdom. Even (especially?) some designated as "best practices" by the popular business press and consultant types. In other words, these practices may produce some desirable results under certain circumstances, in our broken world's system. Many, however, are actually inconsistent with, inferior to, or counter to the way things work in the eternal Kingdom. Meanwhile, there are some Kingdom practices that sound counter-intuitive in light of your business training, but which may well revolutionize the results you see.

In Your Workplace as in Heaven?

If you've never thought this way, I know it sounds like I'm just speaking in abstractions, but as you'll see in Sections 3 and 4, this Kingdom mindset is a powerful tool for navigating the real-world activities businesses engage in every day. Matters such as sales, marketing, accounting, engineering,

IT, customer service, installation, administration, operations, channels and partnerships, shipping and receiving. Whatever your line of business, whatever your processes—there's a way the world does it, and there's a way it works differently in the Kingdom... *if* you have "eyes to see and ears to hear" (Matthew 13:9-16).

Note we're not talking about doing church stuff at work. When I refer to "Kingdom business practices" I'm not talking about holding Bible studies at lunch, or leaving tracts on employees' desks or quoting scripture in your meetings. I'm not saying you *should never* do these things—who knows, maybe God has explicitly called some of you to do these very things. What I'm saying is that's not what this book is about. It's about conducting business operations from a *Kingdom perspective* rather than a worldly one.

Once you've set your heart to seeing your area of influence look more like God's Kingdom, how do you actually go about doing it?

Well, first, I'll propose you need to believe it's possible for normal people, like you and me. By the time we're done with this book, I hope you'll see you don't need to be a famous business giant (like Steve Jobs, Mark Zuckerberg or Elon Musk) or a spiritual or religious giant (like Bill Johnson, Billy Graham, or the Pope) to radically transform your own area of influence. It's for everyone. Accordingly, what you *will* find in this book is a collection of stories from a normal small-town guy with a modest but successful company, who loves God and wants Him involved in the business. That means this book shares stories likely to be a lot closer to your everyday work-life reality than what you would typically read in the business press.

Next, I believe there are two aspects of accomplishing such a vision: a natural aspect, and a supernatural aspect. In the natural aspect, you can start by following some (biblical) principles. These could even be basic ones, like the "Golden Rule" (treat others as you would like others to treat you). Surprisingly, such basics are all too *uncommon* in the business community at large, so imparting this simple concept to your workplace would be a great start. At Yakabod, we started out by applying biblical principles like this in our early days, and progressed from there. This is something anyone can do, regardless of their spiritual posture or religious convictions.

To really make things look like Kingdom, though, you need God's presence. Not only to do stuff *for* Him, but to do stuff *with* Him—as a "friend of God," who "does what you see the Father doing and says what you hear the Father saying." You can't go too far without His supernatural grace, provision, and intervention. (Plus, you can't really bring the Kingdom into your workplace if you don't know the ways of the King!) The good news is He'd love to partner with you in that way.

> *To really make things look like Kingdom, you need God's presence.*

Especially in your workplace. Just invite Him into what you are doing, and ask Him what He'd like to do about it. He can and will supernaturally clean up the broken kingdom stuff, often working through you and those around you to make it look more like His Kingdom. If you don't believe me, just ask Him. What do you have to lose?

For My Jesus-Following Friends

If you're anxious to get to the "business stuff" because this "spiritual stuff" isn't your thing, you can safely skip ahead to the next chapter. However, before I let my Jesus-following friends move on, there are a few things we should address.

First, let me explicitly state: I'm an entrepreneur who loves Jesus, not a theologian. I make no claims to the contrary. I certainly believe sound doctrine is important, but developing, refining, or defending it is not my call—nor is it the purpose of this book. I give scriptural references where appropriate, but honestly, most of my references will be self-apparent if you have spent any time reading your Bible. For example, if you are wrestling with my assertion in the Introduction that Heaven is marked by peace and joy because I didn't give a scriptural reference (see Romans 14:17), or you're upset I didn't explicitly include "righteousness," in the initial discussion, then this may not be the book for you.

I'll trust you to search the scriptures for yourself if you're questioning something I've said, and I'll trust your pastor to help you develop doctrinal rigor and refine your theological positions. *This book is more practically aimed at that issue you will be dealing with next Tuesday afternoon at your workplace.* If I equip you with some examples to get you thinking about how your own faith journey might apply to the situation, and you're encouraged to ask God what He's saying about it, then you're already starting to bring His Kingdom into the situation, aren't you? I know He would absolutely love that. Likewise, if you can't remember a single one of my examples, but you find yourself asking or praying, "This thing we're doing, is that the way things work in the Kingdom?" then I will consider this book worth the considerable investment it required.

Let me also explicitly state: most of the theological insights I draw on are not my original thinking, but rather, I am standing on the proverbial shoulders of giants. For example, seeing that verse in the Lord's Prayer about "bringing Heaven to Earth" differently (though I have seen it differently) is not my contribution; other Spirit-led believers have discerned, emphasized, and taught extensively on this concept. Likewise, with the transformational call embedded in the word "apostle." While these may be new to you, as they were to me at one point in my faith journey, these insights aren't uniquely mine. Instead, I'm a practitioner. I've spent years devouring books, podcasts, sermons, and of course scripture, wrestling through—in partnership with the Spirit—what insights like the above mean in real, practical terms for our business on a given Tuesday afternoon. I provided some background above so we're "speaking the same language." This is expressed in my own words as I understand things, not plagiarized from others' books or podcasts, but please don't attribute the concepts to me. My contribution comes in the successive sections, where I offer some unique insights into the "how" from my own experiences.

Maybe that leaves you wondering what kind of company or team it requires to actually pursue the lofty concept of God's Kingdom being "at work as in Heaven"? As you will discover, it only takes a rather normal team of people...

THIS WORKS FOR NORMAL PEOPLE

I'll tell you more about my personal journey, and Yakabod's journey, in Section 2, but suffice it to say, by the time you're done reading that section, you'll likely agree it would all be considered fairly "normal" or "modest" by most standards. Sure, it's great reading about the twenty-year-old wunderkind who sketched out the next tech revolution on a napkin and had a $10B company and his own island two years later. But that's not this book or my story. This should be good news, because it means the stories, perspectives, successes, insights, and hard lessons I share in this book work for normal people in everyday circumstances—like you and me!

Allow me to provide some quick background at this stage: Yakabod is a software company that builds secure case management solutions for business enterprises. It wasn't exactly what we pictured when we started in 2001, right at the very peak of dot-com mania. For a brief period back then, we thought—just like everyone else did—that with enough "eyeballs" and some venture capital, we would soon be dot-com quadrillionaires. (If the "eyeballs" reference doesn't click for you—don't bother Googling. It was foolishness anyway.)

Our board wisely counseled us in those early days to sell to customers—not investors, which means we got over that brief period of youthful exuberance rather quickly. I can't remember if our pragmatism took over before or after the market totally cratered in April 2001. Either way, that focus helped us survive long enough to slowly build a solid, sustainable business you would probably consider modest. We're still not quadrillionaires. Even so, if we're honest, I don't think we would ever have imagined being as outright blessed as we've been over the years since.

It's an anomaly for a niche software company like ours, but after two decades we truly feel like we're just getting started, and our best days are still ahead. We recently upgraded from a great workplace into an absolute showplace of an office, and we are well respected in our community. We have a great team of people who all love working together, and who feel more or less like a family now. We have created many stable, fulfilling careers, which have blessed dozens of families, and numerous neighborhoods in ways far more expansive than basic financial provision. (If you're kicking the dog and yelling at the kids when you go home, we can safely say it's unlikely to be our fault.)

More Kingdom, Less kingdom

If you ever visited our office building, you would very likely want to spend more time here. Something about it just feels different—welcoming, peaceful, comfortable. It's the kind of place you would love to be every day. We have had many hundreds of visitors, perhaps even in the low thousands by now, say exactly that. If you're a believer in Jesus you might understand that part of what you're feeling is the presence of God. This makes perfect sense since the principal owners are, after all, praying in the space most days, welcoming Him.

On further reflection, you might conclude it looks and feels more like the Kingdom of Heaven than the kingdom of this world. It's not perfect here of course, and surely there are things to be improved, but in general, you would be correct in your conclusion. This awareness of God's presence in our workplace isn't limited to hardcore Jesus-freaks though; people from all spiritual walks (including self-proclaimed atheists) feel it too, even if they use different language to describe it.

In successive chapters I present in more detail how this has been precisely the call God has placed on our company—to wrestle with the process of making Yakabod look and feel a little more like His Kingdom every day. Recently, He has challenged us to think even bigger than we have been. If a humble little company like ours can expose our employees, customers, and stakeholders to an experience that feels more like His Kingdom, and even build a culture around this aspiration, could it be possible an ecosystem of such companies can bring a Kingdom experience and culture to a whole community? Now *that's* a Big Hairy Audacious Goal![2]

From what I've shared so far, I hope you're getting the big picture. God has blessed us with a great little company, which has in turn blessed scores of grateful individuals and families, and influenced countless more. Likewise, Yakabod has already proven to be of significant importance to our community, as well as having had a considerable influence on it. This is reflected not only in who this community is, but in who it's *becoming.*

Yaka-Who?

Even so, I can be reasonably certain—unless you live here in Frederick (Maryland), or you are somehow connected with our modest base of customers or employees, *you have never actually heard of Yakabod.* You didn't see us in Fast Company business magazine or hear a talk on us at SXSW (South by Southwest). We never showed up in the Inc. 5000 (a who's-who list of hot companies according to Inc. Magazine), let alone the Fortune 500. There is no Harvard Business Review case study on our practices, and you would not discover us on the Best Places to Work list. Not even the Frederick County list, because we don't bother to apply.

Hyper-growth companies like Facebook, Uber, and the next-hot-new-thing, are the firms that get all the business press. The hype is so pervasive, communities build entire conferences or festivals (e.g. SXSW, TomTom Festival) just to position the host community as the "next Silicon Valley." The popular business press might have convinced you that if you're not starting one of these unicorn companies, you should at least work in one. I too fell prey to that mindset in Yakabod's earliest days. When we had been in business for six months and hadn't yet raised a $5 million Series-A round, or grown to fifty people yet, I'd feel pressure to apologize at all the networking events because we weren't growing quite as fast as Google was in those days.

Fortunately, I accepted long ago that we're not one of those companies, and we may never be. The beautiful thing is, *we don't need to be.* That's simply not our primary mission. *You* don't need to be either, unless, of course, God has explicitly called you to develop such a company. Please understand, I am by no means belittling Yakabod's achievements and I am

> **We don't need to be famous to have a profound and eternally significant impact.**

not the slightest bit ungrateful for our relatively modest size as companies go. Neither am I trying to shortchange the power of God to lead you into absolutely amazing things, beyond anything you can hope or imagine in your "normal" career or your "normal" company. Likewise, I would never encourage you to dream smaller. Maybe you really are the next Elon Musk or Mark Zuckerberg or Steve Jobs. I'm just saying, no matter what you're reading in the business press, neither you nor I have to be someone famous to have a profound and eternally significant impact on the people and culture surrounding each of us. Take, for example, my friend Jim.

Cleaning Toilets for the Glory of Jesus

Jim was a maintenance worker at a regional county park featuring a small lake in a woodland setting. Being a fisherman, Jim loved that job, but one day the county government reassigned him to janitorial duty at a middle school some distance away. After seeking the Lord in prayer, Jim resolved that if his new assignment was to clean toilets, then he'd clean them for the glory of Jesus. You might imagine what he stepped into when he began working at the school.

The other janitors hated their jobs, didn't like the teachers (nor did the teachers like them), and the janitors really didn't like students. They did their work half-heartedly, doing just enough to get to the next smoke break where they'd go outside and complain about everyone and everything. They'd then take their misery home to share with their families. Things weren't much better with the teachers and administrative staff either. In short, the workplace was full of disgruntled, unmotivated staff, rampant cynicism, and was a totally negative, toxic environment.

Right away, Jim just set about worshipping Jesus with his work. Sometimes this meant quietly singing a worship song to himself as he worked, finding things in his life for which to be grateful, or just thinking about all Jesus had done for him. At other times, Jim's attitude of worship was simply reflected in being pleasant to people, and genuinely caring about them.

Of course, these attitudes also meant the toilets *were* actually kept clean—at least, cleaner than they had been, perhaps in a very long time. Since Jim's a Jesus follower, he carries the Holy Spirit around with him, and the fruit of the Spirit—peace, righteousness, and joy—just started leaking out of him. Now Jim wasn't passing out tracts, holding Bible studies, or forcing Jesus into conversations; he certainly wasn't calling out people's sins. Jim is "*in* the world, not *of* the world," so he also wasn't complaining, grumbling, talking badly about people, or skimping on his duties... he simply worshipped Jesus while he worked.

As a result, the whole atmosphere in his workplace shifted, slowly but surely. Before long people were asking him why he was so happy. Jim didn't give them a sermon, he just replied with something simple like: "Because Jesus loves me, man, so today's gonna be a good day." This continued, and following Jim's lead, people started treating each other a little better, complained a little less, and began laughing a little more.

Before long, a few people approached Jim to ask him deeper questions. One guy had some marital issues so he approached Jim for advice. Jim was able to respond with some practical biblical wisdom, for which the guy would never have opened a Bible to find. Another guy was in some trouble and feeling conviction in his soul; he didn't know he was feeling the Holy Spirit, but Jim did, and Jim was able to share the gospel with a man who would never have stepped into a church to hear it.

In the three short months Jim was at the school, he totally shifted the atmosphere. Ultimately, Jim had the opportunity to explicitly share his faith with a dozen pre-believers, and have much deeper conversations with several of them around biblical principles applied to their specific challenges. He caused the place to look a little more like the Kingdom of Heaven and a little less like the wrong one.

Later, Jim would discover the little taste of God's goodness he had introduced to the school had ultimately brought conviction and a sense of their need for God to many more people—even those with whom Jim had never explicitly discussed his faith. Jim's is a textbook example of Kingdom influence, and my friend Jim brought more of it into his area of influence as a janitor than most CEOs and high-powered executives I know.

If We Can Do It, You Can Too!

My hope is this book will inspire you and provide some practical ideas to help you start making your workplace look a little more like His Kingdom every day too. I'll tell you upfront, we don't have a formula for this process.

We simply have access to the world's most awesome Creator and Innovator. As you consider our examples and start praying, I am confident He will show you many additional ways to make your own area of influence more like His Kingdom. (Maybe you'll be gracious enough to email those testimonies and insights to me at **scott@atworkasinheaven.com**.) Likewise, as Jim demonstrated, you don't have to do anything fancy or complicated to get started. Over the course of this book, I hope to save you the twenty years it took me to learn some of the "higher level" approaches and clarifying questions we're now using, but if you are just intentional and committed to bringing Jesus into your Tuesday like Jim was, you've already taken the most important step.

Some of you don't need convincing to pursue the concept of "at work as in Heaven," because you work in the kind of place where any taste of the goodness of the Kingdom would be a welcome relief. I worked in some of those places too. That's how I got started on this whole Kingdom adventure…

SECTION 2: ADVENTURE BY GOD

IT BETTER WORK ON TUESDAY (OR WHY BOTHER WITH SUNDAY?)

I have completed many big adventures in my life, from trekking the John Muir Trail in the High Sierra to bikepacking the length of the Blue Ridge Parkway. Well, they're pretty tame if you're an Alex Honnold[3] type, but to me they're real adventures. God willing, I plan to undertake plenty more adventures before I'm done. Honestly, though, none of them compares to some of the adventures you find yourself in when you partner with God and let Him make the plans...

I was raised in small-town Ohio, a solid working-class town. It was a great place to grow up, a lot like my current hometown of Frederick, only quite a bit smaller. There was a strong work ethic among the town's residents, and a deep sense of community. A general respect for people was also observed in a "golden rule" sort of way. The people in the community were *for* each other, not against each other, and there was a solid foundation of Judeo-Christian morals. Sadly, like much of the Rust Belt, the town has been mired in economic decay and related issues over the past few decades, but when I was growing up there it was Mayberry[4]. Well, actually, the town was probably past its peak of prosperity and already in decline, but we didn't realize it at the time.

A good portion of the community went to church—not everyone, of course—but the traditional, mainline, denominational Protestant Churches were well represented, and there was a well-attended Catholic Church. There were some radical "Jesus-freaks" out on the fringes of town too, but they made the rest of us nervous. "That's okay for you," seemed to be the prevailing mindset in town, at least in the circles I moved in. "Just leave us alone," was the general sentiment. "Let us go to our little neighborhood churches where we keep religion and politics out of our conversations, and you keep the *holy-roller* stuff to yourselves." I was going to church several times a week myself—youth group on Wednesdays when I was younger, then on Sunday evenings in high school. I would sing with the choir on Sunday morning, attend the Sunday school session, then often hang out with other youth group kids throughout the weekend. On yet another night of the week, I would be there for choir practice if I remember correctly.

A Good Life—as in Good and Empty

My experiential learning as I grew up in this setting was that if I was a good member of the community and did my part, I would have a pretty good life, and everything would be fine. During that period, a few different friends asked me questions like, "Is Jesus your Lord and Savior?" or "Do you know what's going to happen when you die?" I think I was even asked, "Don't you want to be born-again?" I can see now they'd each had an encounter with Jesus, which they were trying to share with me, but I had no clue what they were talking about back then. I would squirm inside and say something like, "Well, I don't know about all that, but I'm a good citizen, I go to church, I'm nice to people—I have it covered. I don't think I need that stuff. Really... I'm good."

26

After I finished school, right on schedule I went off to college, got a degree, and started a career. By that stage, I had fully bought into what you might characterize as western consumerism. All I needed was more. If I wasn't happy, I just needed an upgrade. My parents had given me their old Renault Le Car to get through college, so when I started earning a real paycheck I knew I'd buy a better car, and then eventually trade up to a convertible.

Then once I started working, I moved out of the frat-house style rental in college, into a better apartment with a few guys. Before long, I bought my own townhouse. The cheap beer I drank in college was upgraded to microbrews, and eventually to semi-fine wine. If I had a cute girlfriend and I got bored with her (or more likely, she dumped me) then I would just find a cuter one. In short, I was doing everything society was telling me I should do to have a good life, and I was doing it well. But no matter how many upgrades I made, I started feeling more and more empty and unsettled inside. I didn't realize it for a long time, but I was growing desperately tired of running from the emptiness.

During that period, in my late twenties, I had a girlfriend who was extremely beautiful on the outside. She was the kind of stunner that caused even sixteen-year-old boys to stare wide-eyed when we walked by. We were physically doing what younger couples do, in fact, that was more or less the basis for our relationship (I'm sure you can figure it out.) I would now recognize our activities as sin, but back then the self-gratification temporarily anesthetized my growing internal discomfort. Then one day she surprised me by saying, "I can't do that anymore; I'm a Christian."

"Christian?" I replied, confused, "Well… I'm one of those too. What's that got to do with it?" Never mind that I hadn't been to my old church in a decade; I was still getting their newsletter, so I was still in the club, right?

"No," she said firmly, shaking her head, "I cannot do that anymore. The Bible says it is sin."

"Bible?" I asked, frowning, "You can make that say anything you want; it's just a bunch of stuff made up by men."

"No it is not," she chided. "That is the Word of God!"

"Word of God? That's just crazy," I snickered.

Looking back on it, I imagine the Father watching this scene, gleefully gathering some witnesses around and saying, "Hey guys, watch this!" He knew precisely what He was doing. He used my own hunger for sin to reel me in, and He knew exactly what I was going to do next. After all those years I spent in church I knew I should have had some argument, some verses I could quote back to persuade my girlfriend to resume our indulgences, but I had *nothing.* It made me just mad enough, and I was just desperate enough, that I went out that night to the nearest bookstore and bought the "best" Bible I could find. I resolved to read the whole book from beginning to end so I would be able to find the ammunition I needed to debate things back to the way they were. I started reading my new Bible that very evening.

> *God used my own hunger for sin to reel me in, and He knew exactly what I was going to do next.*

An Eternal Change

The first couple of nights reading the Bible I was fascinated by the stories. Who knew the Bible was such a page-turner? Some nights I read several chapters at a time, unable to put it down. Other nights I remember—probably in Numbers or Deuteronomy—I would read about three sentences before my eyes glazed over, and my head hit the pillow.

Meanwhile, the girlfriend had decided three days of abstinence was long enough, and we were back to our shenanigans. Even so, I was stubborn enough to keep reading every night. I was going to be ready the next time she pulled that nonsense. For half of the Old Testament, I ignored the nagging

28

little voice that kept whispering in my ear, telling me I was *enjoying* the reading. By the time I had read as far as the life of King David, probably somewhere in the upper chapters of 1 Samuel, I realized my girlfriend had been right after all: this book I was reading *had* to be the Word of God. The stories were too real, the characters too authentic, the themes too consistent across generations and centuries, and the words just too *alive*. There was no way it could be the "made-up words of men" I had naively accepted as the truth. I simply could no longer deny the reality that the Bible is the Word of God.

The problem was, this awareness left me facing a critical decision.

I came to the realization I had been living my life completely devoid of God, which was the cause of my life's total emptiness. In fact, I realized the emptiness was getting worse. I knew if I continued on the same path, I was heading toward an eternity of this terrible emptiness… quite literally hell. I had already been getting little tastes of this realization in my quieter moments, and I knew I didn't want any part of it. I wrestled with the decision a little while longer, kept reading my Bible (I ended up reading it to

> *I could no longer deny that the Bible is the Word of God. That left me facing a critical decision…*

the end, then started over), and began talking to friends who claimed to be Christians… but I just wasn't sure I could give up my sin. Yet I also knew what I was doing wasn't working. I had no understanding of grace back then, not realizing that you don't get cleaned up to take a bath—if I had just gone to God as I was, He would have helped me to move away from the sin in my life.

One day, while driving down the road, the conviction in my heart increasing to a point of total consumption, I knew it was time to make the decision "official." I pulled over, said a quick prayer, and asked God to take control of my life; I asked Him to steer it in the direction He chose for me.

There was no flash of light, no choir of angels singing in harmony (that I could hear anyway), but the decision to live for God was confirmed; I was all in. Not just in terms of believing in Him, but in my whole approach to life. I knew I wasn't just making a decision about my time on Sunday—I had already done that and had never met God. No, I knew I was making a decision on what my Tuesday and Wednesday and Thursday were going to be. If this God thing didn't work on those days, I really had no need to bother with church on Sunday. If my new life with God wasn't equally valid when I was at work every day—or out rock climbing or hanging with my friends, or maybe even sitting in church—I wanted none of it. But I had just enough simple faith to believe it had to work, because I now knew God was very, very real.

Ironically, to this day, I have no idea whether that girlfriend really was a Jesus follower, or had just expressed the temporary feeling of some religious shame or guilt. Long after our relationship was over, I saw little fruit of the Kingdom from her. That is between her and God, of course, but whatever the case, thank God He used her temporary decision to eternally change my life. Slowly but surely, I found myself thinking differently than I had just a few months prior.

The Birth of an Adventure

There were some notions Jesus had to unwind in me in those early days. I deeply believed some things that were generally accepted in our culture at large, but simply weren't true. Perhaps the biggest lie I had bought into was that I had to turn my brain off to be a "Jesus-guy." From the time I started attending engineering school, it was understood in those circles that I could do science, engineering, and math stuff, or I could do "God stuff," but under no circumstances could I do both. Fortunately, Jesus dispelled that myth almost immediately as I stumbled into a category of books called "apologetics." I read everything on apologetics I could get my hands on, and it blew me away.

Before long, it became obvious I must have had my brain turned *off* before I decided to live for God. Everything God showed me about His character, His ways, His creation and His Kingdom just made so much more sense. It was far more tractable intellectually; everything hung together and made sense in a way that most of the scientific or humanistic explanations didn't. Maybe because I was a systems engineer, I could see how God's systems all worked together, whereas the systems fashioned without Him seldom did. He began to show me almost immediately in my faith journey, there was a difference between what was "common knowledge," and what was Truth.

There is plenty more to my story as an emerging Christian, of course, but that's enough for this context. It's clear now, even in my earliest days as a believer, God was building the foundation for what was to come. Before I ever got the chance to start my own company, and before I knew it would be called Yakabod, He had already firmly entrenched in me that:

a) He was going to be part of it, because He was supposed to be part of everything I was doing, and,

b) His ways were often very different than the world's ways, and His ways made a whole lot more sense, anyway.

I soon discovered that fitting my understanding of biblical principles— even though they now made more sense—into a system designed by the world, was an entirely new and complicated challenge. I also realized how, in choosing to remain committed to honoring God with my company, I had potentially put at risk—at least in worldly terms—the very business with which I had decided to honor God.

I WILL HONOR THOSE WHO HONOR ME (OR WHY WE'RE UNASHAMED)

Have you ever looked back and realized a moment carried a whole lot more significance than you ever imagined it did? A split second of time that could well have changed the course of your last few decades? God teed up one of those moments for me in the earliest stages of Yakabod. Fortunately, I had already decided that if my faith didn't work on Tuesday, I wasn't going to bother with Sunday. That was a bit of a challenge when I was working as an employee at other companies, especially when a company's established practices conflicted with my faith. But I would soon learn it was a different thing altogether when that faith-driven decision on a Tuesday would mean the death of a lifelong dream...

Somehow, from the earliest stages of my career, I knew I would launch—in fact, *needed* to launch—my own company. As a youngster, I was always the one starting things, which was a characteristic that didn't really fit the contemporary cultural ethos in my small rust-belt hometown. The prevailing philosophy in that time and place was to keep your head down, do your part, and never take unnecessary risks. So it's safe to say, I never had any real entrepreneurial training. I doubt I even knew what the word "entrepreneur" meant back then. Even so, I would somehow start, launch, and organize projects, events, or activities that were rather ambitious in retrospect.

One example that sticks with me is when I was "volunteered" to be the leader of the teen social committee at the blue-collar country club outside of town, to which my family belonged. I was given a modest budget to organize three summer evening dances in the clubhouse, booking three inexpensive DJs for music. It sounded rather pedestrian to my ambitious young self, so I risked a good chunk of the budget on the first event, negotiating a hefty discount with a respected local cover band. I then convinced a bunch of friends to help market it, which of course took some serious groundwork in the days long before social media.

The first event packed out the clubhouse and resulted in a profit for the event. That left two more dances to plan, with a bigger total budget than I had started with. The second event turned an even bigger profit, which provided enough funds to book a regional headliner for the final event, and again pack the clubhouse to overflowing. I was around fifteen years old at the time, so it was the equivalent, at this point of my career, of starting with a $10,000 budget and running summer programming at Frederick's 1200-seat Weinberg Theatre, ultimately managing to book U2 for the season closer. Well, maybe it wasn't quite *that* big. Still, looking back I have no idea how I pulled it off, except to understand in hindsight that's just the way God made me. I didn't realize it at the time, of course, but in retrospect it's clear God had equipped me, and was refining in me the skills, to launch new ventures.

False Starts

Gifting or not, at first I experienced many false starts launching a company. I didn't say failed companies—I couldn't even *launch* them. Working with some teammates and the backing of some supportive bosses, I managed to help launch some new products, business units, or subsidiaries within the larger companies for which I was working. Each would show some very promising initial success, but then top out as it ran into the bureaucracy of the parent organization.

As frustrating as it was at the time, I learned a lot about business on someone else's payroll. Before that process, as an engineer coming up the technical ranks, I didn't even know there were differences between sales, marketing, and business development, let alone what those differences were. I wasn't following God at all back then, so it was probably His divine protection that kept me from launching my own startup, which I would most likely have pursued for my own selfish purposes, rather than any greater good. Who knows how bad that would have turned out, and whether I would ever have recovered?

After I came to faith, the desire to launch a business still burned brightly within me. I continued to look for the right opportunity, exploring various ideas, but things never quite lined up. It seemed I was always missing one piece—and a different piece each time. Somewhere in that struggle, though, I resolved that if God would ever give me the opportunity to launch my own company—and it was becoming quite clear that opportunity would have to come from Him—I would do it for His glory.

In late 2000, the opportunity was finally presented to me. In the fall of 1998, I had taken a day job with a friend who needed help with a large contract he had just been awarded. I took the job with the open understanding I would be there for a year at most, while simultaneously trying to get my own firm launched on the side. I was already assembling the team in my spare time throughout 1999, refining the ideas, and shopping the business

35

plan for launching a company to build custom web applications.

By the fall of 2000, I was two years into the day job and didn't know how much longer I could continue doing it. Things weren't coming together to launch my company yet either.

One day, a former business associate who was by then employed with a software product company, had an opportunity to make a big sale to a very strategic customer. The catch was the strategic customer would sign on only if their software would allow users to enter data, and get the results back on the web.

That's a simple process today, but at the turn of the millennium it was advanced technology. My associate's company had no expertise with this, but he knew our team could successfully deliver the *front-end* web application that would get their *back-end* (database) product online. He brought us into discussions with the product company's senior management, which eventually turned into us providing them with a substantial fixed-price proposal to deliver the solution. The senior management were hesitant to issue such a strategic subcontract to our unknown pre-launch startup, but we had some strong personal references, and they couldn't find anyone more established to take it at a fixed price for anything close to the price we were offering. Getting desperate to make the sale to their customer, they went for it.

Yakabod? What's That Mean?

Early in 2001, somewhere in that proposal and negotiation stage, a launch began feeling real enough that I officially incorporated, and started setting up the company structure. Those were the days of the dot-com domain name land-grab, so everyone, especially tech companies, were making up elaborate names for their

> *I had already resolved to build the company for God's glory.*

companies. Often, they were obscure foreign language words for something of interest to the founder. (I vaguely remember one that was something like "the Persian word for surfer-dude.") I had already resolved to build the company for God's glory, so following the formula of the day, I dug into a concordance as my foreign language source and eventually stumbled on the Old Testament Hebrew word *KBD,*

> ***Yakabod means the heavy, weighty, mighty glory of God.***

transliterated as Kabod or Chabod, meaning the "the weighty heavy mighty glory of God[5]." Prepending Kabod with Ya, for Yahweh, I decided on the name Yakabod, meaning "God's glory" in Hebrew, and sure enough, the URL for Yakabod was readily available.

Branding experts immediately told me it was an awful name. Part of their rationale was because it gave potential customers no clue as to what we offered. "More so," they asserted, "the whole 'God-thing' would be a total turn-off to customers," but I was stubborn enough that I didn't care. One scripture that really resonated with me in those early days was in 1 Samuel 2:30 (NLT,) in which God declares "…I will honor those who honor me..." I had already resolved that if I was going to embed a reference to God on our business card, I would just have to trust He would honor that choice, like He said He would.

Curiously, despite the branding experts' dismissal, I quickly discovered the name really stuck with people, perhaps because of a familiarity with the name Ichabod, as in Ichabod Crane from *The Legend of Sleepy Hollow*. Although, in 1 Samuel 4:21 we see that Ichabod actually means, "The glory has departed" or "no glory[6]." With such an unusual name, everyone—and I mean literally everyone—asked what the name meant… so I would have to tell them. In the beginning, it was often awkward. Encounters at networking events often went something like this: "Hi, I'm Joe from Oracle Corp."

"Hi Joe, I'm Scott with Yakabod."

"Yakabod, that's interesting! What's that mean?"

"Well, it's Old Testament Hebrew. It means God's glory." Joe would frown, or stare condescendingly, then in some cases, "Joe" (or Mary or James) would simply walk away without saying another word.

In time, thanks to the famous implosion of Enron (later detailed in the documentary, *The Smartest Guys in the Room*[7]), I learned to soften it a little. In addition to sharing the literal definition, I would say, "It's our anti-Enron device. It keeps us thinking about something other than our own egos while we build the company." That seemed to let the ones offended by the notion of God's glory sidestep the name issue with a nervous chuckle, while continuing the business conversation.

> *It's our anti-Enron device. It keeps us thinking about something other than our own egos while we build the company.*

Standing Firm

At the time, it sure felt like we were finally going to launch but my commitment to the motivation behind the name Yakabod would be tested immediately. The deal with the product company was lined up, their senior management gave the go-ahead, the end customer was excited to work with us, and we were just a day or two from signing the contract. With that contract in hand, Yakabod would finally be "in business." Then my associate at the product company threw me a curveball. He requested that Yakabod raise our price, so we could include some "third party integration services" he claimed we would need. In my naiveté, I couldn't see why we would need to engage someone else to help with integration, when that was one of our core skills. He awkwardly danced around explanations, but was adamant it had to be part of the deal. It finally dawned on me what he was really asking. He wanted us to cut a check to a fake subcontractor, whose sole purpose was to provide a kickback to him and another sales guy involved in the deal.

I gave him an emphatic "No, that won't work." We simply couldn't do that. It would never stand the light of day if his management ever found out, and I knew I couldn't name the company Yakabod then do something like that, on our first contract, no less. Still, I was crushed. All these years trying to launch… it was right in front of my nose. Yet, I would have to walk away from the entire deal.

Trying to blow off the stress and the crushing disappointment, I went out cycling. I'm not really a "crier," but I can still show you the exact spot on Middletown Road where, overwhelmed with the disappointment, I started sobbing with very real and deeply anguished tears. I figured the deal was my last (and best) chance, and knew I'd probably never get a company launched after that. I kept riding, just pouring my heart out to God, telling him how heartbroken I was because I was sure this was the trigger for our launch. When it hadn't materialized yet again, I had no idea what to do, because there wasn't anything else in the pipeline. "I know I can't do the kickback, Lord," I half-prayed, half-complained, "I have no argument there, but I desperately need to launch *now*. I just can't keep working the day job anymore. It is too soul-crushing!" The mere thought of looking for another day job was even more devastating.

It doesn't always work out this way or this quickly, but God used that situation to teach me a very valuable and immediate lesson in what a Jesus follower would call "walking by faith not by sight." He patiently listened to my moaning and wailing for a few hours on my ride, then two days later, my associate at the software product company called back. They dropped the demand for the kickback and we got the contract on our terms, exactly as we proposed it. *God would indeed honor those who honor Him!* If I would simply continue to *seek His Kingdom first* according to Matthew 6:33, the rest would be provided as well. This was another verse I learned to tightly cling to in those early days.

> *Before the company was fully launched, God was already teaching me I needed to "walk by faith, not by sight.*

Open... but for How Long?

With that, Yakabod was officially in business in early 2001. My business partner at the time, a software engineer, who was and still is, a dear friend, focused on building the application with a handful of other developers we enlisted, while I did just about everything else: project management, requirements definition, systems engineering, and company infrastructure. Then, shortly after the fixed-price development contract was signed, a long-term, consulting gig "miraculously" appeared. Another associate had a non-competitive technology services startup, and he wanted me to be his "virtual CTO"—an offsite Chief Technology Officer, until he scaled his company. He also understood it would be an interim thing until I could scale Yakabod. Although Yakabod was still a side-hustle for everyone else at the time, by running the consulting gig through Yakabod, there was sufficient cash flow for me to quit my day job and focus full time on building the company.

When we successfully completed the development project and collected on all our payment milestones, we were able to pay all the moonlighting developers and the infrastructure costs, and still retain a substantial profit in Yakabod's` coffers. My business partner decided he wanted to cash out and invest his share of the profits into real estate, which was a good choice for him since that's what he knew and was passionate about. As part of that agreement, I left my share of the profits in the company to bootstrap it, and thus retained all the equity.

After a short while, however, my investment wasn't looking so smart. My buddy had bought some rental condos in a hot market, and they were generating some real income while also appreciating rapidly. Yakabod? Not so much. But at least we were launched. The revenue and cash flow from the consulting gig I ran through Yakabod provided a modest salary for me, while I invested Yakabod's seed funding (the retained profits) into sales and marketing. We met with many interested people, and some good things were happening, but plenty of cash was going out the door, and new sales weren't coming in yet.

I had a new wife, a new three-year-old son (stepson), and a mortgage far more appropriate to a steady day job. My wife and I had already agreed when we married six months prior that she would stay home with our son to manage the household, thus providing some much-needed stability for both us boys. To do so, she had quit her teaching job—the one with the reliable income, the great healthcare benefits, and the pension plan. It was a big, risky step, but Yakabod was at least treading water, and things seemed stable.

When a Cash Flow Crisis Is a Blessing

Then the dot-com bubble suddenly burst, and the bottom totally fell out of the market. Large, well-capitalized, long-established companies began disappearing overnight. By late summer 2001, I was watching Yakabod's cash dwindle, and the brick wall—the projected date at which we would run out of cash—loomed closer and larger. We hadn't sold any more software delivery engagements, but at least the consulting gig helped slow the bleeding. That is, until that associate stopped paying his bills.

He called me the afternoon of September 10, imploring me to hop on a train to Manhattan and set up at the World Trade Center the next morning. He was hoping to line up an impromptu sales call with an executive or two he knew in the buildings. At that point, he owed me close to $10,000 in unpaid expenses, and I didn't know if I would ever collect. I told him if he had a firm meeting booked, I would consider going in the hope of closing a deal, so he could pay me. I made it clear I wasn't traveling at my expense for a speculative meeting until he made good on his debt. What followed might be the only time I ever saw a Yakabod cash-flow crunch as a major blessing.

He managed to convince a few others to scramble to Manhattan that evening of September 10. They were near, but thankfully, not yet in the Towers when the planes hit the next morning. They all eventually managed to safely evacuate the city and get back home, but only after an extended ordeal, as you can imagine.

41

Through the turbulence, I was still holding onto God's promise of, "I will honor those who honor me." When the brick wall came too painfully close, I was filled with remorse as the Board told me I'd have to take the obvious step I'd been avoiding—if I wanted to survive, I would have to terminate the sales consulting contract of a dear friend, Dave, who was an influential part of our early journey (and to this day continues to be a real encourager!).

I had spent a good portion of my earlier career in the Intelligence Community market, and fortunately still had a professional network in that space. It was the last market I imagined Yakabod would ever focus on when we started, but the nation's response to the tragic events of 9/11, and subsequent investment into the Intelligence Community, caused significant demand for precisely the skills I was able to offer through the company. Consequently, some friends in the space began referring their government customers to us. The result was a series of small consulting opportunities for Yakabod to design web-based knowledge-sharing solutions, which eventually led to the opportunity for us to build the solutions we were designing.

> *In my naively blissful ignorance, I had just enough faith to trust that if God was in it, it would work.*

In retrospect, there's no way I would have had enough faith to launch the company if I had really known how little I knew, and just how unlikely our corporate survival was. We honestly weren't even sure what we were selling in those early days. In my naively blissful ignorance, I had just enough faith to trust that if God was in it, it would work, because *He honors those who honor Him.*

Later I would get a much broader picture of what it means to build a company for God's glory, and I'd understand how my actions, the corporate culture, and His presence, were all factors that bore witness to His glory.

Back then, though, all I had in my toolkit were my words, so I upheld my end of God's promise to honor Him. If someone asked what Yakabod meant, I would tell them, no matter how awkward the situation, or how likely it was to torpedo a potential deal. God, of course, more than upheld His end of the equation. Somehow, every time the brick wall got a little too close for comfort, another consulting contract would appear, or some unexpected referral would bring in enough cash to keep the lights on a bit longer while we continued to build the corporate foundation.

During this time, Scott Williamson, a man with whom I was destined to cross paths, was a pioneering developer in the early Internet community, leading the development of domain name registration technology. Cashing out as the market ran up, Scott launched his own startup with some of the proceeds, building a flexible software engine. Just before the market peaked, a venture-backed firm acquired Scott's little startup, and his software, with the aim of turning one of their investments around. Scott managed to accomplish this, but when the market collapsed the investors pulled out and Scott was able to retain his software engine as part of the severance package. He set up his own company, and set about building an innovative early e-commerce platform, without any customers as yet. At that time, Yakabod had consulting customers requiring software solutions, but we had no real software of our own. Sometime in 2003, one of my mentors introduced me to one of Scott Williamson's mentors, who told me, "You two really need to meet."

Two Are Stronger Than One

At our very first meeting, Scott and I discussed the name Yakabod and what it meant, and I discovered both he and his wife Debbie were committed believers. The Lord had been tugging on their hearts to explore how their faith impacted their Tuesdays and Wednesdays as well. We had several subsequent discussions, and during that period, a customer notified me she was ready to issue Yakabod a contract to build a web-based collaboration solution (still advanced technology at that point). Scott's software was the perfect platform on which to build it. We decided to merge, and we've been business partners since.

Interestingly, it was Debbie, Scott's wife, who first committed to the idea of a partnership. (Scott might still be wondering whether it was a good idea!) By nature of our roles and personalities Scott was never in front of the business ecosystem (customers, prospects, partners, etc.) as much as I was, but if anyone asked Scott what Yakabod meant, he never hesitated to explain either.

We're now approaching two decades since those humble first steps. People stopped caring about made-up internet company names at least a decade and a half ago, yet we are still quite frequently asked, "What's that mean?", and we still tell them, of course. By "we" I mean Scott and I, because we don't put that burden on our team. If the staff are asked, they know they can simply deflect to me, Scott, or the website, if they're uncomfortable answering the question. We're not consciously thinking about the "honor" scripture anymore, it's just an unspoken, but deeply embedded element of our culture and business practice. God has so blessed us over the years, there is no way we're going to consciously dishonor Him or His place in our business.

Naturally, there have been many scriptures which have come in and out of focus for a season since then. At one point, we found ourselves in an Isaiah 54:1-3 season, as we had been "enlarging the place of our tent," "lengthening our cords" and "strengthening our stakes," all "without holding back" (paraphrase of Isaiah 54:2). Soon, it became apparent the verse was literal for us, and not just figurative. We were bursting at the seams of our beloved office and needed to find a new one.

Somewhere during the search for a new office my friend Victor came out to pray with me. It is worth noting that Victor is a Spirit-filled believer originally from Egypt—God actually sent him to the United States as a missionary. He says God told him He was honoring America for all the missionaries we've invested in sending over the years, so He's sending some back to us. Praise God!

The first time Victor walked into our old office, he strongly felt God's presence, and carried some great encouragement to us. In meetings since, Victor and I have talked about and prayed into our Isaiah 54 season together. The journey of finding our new office was an intense one filled with some real spiritual battles, which I will discuss later in the book, and Victor faithfully helped pray us through those battles and into our new home.

Once we had moved into our new office it was time for Victor to visit again, to see for himself the beautiful outcome. As he walked up the stairs to our third floor space he felt the presence of God strongly again. Victor and I had only met a few years earlier, so while he certainly knew the "honor" verse, he didn't know the significance of that verse in the Yakabod story back to our earliest days. As Victor walked through the front door, struck by the magnificence of the first impression, Victor heard God ask him, "You know why My presence is here, don't you?"

"Why is that, Lord?" Victor asked.

"They have honored Me, so I have honored them." (Nobody's mastered the mic-drop moment quite like our Father, have they?)

If the launch of Yakabod came through a *moment,* of standing firm against the temptation to compromise, the growth of Yakabod came more through a *season* of faithfully standing firm. In what appeared to be a divine conspiracy, I found myself getting hungrier for more of God's presence, especially in my daily work-life, on any given Tuesday. I knew there had to be more to this "God's glory" thing than integrity and ethics, especially since I knew our call was to influence the marketplace at large, to be "in it" not "of it." It became apparent if the company was going to be live up to its name, "God's glory," we were uncovering more questions on how to do that than the answers we had yet received.

NO LONGER SERVANT, BUT FRIEND (BEYOND WORKING FOR HIM AND INTO WORKING WITH HIM)

When I started the company I knew it had to be for God's glory, and I was willing to embed that right into the company's name and put it on the side of the office building. When my business partner, Scott, merged his company with mine to form the current Yakabod he was in full agreement, but what does building a company for God's glory mean exactly?

We've spent nearly two decades wrestling with that question and honestly, I'm still not sure we have anything close to the whole picture. You need to have strong corporate ethics of course, and deep personal integrity, but we knew it was about more than ethics and integrity—those are table stakes. In the early days of wrestling with this I ran into a few companies building their brand on integrity, and it struck me that they were trying too hard. Their efforts came across almost as self-righteous. Aside from the seemingly ironic touch of hubris, if you have to tell everyone how ethical and integrity-filled your company is then perhaps it's a case of, "Methinks the lady doth protest too much."

In that same period, Enron would experience their spectacular collapse, while simultaneously proclaiming on their website and in their communications that they operated with the utmost integrity.[8] That did it for me. I knew there had to be more to this "God's glory" thing in the context of building a company than merely upholding integrity.

Our dilemma, though, was we also knew we weren't called to be a "Christian company." I actually wasn't sure what that was, but I had run into some of those companies in our formative years. Did it mean they only hired or did business with Christians? Is that even legal? I didn't understand it, but decided I wouldn't judge their call. *Maybe they're doing exactly what God called them to do*, I thought. As we pushed into "building a business for God's glory,"

> *We knew there was more to it than "integrity"—that's table stakes—but we also knew we weren't a "Christian company."*

however, it became apparent we were being called to something different. Our call was to build a business, not a church. In other words, it wasn't about holding Bible studies at lunchtime, posting tracts on the lunchroom bulletin board, or signing up volunteers for mission trips. I'm not saying that's wrong, or not somebody else's call for their business, but it *clearly* wasn't our call to replicate church functions in a business. Our call was to influence the marketplace at large, by operating as a business doing business activities for God's glory. To be *"in"* the secular marketplace as a light, but not *"of"* it. If we only hired Christians, or built our software for Christian organizations, we knew we'd totally miss that call.

Scott and I prayed together privately just about every day. In those days, our prayers were usually about the business or our team, and often for our customers as well. As the leaders of the company, we also knew it was important to carry a heart of gratitude, and to trust God as a matter of practice. We appointed a Board of Directors with members we trusted to hold us accountable to our faith in our business conduct. (Unfortunately, we had a major misstep there in the context of bringing our faith into Tuesday, but that's a story for later…)

Building on Core Values

As leaders, aside from the steps taken above, we weren't quite sure how to carry our faith over into the daily work life and operations of our small team… until we stumbled onto the notion of core values. Scott and I defined our company's core values very early on, even before we hired any full-time employees. We stated openly that Yakabod's core values were derived from our Jesus-centered faith, and they were non-negotiable in our corporate culture. We also acknowledged that employees were free to pursue whatever spiritual path (if any) they desired. If an employee felt the core values had been delivered by Martians for example, that was fine as long as they lived those values out at work. A prime benefit of having core

> *Core values became a key tool in building Kingdom culture while hiring people from all walks.*

values is they allowed us to effectively hire people from all walks, while still building a culture that honored God's glory. We will explore this intriguing concept in more depth in Chapter 11.

We determined one of our company core values was grace. It's fairly unique to see the word "grace" on a corporate website, and I guess it was an unwitting code word to other believers because we'd get résumés from Christians who assumed we were a "Christian company." They further assumed we should hire them on that basis alone, regardless of the required technical skills. (I'll rant a bit more on this topic in Chapter 13.) This just confirmed the understanding of our call—to build a business for God's glory, which is far different in ideology and practice than a church or a "Christian company."

Scott and I wrestled with what this meant, while proceeding in practice to build a team and culture based on core values. One of the challenges was we really didn't know where most of our team stood spiritually, except for a few who had told us they were believers. The team all knew where Scott and I stood, of course. The definition of Yakabod was on the website, after all. They had also heard me say it plenty in front of customers or partners who would ask about the company name. The team were also crystal-clear this burden to explain our name rested on Scott and I, not on them. While we never shied away from sharing a lesson rooted in our faith with the team, we were careful to use common business language to convey those lessons.

Occasionally I'd pray at a team function, but it would typically be at an off-hours event like a Christmas or holiday party, and always with the disclaimer, "I know God has blessed us, and I need to give thanks… but if that's not your thing, you're free to ignore me or slip out for a few minutes; and I won't even know because I'll have my eyes closed."

We never had a single issue in this regard because our employees never felt put-upon or pressured. There was no insider language, no Christian clique, and they were experiencing the effects of grace every day as defined in our business context. Who doesn't want to be treated with respect, honor, and dignity? I understand there are different levels of "overtness" that make sense in each work situation—and in some circumstances, *how* the Kingdom is carried into a situation has to be covert—but my point is, God will guide you to that level, and if you operate there it will likely be attractive to those around you.[9] (We'll unpack that more in Section 4.)

Over time, we began to understand it wasn't only our *words* that would give God glory in our context—not that we were afraid to speak about our faith—but our *actions* proved far more powerful to that end. We were giving God glory through the systemic, long-term, consistent pattern of our interactions with employees, customers, and stakeholders, as well as in the decisions we would make. There was no need to constantly remind our employees that the founders saw Yakabod's highest purpose as giving God glory. It was more important they could see this demonstrated in our actions over a long period of time, enabling them to translate that into their own context.

During that period we had one employee who was a self-proclaimed atheist (science and reason were his gods), but when he left us on good terms after a few years, he told his team leader he was really confused. It turns out he just couldn't reconcile what he'd experienced from Scott and me at work every day with the stereotypical Christian as portrayed by mainstream media. He had to reconsider his preconception that faith was a crutch for people who weren't smart enough to think for themselves.

The Divine Conspiracy

Just as I was settling into our "way of doing business," God engaged me in what the other Scott calls "the divine conspiracy." If you are a Jesus follower, you know exactly what I'm talking about. Something was stirring in my life, and it just seemed to come at me from all angles—the music I listened to, the podcast that popped up on my drive into work, an email from a coworker, a book referral from a friend—it all pointed to something in me, which God was working on. I didn't have language for it at first, I just knew it was about wanting more of His presence. Not in a theological sense, but in my every day, every hour, even every moment experience in my relationship with Him. Simply stated, I was hungry, and getting hungrier, for a deeper level of connection with God.

During that period I found myself wrestling with the interpretation of the company name. The name, technically, translated as "God's glory," but I told everyone who asked that we were building a company to "bring God glory." For some reason, the missing apostrophe "s" in my explanation really began to bother me. After a month or so, I was walking down East Street here in town when God hit me with, "The apostrophe 's' is supposed to be there, because you're supposed to bring God's glory."

I suddenly understood what He meant and exactly what the "stirring" was. He was calling us into a new season.

> *God was calling us to move beyond working for Him, and into working with Him.*

We had been trying our best to work for Him. Now it was time to work *with* Him. It was time to *carry* His glory into all situations, not to just honor Him with our actions. In other words, He was saying "I no longer call you servant, but friend" (a paraphrase of John 15:15).

This revelation shifted Yakabod into a whole new journey, accompanied by an entirely new set of questions. What does it look like to work with God as a Partner in your workplace? Would that even be possible? We came to realize that Jesus clearly felt it was possible. In fact, that's exactly what Jesus did. He said, "I only do what I see my Father doing, and only say what I hear my Father saying" (paraphrase of John 5:19 and 12:50b). That was Jesus, 24/7, partnering with His Father.

Well, you're probably thinking, *I'm not Jesus*. True, neither am I, but as Jesus followers, we do have "the mind of Christ," and we know we have the Holy Spirit inside of us, who is continually at work transforming us into the image of Christ. Just as John 15:15 tells us: while servants don't know what the master is doing, friends do! And we are called friends, even sons of God. The evidence revealing it's possible to partner with God is compelling. What if we could do what Jesus did for twenty minutes a day, where we are so connected with the Father we are emulating Him in our activities? That would change everything, wouldn't it? If we just did this for twenty minutes a day, much less an hour, imagine how different our workplace would be!

As we started pushing into that concept I'm not sure we figured out a lot of answers, but we sure kept running into more questions. If we're partnered with God, for example, He plays by a different set of rules to us, and His Kingdom works totally different than the worldly one. What would that look like, if His Kingdom, operating on His rules, showed up at your workplace next Tuesday?

For example, say you're a restaurant owner, it would be pretty cool if you could take a few fish and some bread and turn them into a meal for the whole evening's seating. Imagine the profit margin! On second thought, the revenue model may not work out so well, because Jesus didn't charge for that meal.

Joking aside, though, as we dug into the idea, more practical examples of the differences between this worldly kingdom and God's Kingdom arose. The typical workplace is marked by stress, chaos, anxiety, shame, guilt, manipulation, and plenty more undesirable attributes. Even with a great boss, not many people love going to work every day (there's a reason happy hour was invented). The question to ask is, which kingdom are all those undesirable attributes coming from? Certainly not God's Kingdom. You can tell by the markers: His Kingdom is marked by peace and joy. What if your workplace was predominantly marked by peace instead of stress? What if your workplace was marked predominantly by joy, instead of bitter envy and backbiting? I won't say we've mastered it, but it sure feels different in our office. We'll go into this more in Chapter 17, but it's different enough in our office that people very often remark about it; even those who aren't spiritually inclined.

I understand if many of you are thinking, *That's okay for you, you're the CEO! I don't have that kind of authority at my workplace. At my level, how can I have any bearing on whether my workplace looks more like the Kingdom?* If that is what you're thinking, I'd challenge you to get your faith out of Sunday, and into Tuesday and Wednesday and Thursday! You're underestimating your potential for *exponential* influence.

All Authority

The consequence of the resurrection is that Jesus has been given *all* authority in Heaven and on Earth. Not just some authority. Not just in the Church or only in "spiritual matters." Jesus has *all* authority. That means in your workplace too. Look at what Matthew 28:18-20 (KJV) says:

> "[18] And Jesus came and spoke to them, saying, 'All authority has been given to Me in heaven and on earth. [19] Go therefore and make disciples of all the nations, baptizing them in the name of the Father and of the Son and of the Holy Spirit, [20] teaching them to observe all things that I have commanded you; and lo, I am with you always, *even* to the end of the age." Amen.'"

Here Jesus is *delegating* His authority to those who believe in Him. This means you carry His spiritual authority with you wherever you are. In a practical sense, if you put peace and chaos in a room together, guess which one wins—no matter who the CEO is? Peace comes from the superior Kingdom. If there is a clash between Kingdom and kingdom, Kingdom always wins. If you're a member of that Kingdom, Jesus has already delegated to you all the authority you need to carry that Kingdom attribute of peace into your office and into the conference room. Even if the only influence you ever have on your workplace is making your cubicle, office space, or workbench, look more like peace and love than stress, anxiety, and anguish every day, wouldn't that still be awesome? Not to mention how amazingly attractive it would be to those around you.

We're still trying to figure out how a company can look more like the Kingdom each day, but recently God's given us even bigger questions, or at least He's given them to me. (I'm sure this is the next step in my call, but after much prayer, Scott realizes it's probably not his.) Those bigger questions are, if a company can look more like His Kingdom, can that spill out into the community? In other words, can a whole community look more like the Kingdom of our Lord than the kingdom of this world? If so, can a company—or an ecosystem of companies—play a role in that? Can a group

54

of companies working together, change the culture of a city?

Is that possible? Jesus seemed to think so…

Many of you, maybe most, are familiar with the Lord's Prayer found in Matthew 6:9-13. You probably also know the backstory of how the disciples asked Jesus to teach them how to pray. That's interesting in itself, because by that point they had been watching Jesus, and listening to Him pray for quite a while. You'd have thought they would have noticed the conversational intimacy He had with His Father by then; how He didn't really need a script. In any case, Jesus instructs His disciples with an example we know as the Lord's Prayer, the only structured prayer the Bible records Him teaching.

In the middle of this prayer, He says to pray that the Father's Kingdom come and His will be done, on Earth as it is in Heaven. I learned this prayer as a youngster and prayed it for decades, even before I knew Jesus, without thinking too deeply about it. I would encourage you to pause, however, and think about what Jesus is actually saying. He is telling us to pray that things on Earth would look like they do in Heaven. I've heard a noted pastor explain that Jesus wasn't saying to pray that you'd get to Heaven. *He said to pray Heaven would come here, to Earth!*

It made me wonder about such a possibility; could things here on Earth be as they are in Heaven? I'm no theologian, but I don't think Jesus would teach us a prayer that's not possible, or one that doesn't work. In fact, you don't have to read much of the historical account to quickly realize that everywhere Jesus went the sick were healed, the lame walked, the deaf heard, the blind saw, and even

> *Jesus proved it's entirely possible to bring Heaven to Earth. Then told us to do the same.*

the dead were raised to life again. It seems Jesus proved it's entirely possible to bring Heaven to Earth, and He started to fulfill the prayer Himself. In other words, as there's no deafness in Heaven, when Jesus showed up in a village, for whoever would receive it, there was no longer deafness in that village either.

You might be thinking, *Well, of course that's possible for Jesus, but how is that possible for me?* Jesus already answered this question. When He sent the twelve apostles out and later the seventy disciples in Luke chapters 9 and 10, He gave them dangerously few instructions: "Preach the Kingdom of God, and heal the sick…" In essence, He was saying, "Do all the things you saw me doing." To put it another way, He said, "Get busy making the Earth more like the Kingdom of Heaven, and when people wonder what's going on, tell them the superior Kingdom has arrived."

For many of you, this revelation changes everything, as it did for me. I understand it may be different to what you've grown up believing, so don't take my word for it. There have been several books written on this topic, so you can and *should* dig deeper, in prayerful contemplation. I can highly recommend one book that was transformative in my own journey; namely, *When Heaven Invades Earth*, by Bill Johnson,[10] though there are many other books on the subject too.

When we talk about "bringing the Kingdom" or some similar phrase, this is exactly what we're talking about. We're not talking about imparting any sort of religious structures or functions to a corporate environment. It's simply praying and doing what Jesus instructed us to do—to make things look more like Heaven than Earth in our sphere of influence.

Part of that is achieved in the realm of the natural. You don't have to be a Jesus follower to make some things look more like Heaven than Earth. For example, treating employees with respect and honor, rather than as assets to be leveraged for your personal advancement—that's Kingdom instead of kingdom. Anybody can treat others with respect and honor, and anyone you would consider for hire would agree that's good, no matter their spiritual standing.

A major part of this, though, is attained in the realm of the supernatural, and available only through a relationship with God. For instance, when Jesus sent the seventy disciples out in Luke 10, the ability to release their peace and take it back up again is all about an overflow of the presence of

God with them in the place. It is as though peace is a tangible presence, and a marker of the Kingdom of Heaven being at hand. If each of the seventy could release peace into a village, why couldn't you carry it into your conference room? You can try all you want of your own accord, but you can't release and take back peace without first establishing a relationship with God. The supernatural part of bringing the Kingdom is the ability for the believer to:

a) know what the Father is doing and/or would have you do in the situation at hand,

b) allow Him to do things through you that you can't do for yourself, and

c) trust that He'll do some miraculous things that only He can do.

I get that Jesus did this perfectly, and most of us are still learning how to walk in that reality... but the reason we don't see it more in our workplaces is not because it isn't available to us.

If you don't know Jesus, I pray today would be the day you see His goodness, and want more of it. That you would begin to understand (as I did back in Chapter 3), all He has saved you from if you will only believe in Him. I pray you see life without Him is emptiness, and an eternity without Him is quite literally hell. He's ready and willing to save you from all that. There's no magic prayer to memorize—simply ask Him.

Meanwhile, if you're a believer in Jesus you already know what He's saved you from, so I pray this is the day you would see all He's saved you *to!* That you'd find Him in your Tuesday, and every other day of the week. That He'd show you *how* you can make your own workplace look a little more like His Kingdom every day.

Okay, you have the backstory! We're now ready to look at some practical examples of "at work as in Heaven" we've gleaned from nearly two decades of trying to make our faith work on Tuesday...

SECTION 3: Lessons from Two Decades of Tuesdays

SECTION 3.1 INTRODUCTION

SECTION 4. INTRODUCTION

THINGS JUST WORK DIFFERENTLY IN THE KINGDOM

Any good adventure has a planning and preparation stage, sometimes an extensive one, before the actual adventure unfolds. The previous section focused on the former stage, as I shared how God positioned, called, and equipped me to launch and build our company, Yakabod. By the time I started, I knew He'd be a non-negotiable part of my Tuesday not just my Sunday; and I had some vague awareness that the conventional ways often ran counter to the Kingdom's ways. In this section, I'll share stories, experiences, and lessons learned from nearly two decades of the adventure itself—of building a company in a way that seeks to fully integrate my faith.

I've hinted in previous chapters—or maybe outright declared—that many so-called "best practices" are only so in an inferior kingdom, and that an approach taken in pursuit of the superior Kingdom may even be counter-intuitive to your business training. I'd love to tell you I started with a big list of these differences, and that we just went down the list to make sure we were doing the Kingdom practice instead of the kingdom one. For example, how are we going to approach software development as we grow to a team of ten instead of two people? Kingdom way is x, kingdom way is y, so clearly we'll do x. Check. As with any adventure, though, the path wasn't quite that clear. In fact, it's still not. In the early drafts of this book, I really figured I'd take a specific functional area, like marketing or engineering, and then contrast Kingdom business practices with kingdom one, so you'd have an extensive, if not exhaustive, list to get started. The more I got into it, however, the more I realized things aren't so neatly partitioned in real life, and neither have they been in our own adventure.

Making Sunday's Lessons Work on Tuesday

Do you remember the story of my friend Jim in Chapter 2, who took on his unwanted re-assignment by simply resolving that if he had to clean toilets then he'd clean them for the glory of Jesus? Unlike Jim, my assignment in starting a company was not unwanted. However, like Jim, in those early days of trying to make my Sunday work on Tuesday, I started very much as he did. I simply resolved if the Lord would give me the opportunity to start and build a company, I'd do it for His glory.

As I tried to figure out what that meant, the books and material available back then were good, but not necessarily plentiful. Perhaps I'm over-generalizing, but it seems with hindsight the authors, at least the ones I read back then, generally focused on biblical principles. You look at the circumstances in front of you, draw on your understanding of biblical principles, using reason and logic, to figure out how to apply the principles. The limitation is that this is all "natural." You are starting from a picture of this world, and attempting to influence circumstances or reshape outcomes to adhere to the biblical principles you think apply. Of course, you can also do that prayerfully, which may help supplement your own logic and reason with some divine wisdom. That's where we started, and if that's where you start, that's great. You have at least started. It's *way* better than keeping your faith locked up in Sunday. The problem is, this approach tops out. It's limited by the realm you're playing in. You can only make the kingdom as good as the kingdom can be.

"At work as in Heaven" is an entirely different approach. It starts with Heaven as the model. The one clarifying question becomes, "Is this the way things work in the Kingdom of Heaven?" If not, you partner with God to transform the situations so they do. You're not working only from principle, but rather from relationship. Almost by definition you're shifting beyond natural into "supernatural." Since you're after Kingdom (the ideal

> *The one clarifying question becomes, "Is this the way things work in the Kingdom of Heaven?"*

situation, the way God's perfect design intends it to be) as opposed to kingdom (the best it's going to be in a fallen world), it's almost certainly going to require some supernatural intervention to transform things in that way. It might be some prophetic wisdom or insight, maybe it's some of His grace at work through you, maybe it's some improbable thing "coincidentally" working out, or possibly it's an outright miracle where He intervenes to do the things only He can do, but it's likely going to involve the supernatural in some way. That doesn't mean principles don't matter. It just means they are set in a much higher context.

We didn't start out with the concept of "at work as in Heaven" and we'd not claim to be experts at it yet. I've intentionally retained the sense of that progression as this section unfolds. For example, we solidified our approach to cash flow in the earliest days of the company. I'd seen and experienced some things in other companies that just didn't seem right or make sense, so I knew I wasn't going to do those things in any company of mine. Meanwhile, I understood some basic biblical principles and let those guide me. There was certainly a lot of prayer involved, but back in those early days I don't remember us actively dialoguing with the Lord around the question, "Is this the way cash flow works in Your Kingdom?" Now with the benefit of hindsight I can look at our approach, articulate it with clarity in a Kingdom-versus-kingdom context, and see why the approach we took— using our intuition—actually worked! (I can't say it happens that way all the time...) Likewise, we're now able to make hard decisions around cash flow and refine our approach, if needed, from a broader and deeper faith in the promises and ways of the Kingdom.

A bit later in our journey, as you'll see in the middle chapters of the section, we were starting to understand the notion of partnering with God and the Kingdom context. Even so, we still didn't have a big list of contrasts between Kingdom and kingdom business practices to draw from. In fact, looking back now, I can see we really only had a clear grasp on a few such contrasts. It's just that once we "got it," and really internalized one of those concepts, we applied that understanding to *everything* we did. You might say that when we were "transformed by the renewing of our mind" we made sure we did the same thing to our business practices. For example, when we fully "owned" the sense of living from God-given identity rather than from others' perceptions or expectations (i.e. authenticity), we made sure it flowed through everything.

We're a software company, so of course that meant our authenticity had to be evident in the way we built software and the functionality of our software. To a greater extent, though, that meant our sales, marketing, operations, project management, customer interactions, hiring processes, and even our coffee. It all came from who God made us to be, rather than being driven by external expectations or a desire to shape others' perceptions. (Before you think that makes it "all about us," remember that part of who God made us to be is an active, intentional blessing to someone else...) That's an ongoing process, by the way, as we hire new people, expand our team, and scale into new markets. It's still an active process of pursuing authenticity to our God-given identity as the company grows, and continuing to refine practices as we become aware of discrepancies.

As you'll read in the later chapters in this section, like "Not in My Town" or "Kingdom Culture," at this point of our ongoing adventure, we now do our best to start in prayerful dialog with the Lord around the key question "How would this work in Your Kingdom?" When we do it right, that's our starting point now in determining the approach we take and the decisions we make. It's a wonderfully clarifying concept because there's just one question to ask. Everything else unfolds from there.

Come up Higher

Let me show you how this has played out in practice. As you'll see, it's been evolutionary, not a few discrete steps. There's so much nuance here, I hope I haven't obscured the profound implications of this shift from intuitive and/or principle-based decisions to the identity and presence-based decisions of "at work as in Heaven." In a later chapter, I'll unpack how a minor little operational detail—serving our own locally-roasted Yakablend coffee—actually matters. It might seem odd, but it really is a Kingdom thing.

Initially we were just acting intuitively. We loved great coffee and thought it would be cool to have our own. We didn't understand any tie-in to core values, we certainly didn't do it to express our core values, but it is true it happened organically *from* our core values. If budgets had ever become so lean back then that we needed to cut deep on expenses I would have never even considered slashing the coffee spend. Software teams work better when caffeinated, and the hit to team morale would far outweigh what little we'd save. In other words, I would have made the decision back then based on both tangible and intangible costs. (I've been places where executives cut company-supplied coffee at the first hint of fiscal turbulence without ever considering the intangible costs. So I considered this a more "elevated view" in decision making back then.) Sometime later, I realized the connection between coffee and core values—that providing good coffee was actually an expression of our core values.

Some time after that, I realized the connection from coffee and core values was actually a connection to identity and authenticity. In other words, our coffee was not just one little marker we were adhering to our core values, it was a simple but important element in a visitor or employee experiencing our core values! We weren't trying to artificially shape your experience of us, but rather it was one small act in transparently communicating who we are.

Now I can see this all relates to Kingdom and presence. It's not just the way someone experiences us, it's even more. It's a component in your relationship with us, something that attracts you, forming a small little bond, one of those reasons you want to be here. In some offices, you might bond over a sports team ("How about them Orioles?"). In our office, that little bond starts from hospitality in which you experience a little of the grace in our culture, which most likely includes coffee. So now, no matter how lean things might get, I'd *never* cut the coffee budget, because I understand the connection to Kingdom and "at work as in Heaven."

Can you see the nuance in the progression? I wouldn't have cut the coffee budget fifteen years ago—the same decision, the same outcome. At each of those stages I described—understanding the connection to core values, then to identity and authenticity—it would still have been the same decision and the same outcome, but from a progressively broader and higher perspective. The nuance, and power, is that my decision now, on this simple little thing, would come from an entirely different and higher plane. It's now in the context of the Kingdom, in full consideration of spiritual implications, rather than purely practical or earthly considerations.

Which means in this one matter I'm that much closer to "taking my heavenly seat," that much closer to seeing things from the Lord's perspective on this. I doubt I have to remind you His ways are infinitely higher than our ways! Accordingly, decisions I make from a Kingdom perspective are authentic, powerful, authoritative, and there's a freedom in those decisions! If you're thinking I've made way too much fuss over a hypothetical decision about a coffee budget, then perhaps I've inadequately explained the profound thing at play here. If I were forced to make the hypothetical decision above I wouldn't be agonizing over it, stewing on it, wondering what God is saying about it, deliberating how I "give Him glory" in it, worried about getting it wrong… I wouldn't even really think much about it. I'd know this little thing is aligned with the Kingdom and I'd press ahead in joyful confidence.

> *Decisions made from a Kingdom perspective are authentic, powerful, and authoritative.*

How often have you experienced that in your decisions? (I'm not suggesting I have this level of clarity all the time. Even most of the time. I am, however, hungry for the joy, freedom, and perspective my "heavenly seat" brings when I manage to sit in it!)

Only Took Me Twenty Years

Of course, we didn't have any of that clarity when we started nearly twenty years ago. I'm showing you this progression to encourage you that getting started is easier than you think. I hope the subsequent chapters in this section will encourage you to *just get started!* If you want to start by simply applying some biblical principle to the thing you're facing at work, the "golden rule" perhaps, that's great. It's one small little step closer to "at work as in Heaven" and a great place to start. You don't need to see the whole path or nuance I described above to start taking steps.

Ultimately, though, I hope to save you the twenty years of slow learning, missteps, and confusion I pushed through to finally "get it," so you can jump right to the clarity it took me so long to settle into. Namely, that you would have the awareness and sensitivity to look at specific situations in your workplace— the real stuff you are doing every day—whether that means cleaning toilets or running a major corporation. I would like you to ask, whether proactively or reactively, "Is this the way things work in the Kingdom of Heaven?" then have some conversation with the Lord to figure it out. You don't have to start at this more advanced level of course, but there's no reason not to either.

I'll highlight specific Kingdom-versus-kingdom contrasts which we've applied to our business practices as the chapters in the section unfold. Those contrasts serve as examples you can consider and perhaps use alongside your workplace situations. Likewise, in the final chapter in this section I'll offer several more contrasts for you to consider. These contrasts are clearly relevant to Kingdom business but we don't fully understand how to apply them to everything we do yet. We're experimenting of course, but at this point we know a lot more about the questions than the answers. The fact that things work differently in the Kingdom of Heaven is a rich topic, and we're only scratching the surface.

> *You don't need a checklist or a principle, only an open heart to seek God's Kingdom for the workplace issue facing you.*

As I mentioned earlier, you don't need a big, comprehensive checklist of contrasts. You simply need an open heart to seek God's Kingdom for that workplace issue in front of you, and the resolve to apply what He shows you.

Hike Your Own Hike

There's an expression amongst those who hike the entire Appalachian or Pacific Crest Trail in a season that says, "hike your own hike." It's meant to convey that we each may employ different methods and have different experiences on our respective thru-hikes, and that's okay. This is sage advice for Kingdom business as well. I would like to be very clear on this point—I'm not suggesting we have this all figured out, or that you have to follow our examples in the subsequent chapters to do it right. I'm just sharing some experiences we've had and lessons we've learned in wrestling through real business problems, while dialed into the spiritual implications of the decisions we're making. I'm not offering a prescribed set of rules, principles, or formulas; in fact, I would consider it surprising if everything worked out exactly the same way for you.

Principles may lend themselves to formulas and repeatable results whereas relationships don't. Ultimately, this is all about your relationship with the Lord. He's made you different to me, and He has a different purpose and destiny for your organization than He does for ours. That's why you need to partner with Him. That's also why I've made a point of including stories and practices where relevant, from other friends pushing into this concept; because you'll see something a little different in their businesses, but no less Kingdom-based!

Does Kingdom Business Actually Work?

The obvious question is, does all this Kingdom stuff work? It's a fair question since we've all seen some typical business school best practices produce some measurable, positive results. There's a reason they were designated best practices, after all. So if Kingdom business practices are supposed to be superior, do they actually produce superior results? Like right now, in your real world business? Not in some future Heaven-like place, but in your normal everyday have-to-go-to-work-to-collect-a-paycheck workplace?

As you'll see in this section, our experience proved this to be a resounding *yes*. At Yakabod we've realized some very practical benefits by pursuing "at work as in Heaven" within various aspects of our business administration. These include our recruiting, retention, productivity, marketing and sales, customer engagement, corporate financial posture, and many more. For example, we've found our Kingdom culture gives us an obvious home-court advantage with customers, and in recruiting candidates. Following Kingdom practices for cash management that were generally counter-intuitive to "best practices" we've bootstrapped, self-funded, and never had to use "other people's money" to build a successful technology business. We also have an uncharacteristically low employee turnover rate for our market segment. I understand success can be measured many ways, and we'll explore that topic specifically in Chapter 28, but in terms of the things important to us, Yakabod provides all the proof *we* need to know that Kingdom business practices work. We will certainly continue to build our business on them.

While Kingdom practices undoubtedly work to the advantage of a corporate entity, don't be surprised if these practices are opposed! Christ

> *Kingdom practices definitely work, but don't be surprised if they're opposed.*

has all authority, and His is the superior Kingdom, but there remains an ongoing rebellion. For more insight, re-read Daniel 10, which provides some insight into the unseen battle often influencing our tangible experience. In Daniel's case, it was a twenty one day delay. The beauty of practicing Kingdom vision within your workplace is that the will of God always supersedes any opposition. Perseverance is usually the key.

All about the "How"

I need to reiterate that most of the Kingdom concepts highlighted in the following chapters are not some unique revelation or even my own original research. In the "inflection point period" I talked about in Chapter 5, I had a forty-minute commute to work each way. Every day I was devouring podcasts, books, conference replays—anything I could find that was even tangentially related to Kingdom culture, the 7 Mountain Mandate, or partnering with God in daily life.

To be clear, I am standing on the shoulders of spiritual giants when I share certain techniques, principles, and deep truths. More specifically, I have been influenced by a myriad of great teachings, many coming from Bethel Church Redding. I can point to some specific sermons by Bill Johnson, Kris Vallotton, and Eric Johnson, along with guest presenters like Steve Thompson, Andy Mason (of the Heaven in Business ministry), and various other conference speakers. As I mentioned in chapter 1, the Lord has also used great content from other leaders like Ed Silvoso, Lance Wallnau, John Eldredge and Ransomed Heart Ministries, Johnny Enlow, and many others to help shape my thinking on this.

Naturally, none of this is relevant without the foundational basis of scripture and the illuminating voice of the Holy Spirit. I'm also not claiming any of the "what" or "why" is somehow my original work, or that I know the authors and speakers mentioned, or that they somehow endorse this book. None of the above! I'm just saying plenty of people smarter than me have been focused on the theological foundations from which I draw. My contribution is simply the active experience of prayerfully wrestling to put all this into practice at work every day.

Ultimately, I pray our experiences in the succeeding chapters give you a sense that things really do work differently in the Kingdom, and fill you with a confidence that the Kingdom has practical application to your workplace every day too. As you discover specific examples from your own workplace, I'd love to hear the before and after (scott@atworkasinheaven.com).

With that, let's get practical and start with the topic almost every business worries about most—cash.

SECTION 3.2: CASH

CASH IS KING (BUT NOT NECESSARILY KINGDOM)

I know we aren't all called to be entrepreneurs or to run business operations, but if you are, you can't do it without thinking about cash often (or maybe even all the time). There's a reason for the startup ecosystem cliché that declares "cash is king."

When I ventured out on my own, I was somewhat ill prepared to build or run the financial operations for a company, since I progressed in my career through an engineering track. I pursued an MSEE degree (Masters of Science in Electrical Engineering) in the evenings, in parallel with the first few years of my career. I already had some inclination by then that I'd start or run a business someday. With a little more foresight, I'd have been wise to pursue an MBA during those years, but by the time I finished the MSEE program I was emotionally done with school.

Better Than an MBA

So, with no formal training in financial or business operations, my knowledge of such matters had to be gleaned from first-hand experience in some of the companies in which I was employed. I'll share some of the more formative lessons I learned, related to cash flow:

Lesson 1: We're an innovative, creative, breakthrough kind-of company—even though we make our employees ask permission for potty breaks! I'm sure you've heard tech companies brag about their technical prowess while also proudly asserting "our employees are our most important asset." While working for one of my mentors in one of these companies, a large technology services firm, my mentor called a meeting and brought in a working lunch; no caviar or foie gras, just some deli sandwiches and chips. Later, he filled in the details on his expense report, including names of the attendees, as required. When the expense report came back from the accounting department, it had been rejected. The reason? His receipt showed charges for a full twelve-pack of Coke—but there were only eleven people enumerated on his expense report. So the whole report was rejected as non-reimbursable. Never mind that he was running a hundred-million-dollar division of the company at the time.

Lesson 2: We're all in this together. Except for me. I worked in another technology firm that struck a somber tone and delivered this message: times are tough, but we're all in this together, so we all need to suck it up, get more done with less, put in more hours for the same pay, sacrifice for each other and the team, and charge ahead. The research and development budget, as well as the business development budgets were cut, support staff were laid off, the coffee mess was shut down, and more. Yet, in that very same quarter, the business unit chief embarked on a luxurious remodel of his multi-room office suite. I'm not talking about a paint job and a few new pictures, but a multi-month, wall-moving overhaul costing several hundred-thousand dollars (in a leased building, no less).

Lesson 3: *Cash is tight. So you're going to lend us some at no interest.* One firm had some projects overseas, which meant key people often traveled for extended durations (while incurring significant expenses). For some reason, the company decided they would no longer issue cash travel advances to those employees, even though travel was mandatory. Employees would be required to front all the expenses from their personal funds, and would be reimbursed after they submitted an expense report following the completion of their trip. About the same time, the company decided thirty days was insufficient to accurately process those expense reports, so the employees would often be reimbursed between sixty and ninety days later.

Lesson 4: *Congratulations. You're Promoted! Hope You Like Your Pay Cut.* This example happened more recently, but it's similar to many I experienced in earlier years. A friend's wife was a sales account executive who spent two years pursuing a large, company-changing deal from which she was entitled to a generous commission. Shortly after the customer announced her team had won the deal, she was called into her boss's office to be rewarded with a big promotion for her extensive contributions to the company's growth. In addition to the powerful new title, she'd also receive an increase in her salary by a few percentage points. The catch? Commissions were for sales reps, not executives, so naturally she would no longer receive the commission for the big contract she had just brought in. (More explicitly—the commission she was due was worth three-to-five times the amount they were proposing for the raise.) She pretty quickly said, "No thanks! I'll keep my current role, responsibilities, and the commission." So, just as quickly, they fired her on some made-up charges—all to avoid paying the commission they'd promised her, and which she had rightfully earned.

If you've spent any time in the corporate world, you've probably seen all of the above—and a whole lot worse. I may have an engineering degree, not an MBA, but even I understood the experiences related above formed a "what *not* to do" list. I wasn't thinking from a Kingdom-versus-kingdom lens while many of those lessons were unfolding, in fact I wasn't even a Jesus follower at the time, but it doesn't take much discernment to realize which kingdom the examples above illustrate.

No Paycheck for You, Because It's "Ministry"

We expect churches and non-profit organizations to behave with integrity, but a cautionary note, Jesus people, before you point the finger at "evil corporate America," my experiences in the church and non-profit world haven't always been much better...

The church board called for a congregational meeting at a small but growing church I attended early in my faith journey. The agenda was to discuss raising the pastor's salary. Every Sunday the pastor would present a well-planned, excellent, insightful, Holy-Spirit-inspired teaching. More than that, he was also establishing and mentoring a powerful team, not only bringing growth but setting up the infrastructure to sustain it. In other words, this pastor was no solo caregiver to the flock, he was a visionary leader. The board of elders proposed a small increase to his already modest salary. The pastor would have been happy with all this, in spite of having the skills and qualifications to command a much higher salary elsewhere. Even so, the proposed increase was met with some unexpected grumbling amongst the congregation. One guy in particular stood up and even complained about how a pastor shouldn't be growing rich off the church, and asked whether he was there to minister or to make money?

> *You might expect that some corporations behave badly with money. My experience is many churches and non-profits don't do much better.*

The worst part of this ordeal is that the pastor and his family were sitting in the front row, listening to these objections from people they'd been faithfully serving. Eventually, after more grumbling from more congregants, one elder stood up and put his foot down, defending the proposed raise. Matter-of-factly, he said it was consistent with published salary levels for local public school principals—which was the elder team's benchmark—and that's what it was going to be! Discussion over. I really admired that elder's fortitude and resolve, and thought his approach to be good, reasonable, and wise. (Did anyone—especially the pastor—*really* think one would grow rich on a principal's salary?)

I was young in my faith, but I was dumbfounded. I sat there thinking, *Hold it, this is the guy we've entrusted to be our leader and teacher—the spiritual mentor of our families. We can see he's doing an awesome job; don't we want to invest in the absolute best pastor we can find? Forget the principal salary. If we have our priorities straight, shouldn't this guy be the highest paid in the room or perhaps the county?*

I'm sure some of the grumblers considered themselves more spiritual because of their "holy" stance on keeping the church's expenditures low for pastor's pay. Like that money should be spent elsewhere, at the soup kitchen or something. Of course, that was Judas' attitude in John 12:5, too.

I sometimes encountered a similar mindset when I sang lead vocals in a modern Christian rock band. When we played at bars or clubs, there was never any quibbling about our rate—the manager would just pay us our reasonable fee. (Even so, after the considerable investment in gear, travel expenses, time, and administration, the fee was more subsidy than revenue. In other words, we certainly weren't making any money.) Many of the churches that booked us, though, expected us to show up at a church event and play free of charge, which we often did in the early days, until we learned those same churches frequently treated us like we were bothersome background noise for their event.

Cash Works Differently in the Kingdom

At some point we've all heard the expression, "Cash is king!" Before we examine this statement I'd like to be clear, cash is important to any

81

organization, whether business or non-profit. It's even more important to a startup. Unfortunately, there's a worldview lurking beneath the expression, and it's a decidedly self-serving view. Since the goal is to get and keep as much cash as you can, all sorts of manipulative practices, like those described above, are deemed acceptable. In each case, cash was treated as an asset to be hoarded; either on behalf of the organization, or on behalf of individuals.

Sometimes cash is hoarded in the business world so it can later be used as "leverage." Leverage isn't necessarily bad—in fact, it can be useful when properly applied—but it can also be a code word for "manipulate." You can spot the manipulation in the not-to-do list above, because in every case one party benefits at another party's expense. There's a clear winner and clear loser to the transaction.

> *If cash is king, it behaves a whole lot like other kings in the worldly kingdom.*

If cash is king, it behaves a whole lot like other kings in the worldly kingdom in that it abuses its power by "lording over people like the Gentiles do" (paraphrase of Matthew 20:25).

Hoarding and manipulation is just not the way it works in God's Kingdom, because it's unnecessary—God's resources are unlimited! For some reason I've always loved the Psalmist's proclamation that God owns "the cattle on a thousand hills" (Psalm 50:10, NLT). Maybe because it always struck me that He can simply speak the Word to make another thousand hills! Of course, the Bible is filled with examples of God's unlimited resources and His faithful provision in equipping His followers to do what He's called them to do:

- On at least two separate occasions, Jesus fed thousands of people with just a few fish and some loaves of bread. After everyone had eaten their fill, there was way more food left over than there had been before Jesus blessed and multiplied it (see Mark 6 and Mark 8).

- When the Israelites wandered in the wilderness for forty years, God supplied them with manna to eat every day. The people were told not to hoard any for the following day, but only to gather enough for their daily needs. Any extra manna gathered was rotten the following day. The lesson in this was to trust God for provision—for your daily bread every day, as stated in the Lord's Prayer—rather than relying on accumulating for yourself. Take note, however, the people still had to gather their own manna every day (comparable to doing daily work) but they learned to trust God for their supply. In similar fashion, when they had no water God supplied water from a rock.

- When Jesus sent out His twelve disciples, and then the seventy, He told them on both occasions not to take anything with them apart from a cloak, sandals, and a staff, because all their needs would be provided for by God.

- Jesus taught us to consider the ravens (Luke 12:22-31), because they neither sow nor reap, nor do they store up food in barns—yet our heavenly Father feeds them. In other words, ravens aren't strategically investing in their future to become self-sustaining; rather they are constrained to gather what's already available, yet God makes sure there is always plenty available to sustain them.

- In Matthew 7:9-11, Jesus asks "Which of you, if your son asks for bread, will give him a stone? Or if he asks for a fish, will give him a snake? If you, then, though you are evil, know how to give good gifts to your children, how much more will your Father in heaven give good gifts to those who ask him!"

- The scripture says to seek first His Kingdom and His righteousness, and the rest of these will be given to you as well (Matthew 6:33). The "rest of these" being a reference to our daily needs.

- Scripture tells us (Matthew 5:45) God allows the sun to rise on both good and evil people, and He sends rain to the righteous and unrighteous, providing even for those who don't follow Him.

Likewise, because God's Kingdom is one of abundance with unlimited resources to fulfill God's purposes, Jesus followers *have not been given license,* whether it be in business or in their personal dealings, to deal with others within the framework of a poverty (kingdom) mindset. Consider the following principles, based on the assumption the Kingdom is one of abundance:

> *God's Kingdom is one of abundance with unlimited resources to fulfill God's purposes.*

- There is great wisdom in Proverbs 22:7 which advises against borrowing money irresponsibly, explaining "the borrower is slave to the lender."

- The Bible advises us not to "muzzle an ox when it treads out the grain," meaning we are not to manipulate or cheat our workers so we can hoard cash while starving those who labor on our behalf, for "The laborer deserves his wages" (1 Timothy 5:18).

   ○ Likewise, God will send judgment on the rich oppressors who withhold wages from those who "mow their fields" (James 5:1-4).

- Scripture also informs us, "The Lord detests the use of dishonest scales, but he delights in accurate weights" (Proverbs 11:1, NLT). Simply put, God tells us not to manipulate or defraud others for our own gain.

I think a line from Bono in U2's song, "Bullet the Blue Sky"[11] presents an apt summary of all the points above: "Well, the God I believe in isn't short of cash, mister."

Contrast the earlier not-to-do examples with scriptural promises and it becomes clear the root of the problem is a lack of faith in God's promises to provide "seed for the sower and bread for the eater." Perhaps it's because the cash-hoarders have no interest in God, or maybe they're believers who just haven't learned that Sunday matters on Tuesday. In either event, God is a good father who will not only meet your basic needs, but often provides in extravagant abundance so you can use it to be a blessing to others.

This is true for personal finances, and it's equally true for corporations.

Observing the principles above, we can certainly begin to discern some strategies for managing cash as we see the contrast between the abundance of the Kingdom versus the scarcity of the kingdom. Clearly, though, it's a different thing to understand the beautiful promises in the scripture verses above than it is to face the reality of trying to make payroll next Tuesday. We've faced plenty of those situations over the years, so let me share with you what we did. Then we'll explore why it actually worked!

CASH IN THE KINGDOM

Now, as the preceding chapter features the what-not-to-do list, what are you actually *supposed* to do? Long before I saw from a kingdom-versus-Kingdom lens, I had the not-to-do list of experiences coupled with the biblical principles shared in the previous chapter to draw on. As I shared in Chapter 4, I had just enough faith to trust God would honor those who honor Him; that if we were doing what He called us to do, He would provide the resources to do it.

Managing Cash—When There's Little to Manage

Fortunately, I resolved even before Yakabod launched, that if God was in it, I'd have to trust He'd provide everything we required to make it work. Of course, that included cash since I really didn't have much of it stored up when I started. I was holding tightly onto many scriptures that promised exactly that—God would provide. While I grasped the need to understand the market, I didn't need to be consumed by how much money other startups had, or how much "market share" we could grab. I just needed to trust God had more than enough for us. Without having to take it from someone else.

Even before I had "Kingdom language" to describe it, I knew I hated it when companies treated their employees, including me, in the manner shared in the examples I opened with in the previous chapter. I knew any company I was leading couldn't do that. Out of those formative experiences, some basic operating principles regarding cash emerged, and solidified, long before we had much cash to manage:

> *I just needed to trust God had more than enough for us. Without having to take it from someone else.*

- *If we owe it, we pay it.* Whether it was expense reports (or payroll) for employees, or accounts payable for suppliers and partners—we wouldn't manipulate anybody with our cash. This wasn't something we instituted when we had lots of cash. This was our approach in the earliest days of bootstrapping, when our most critical metric was: "days until the brick wall" with regard to when we'd run out of cash—given the current posture. Even when that number shrank dangerously close to zero—if we owed it, we paid it. Early and often. No games.

- *If we can't afford it, we don't buy it.* If you pay what you owe early and often, as advocated above, then you have a pretty clear sense of what you can afford. (There's no looking at all the cash in the bank, and then forgetting all of it had already been specifically allocated.) Likewise, if we didn't think we had enough work to cover a new hire for at least six months, and preferably a year, we didn't hire them. We knew if the business failed it would be difficult enough to go back to a "real job," let alone knowing a good portion of that paycheck would be spent digging our families out from under a pile of debt we incurred in a failed venture. We took that risk off the table. If we couldn't see where the cash was coming from, we simply didn't buy it.

- *We'd much rather spend* our *money, than someone else's.* The corollary to the previous bullet is, if we can't afford it we aren't going to use other people's money to buy it. To be clear, we weren't going to carry bad debt. I'm not saying there's never any reason to borrow money or take an equity investment—in fact there are some legitimate scenarios where it's not only desirable, but more or less required. In our case, though, we weren't going to take on any debt unless it was absolutely necessary, and only as verified through a whole lot of prayer. As a self-funded, bootstrapping startup, we simply didn't want to borrow money under the influence of our own Kool-Aid (i.e. believing our own over-optimistic forecasts), or lose control by selling equity, only to then spend the funds on things we really couldn't afford.

- *We'll pay what things are worth.* It's not that we don't accept discounts, or try to find good value as a buyer. As a seller, however, we never did have a good experience with customers who were looking for fire-sale prices on our services or software. We knew if they didn't value our offerings at our proposed pricing levels, they wouldn't value our employees after we started working a project with them. It was an early warning sign the project had little chance of ever succeeding. Since we didn't want our employees or our company dishonored in that way, we refused to treat our suppliers or partners that way. When you strive for excellence, it's counterintuitive to push for rock-bottom prices as a buyer.

I'm not saying this is the only way to do it. As you consider your own use of cash—whether it be in a business context, or in your own personal finances—you may come up with additional or complementary principles that help your situation work more like the Kingdom than the kingdom.

To clarify and balance the previous chapter, I'd like to be very clear— I'm not saying you should be foolish with cash. Clearly, cash is important. Corporate-survival-level important. You can't start or run a company (or have a job in one) without cash to fuel the operations. That's why at Yakabod, from the beginning we've always known exactly how much cash we had and how long it would last. Likewise, we've always kept a cash reserve of at least two-to-three months on hand. This strategy worked for us because we had long-term, stable contracts. Another local firm, who works largely on smaller, short term contracts, built up to a six-month cash reserve. Clearly, I'm not suggesting you "wing it" with cash. I'm suggesting you view it through a different lens. Cash should be regarded as a resource to be used for the Kingdom rather than an asset to be hoarded.

Similarly, don't be fooled into thinking these principles are an all-inclusive formula. You have to apply discernment to your situation. If you're praying about your finances as you should be, the Holy Spirit might lead you into building a deeper reserve than two-to-three months, as Joseph did to prepare for those seven years of famine (Genesis 41:47-49). Alternatively, He may lead you to invest a chunk of your current reserve on some opportunity He is leading you into. Building a reserve is just wise stewardship, but it doesn't replace seeking out God's ongoing counsel.

> *I'm not suggesting you "wing it" with cash. I'm suggesting you view it through a different lens.*

Harder to Walk Than Talk

I can tell you, treating cash like a Kingdom resource rather than a scarce one, has not always been easy (as you might recall from my "brick wall" stories in Chapter 4). I'll also share some stories later about realizing the Lord was calling me to mentor our team in gratitude and generosity— even as a potential cash crunch approached. At this point, though, our "cash principles" are not normally something we even consciously think about. The Kingdom-aligned principles above are deeply embedded in our corporate culture.

A good example that reflects these Kingdom principles is an incident that occurred a few years back. After we'd extended a lease on our previous office, we discovered we hadn't been paying the escalation on the rent. The renewed lease called for us to pay three percent more in monthly rent for the second year than the first. We'd been faithfully paying our bills to this landlord for ten years at that point so they never noticed, but *we* picked it up and called them immediately. We apologized for having missed the clause, assured them we'd send a check covering the entire discrepancy in the mail immediately, but we'd also FedEx it if they preferred.

They were flabbergasted, and just simply couldn't believe we had actually called them. (The backstory is they had a reputation for being quite "cheap" and slow to pay their own subcontractors; in other words, they'd have never made the call if they were in our shoes.) Fortunately, they were also gracious in accepting our apology. It was our mistake. Honestly, we could have just ignored it, and they'd have never noticed until long after we moved out—but we owed it, so we paid it, without hesitation. We knew we needed to honor them with our cash, not cheat them out of it; and "Integrity" was painted on the walls as one of our core values, after all.

Re-Evaluating from a Kingdom Lens

In Yakabod's early days, we kind of stumbled into our own approach to cash flow, the to-do list above, by learning from our what-not-to-do experiences and some basic biblical principles. I'm pleased to note, in spite of our blissful naiveté back then it worked, and still does! Now that we try to base our approach in situations like this from a Kingdom context, it's interesting to look back to understand *why* our approach actually worked! In business, this type of analysis is often called a "post-mortem" (of course there's no "mortem" in the Kingdom). In my mind, this is like what I imagine happened when, after discovering the theory of relativity, Einstein looked back on Newtonian physics and thought, *Huh, so this is why that all worked.*

Let's look retrospectively at how our early gut-instinct approach to cash actually worked within the higher-level Kingdom by exploring some explicit contrasts.

Abundance, Not Scarcity

The what-not-to-do examples in the previous chapter, in both corporate and church settings, all originated from a spirit of poverty. Worldly wisdom says "cash is king," and accordingly, you should collect as much cash as early as you can, spend as little as late as you can, and in the meantime hoard all you can. In the process, of course, other involved parties—whether employees, partners, suppliers, customers, stakeholders, or pastors—are reduced to "assets" to be manipulated for the sake of extracting or preserving as much cash as possible.

Some people are obvious about their manipulation of others for cash—consider the much-caricatured used-car salesman. Other people are really polite about it—that "friend" you haven't heard from for two years who was "thinking about you" and would love for you to come to a multi-level marketing party they have planned. It's all the same net effect. In both cases, they're viewing you as an asset from whom cash can be extracted.

These people could also be described as having a "poverty mindset." In this view, cash (or resources) are finite. What this means is the more you have, the less there is available for me so I need to grab all I can, by any means possible—even if I have to manipulate (or trample) you or someone else to get it. Maybe the word "manipulation" feels too strong for some readers. Let me put it another way:

> *If your interactions are heavily slanted towards what you can get, rather than what you have to offer, you're operating from a poverty mentality.*

if your interaction with another person (or organization or entity) is heavily slanted towards what you can get from them rather than what you can give them—then that's a poverty mentality busy at work propagating kingdom, not Kingdom.

If the spirit of poverty is the main perpetrator of these kingdom practices, I suspect the spirit of jealousy is a willing accomplice. Since cash is a finite resource in a kingdom view, and we're all competing for that same limited amount, it follows the more you have the less will be available for me. Jealousy comes into play where there's no gratitude for what you *do* have or when you feel entitled to more than you currently have. In the case of the grumbling parishioners, this jealousy surfaced as "I don't have much so the pastor shouldn't either, because that's not 'spiritual.'" (Perhaps that's a part of the reason they didn't have more!)

In contrast, you've likely come across examples of the opposite mindset, where people who have little to nothing are overflowing with joy because of their gratitude and connection with the Lord. These people are operating from an abundance mindset, even if they don't yet possess the material abundance.

If you want your area of influence to look more like the Kingdom of Heaven, it begins with an understanding that Heaven's resources are infinite, and your good Father provides to you in abundance from His great abundance.

While we were definitely concerned with stewardship (more on that next), I hope you see that in our intuitive approach to cash flow we didn't treat cash as a finite resource. There was the cash we had at the time, which was indeed finite and needed to be used wisely, however, in terms of what we required beyond what we had, we also implicitly trusted the Lord had, and would provide, all the resources required to accomplish His plans and purpose for the company we were building to honor Him. We wouldn't have been able to describe it as such back then, but in essence, we started from an abundance mindset. We never felt we had to compete with others for a finite pool of cash. Likewise, after we'd been on the wrong end of manipulative practices earlier in our careers, we were intentional in ensuring we didn't fall into the same practices ourselves. These simple steps resulted in aligning us with Kingdom.

Stewardship, Not Self Indulgence

The Kingdom of Heaven is also marked by stewardship rather than self-indulgence. I'm not suggesting that because the Kingdom of Heaven is one of abundance you have license to operate unrestrained.

Stewardship is marked by thoughtful, intentional, efficient use of resources towards a greater purpose. Exercising stewardship teaches you the discipline required to enable you to handle God's abundance. This equates to how you learn to use the resources, not for self-indulgence, but for the good of those around you. It doesn't mean you don't get to enjoy the fruit of your efforts; it denotes a heart posture of being a blessing rather than falling into the trap of ever greater self-indulgence.

Remember my mentor and the rejected expense report in the previous chapter? Can you imagine having the responsibility and accountability for running a $100M line of business, while knowing you're not trusted to use your judgment with a can of coke? It's mind-blowing to me how that happens, but I'm sure you can imagine how it does. Someone operating from a poverty mindset decided the company was spending too much on meeting expenses and implemented some strict rules that slanted the cash flow practices in the company's favor. In other words, certain executives of the corporation chose to prioritize (or indulge in) additional profits over trusting another key executive to exercise stewardship on behalf of the organization.

This example also illustrates, though, that stewardship is not synonymous with being miserly. I'd propose the company had far more to gain in goodwill and intangible results by allowing their senior executive to extend some very modest hospitality in the form of some deli sandwiches and sodas than they gained in net cash by micromanaging him. Likewise, the church referenced in the previous chapter would have gained far more from encouraging and honoring their skilled pastor with a modest raise than they would have saved by taking a hard stance on budget to appease the grumbling parishioners. Not everything called stewardship is necessarily so. Sometimes it's just a spirit of poverty or jealously hiding behind the label. The Lord provides both "seed for sower and bread for eater." Stewardship recognizes some of this is provision to enjoy now, and some is to be invested in a bigger purpose or a future harvest.

The beauty of approaching this from a Kingdom context is, if you aren't sure about a particular expense that feels to be in a gray area between good stewardship and extravagance or self-indulgence, you can just ask the Lord. As you're learning this, literally ask God before making every significant purchase or investment: "What do you think Lord? Is this a wise use of our cash? Is this aligned with Your purposes?" (Even if you're not hearing some specific guidance in return, if you have gratitude in your heart rather than entitlement, then you're probably moving in the right direction!)

In our early days, stewardship emerged as a natural consequence of our conservative management practices. By maintaining the operational discipline of keeping the cash-flow brick wall at bay and by foregoing debt, we just didn't have excess cash to engage in self-indulgence even if we wanted to. (I guess that's one benefit to being a startup.) At the same time, it doesn't mean we pinched pennies. What we'll explore in the next section is how paying people what they're worth caused us to establish cash as a tool for honor, not manipulation.

Used to thinking in the Kingdom-versus-kingdom grid now, we do what I recommend you do. Not perfectly or all the time, of course, but certainly for any major investment or substantial new expense. We'll pray into it to make sure we're aligned with God's plan and purposes. We just ask Him what He thinks about it and wait until we have peace to move forward. Likewise, for smaller amounts which are clearly discerned as Kingdom-versus-kingdom expenses, we just do it. For example, making a decision to give a modest amount to a worthy charitable cause in our community is clearly stewardship, not self-indulgence. That doesn't mean we don't or won't pray about it. Maybe the Lord would prefer in this time and season we give somewhere else, so we'll certainly ask. It's just that we have no hesitation doing it if we don't feel we're hearing anything in our prayers. Nor do we feel guilty if we just react to the "ask" without having had the opportunity to pray into it first.

Honor, Not Manipulation

By now, it should be clear these Kingdom-versus-kingdom contrasts for cash flow management all go together, and the lines between them tend to blur. For instance, if your worldview is rooted in kingdom and you believe cash to be finite, you will be more apt to manipulate others to gain a greater amount, and more likely to feel entitled to indulge your self-interests.

Another key contrast between Kingdom and kingdom highlights the nuance involved. The first two Kingdom attributes, abundance and stewardship, seem like playing defense—more about what you don't do. Treating cash as a tool for endowing honor or blessing, rather than a means of enabling or justifying manipulation, is more like playing offense—being about what you proactively do.

When we first defined our approach we wouldn't have called it "honor" because we weren't speaking that language back then. I just intuitively knew we weren't going to be on the giving end of the types of manipulation I'd been subjected to. We also understood that a component of stewardship is tithing (a step of obedience), but beyond that is offerings (the outflow of a generous heart). Now, from a Kingdom context, it's easy to see why our approach worked—the Kingdom of Heaven is marked by honor.

Consider that God doesn't see His children for their sins, but rather for who He created them to be. God called David a man after His own heart rather than a murderer and adulterer. That is, God didn't call out David's shortcomings and failings; God identified David by his strengths and victories. Consider Abraham gave his wife, Sarah, to Pharaoh, claiming she was just his sister because he feared for his life. Then he did it again with Abimelech, the king of Gerar. God had to threaten both kings in dreams, so they would return Abraham's wife, but God still counted Abraham's consistent faith as righteousness. In other words, God honors honorable choices.

In deciding to pay a fair price for everything from salaries to commodity purchases, really out of a golden-rule sort of mentality, we fell right into a posture of honor, and away from the need to haggle with people to squeeze a few more pennies out of them.

Also, clear to see now is that if cash is a tool for honor in the Kingdom of Heaven, there are at least two dimensions to this as well. There's paying a fair price under fair terms, like paying your vendors on time without hassle, or reimbursing employee expense reports as soon as possible. Then there's also going above and beyond what's due, with a gift or offering that blesses and honors, like an unexpected performance bonus for your employee or delivering some free features to your customers. Both dimensions are not one-time acts or transactions, they each represent a posture, a consistent way of operating. In other words, if using cash as a tool for honor is an expression of Kingdom, then it's not just what you do, it's who you are.

Moving into Sonship

I know this notion of consistently using cash as a tool for honor is quite a shift in mindset for many. It sure was for me. Even though my parents and grandparents beautifully modeled generosity for me as I was growing up, they were also shaped by difficult economic circumstances. Both grandfathers lived through the Great Depression. My father grew up in poverty, eventually buying out and building a small business in the economically depressed Rust Belt. All of them took their responsibilities as providers for the family very seriously. While I learned much about generosity, I also learned much about thriftiness and contingency saving at the same time. You might understand from this context the notion that cash was finite, and the gnawing fear I wouldn't have enough, were pretty deeply embedded in me.

It was probably ten years into building Yakabod when I finally began to see things differently, as I started to move from servant to friend in my walk with God. It was moving more into sonship—just being able to relate to Him as a good, good Father who loves me as His son. Fortunately, I'd had great models for this in my father and grandfathers, but even so, it took quite a while for me to begin to understand my relationship with the Lord this way, and then to understand how it applied to Kingdom cash.

Think of using cash as a tool for honor like this: suppose while at the dinner table with your family your young son says, "Hey Dad, there's a kid in my class who's been wearing the same torn up t-shirt to class every day. When the other kids make fun of him he looks sad and says it's the only shirt he has. Can we buy him some new shirts to wear?" How would you respond? If it was me, I'd be very proud of my son. Sure, he's asking to give away "my" money, and my bank account is definitely finite. Yet, in comparison to our family's monthly budget, my son has made a small but noble request. I wouldn't tell my son to get a job and earn the funds, or lecture him on either his or his classmate's potential entitlement. I'd give my son the money, not only to bless the classmate, but also to honor my son's caring and generous heart. Context would certainly play into that.

Maybe if my son's a little older it would be a fine opportunity to mentor him in stewardship and sacrifice, and I'd tell him for every dollar he puts in to help his friend, I'd put in five. If my son perhaps asked to give his friend a new PlayStation PS3 and LCD TV, I'd consider the request audacious and have a different response. I'll bet you'd react more or less like I would if it was your son or daughter. Now imagine *you* are the son (or daughter), and you're enjoying a feast in the Kingdom of Heaven. You speak to your Daddy about that need you saw, and how you'd like to be a blessing to someone. How do you think *He's* feeling? We read earlier what Jesus had to say about this:

> "Which of you, if your son asks for bread, will give him a stone? Or if he asks for a fish, will give him a snake? If you, then, though you are evil, know how to give good gifts to your children, how much more will your Father in heaven give good gifts to those who ask him! Matthew 7:9-11 (NIV)

Maybe it's an easier way to cut through some deeply held notions about cash so you can see the Kingdom is built on honor, not manipulation. That God has all the resources necessary for you to "be about His business." (You might also consider this: just *how big* must your request be before it's an audacious one, especially since your Father owns the storehouses of Heaven?)

> *The Kingdom is built on honor, not manipulation. God has all the resources necessary for you to be "about His business."*

Arise and Shine

I know I'm sharing my experiences around cash from the perspective of a founder and leader of an organization, but you can start to bring the Kingdom of Heaven into your workplace no matter where you appear in the organization chart. Jesus describes the Kingdom working like yeast in Luke 13:21, where sometimes a little bit of yeast manages to affect a very large quantity of dough. That's the kind of impact you can have, even as a lower line-level employee in a large organization. Many Jesus followers are comfortable with that concept, and even those with a poverty mindset can still carry much influence by sowing honor, grace, love, excellence, and other markers of the Kingdom.

If you really want to bring the fullness of the Kingdom you have to grasp this statement made by Jesus:

> "You are the light of the world. A town built on a hill cannot be hidden. Neither do people light a lamp and put it under a bowl. Instead they put it on its stand, and it gives light to everyone in the house." Matthew 5:14-15 (NIV)

If you catch hold of the previous Kingdom contrasts—Abundance, Honor, Stewardship—and move in these principles, you could well find yourself with more resources to steward. Sometimes this abundance of resources is an indication of God's favor, a part of Him setting you up on that stand. Now that doesn't mean you must have cash to experience and exhibit God's favor. Likewise, it doesn't mean all the wealthy people in our world have God's favor. It is true, however, many notable figures in the Bible were quite wealthy, and it was sometimes part of God drawing a distinction that others would notice. He was setting them up on a stand, if you will.

The point is, cash is just a tool. You can use it to wield influence that brings the Kingdom of Heaven, or you can use it for selfish purposes. If you're stuck in a mindset where you think God doesn't want you to have any cash, then maybe that's why you don't have any. As in the parable of the servants who received differing amounts of talents, if you use whatever God gives you wisely He often increases the base amount (responsibility) from which you operate. An increase in the resources God gives you demonstrates He can trust you with more to use for His Kingdom purposes.

The ultimate goal, the reason God puts you up on that stand, is so you can shine His light into your area of influence! Not just in your company or workplace, but out into your community as well. The higher the stand God sets you upon, the farther your light will shine and the more darkness it will dispel. (Notice it's God who sets you up on that stand, you don't push other people off the ladder to climb up there!)

Let me boil it down into very practical terms; to reach and influence authority figures in your community you need resources. You need to carry yourself like a king to reach and influence kings. This posture takes some resources and a Kingdom mindset, not a mindset of poverty. That doesn't mean self-indulgence, of course, or trying to impress your neighbors. I'm not saying you can't buy the Lambo if you've been blessed with so much it's not even an extravagance in your budget. I'm saying if you think you *need* it to impress local business leaders you've missed the concept. It does help, however, to have the experience in managing resources at the level of those you're influencing, so you understand the responsibilities, decisions, burdens, and experiences that shape them.

Taking an abundance approach is another example of how all these Kingdom contrasts go together. To be up on a stand, shining at a level of authority and influence in your community, you have to carry an abundance mindset. Confident that everything you need comes from the unlimited Kingdom of Heaven, and you don't need anything from other (worldly) influencers. If they perceive you are connecting with them because you need something, you no longer have influence. I hope you can see that properly stewarding cash as a tool for Kingdom influence might well bring you more of both.

After Two Decades, the Results Are In

There are definite benefits to our company from operating by these Kingdom principles versus their kingdom counterparts. We aren't beholden to anyone, for example. Since we have no debt and have never sold equity, we're under no pressure to prioritize next quarter's numbers over long-term goals, or worse, to pursue someone else's agenda rather than the Lord's. We can show grace to our customers or vendors. We can hold a default posture of generosity with our employees and our community. We can celebrate our competitors' successes, or even refer overflow to them if needed. We were able to join with other firms, unthreatened by competitive considerations, to launch a wildly successful community nonprofit: techfrederick. (Other founding techfrederick members aren't truly competitors with us; but previous attempts at starting this kind of organization in our community failed because many of the tech organizations were afraid of "perceived" competition.)

As wonderful as these benefits are, I know I've shared some practical, but rather unremarkable examples. I wish I had some big testimony to share; some vendor or employee whose life was changed forever from this experience of cash as Kingdom rather than king. Honestly, I'm not sure most of our employees even understand the significance. Many of them have been with us so long—or it's the only post-college "real" job they've ever had—that they haven't recently (or ever) experienced the not-to-do-list type examples so prevalent in corporate America.

Or maybe instead, I'd love to have a story about obvious divine intervention. My friend Vaughn has multiple stories of approaching the financial brick wall, knowing he needs a certain amount of money by a specific Friday to make payroll, save his house, and finally buy some groceries for his family. And that exact amount, to the penny, shows up about ten minutes before the deadline. (On second thought, I'm getting too old to want the opportunity for that kind of story at this point!)

While we don't have anything nearly so dramatic, what we do have is this: we're a successful, self-funded, bootstrapped technology company with no debt. Not just now, but never in our nearly two decades of existence have we been in debt. We self-funded our core software product development. We self-funded several derivative products. We self-funded the launch of a new sister company. We haven't had to give up a single bit of equity (or control) to outsiders, and we've never even touched our floating credit line. Well, we took out some small term loans for furniture each time we moved into a new office—but we could have paid them off at any time with barely a blip to our cash reserves or cash flow.

We've honored the people and organizations in our ecosystem with our cash, paying them all fair value for their services, and never used our cash to manipulate them for some selfish purpose that tied our gain to their loss. In cumulative impact, from inception to the end of 2020, we have invested heavily (over three quarters of a million dollars) in our community's non-profits and key needs. We have compensated our employees generously (over $50 million in payroll and benefits.) Our $75 million+ (and counting) in cumulative revenues have had significant regional economic impact beyond that...

In spite of all that, simply stated: we've *never ever* been short of cash, mister. This must have something to do with the God we believe in...

Summary: Cash
Kingdom

- Resources are abundant; even infinite. There's more than enough to achieve everything in God's call and purpose on your life.

- Cash is a tool to bless or honor others.

- Sow and invest.

- Seed for the sower and bread for the eater.

kingdom

- Resources are finite; if you have more, I have less.

- Cash is a tool to manipulate others for your own personal advantage.

- Stockpile and hoard.

- Self-indulgence.

Key Points

- Cash is important but not more important than faith or the implementation of Kingdom values.

    ◦ if we owe it, we pay it—early and often

    ◦ if we can't afford it, we don't buy it

    ◦ honor: we pay what it's worth (we don't use our position to manipulate).

- Yakabod may not have remarkable stories related to cash, but in seeking first His Kingdom, we've *never ever* not had enough!

SECTION 3.3: REVENUE

WHEN REVENUE RULES

W e spent the previous chapters talking about managing cash, but where does that cash come from? The obvious answer is, "Sales!" That's how it has worked for Yakabod all along. Being self-funded, the company launched and grew on the proceeds of an initial contract, but it could have just as easily not been that way. We were caught up in the early go-go dot-com days, thinking we needed to raise investment capital. (For what, I'm not exactly sure, but that's what everyone else was doing.) Fortunately, our Board counseled us to focus on selling to customers, not investors. That sounds obvious now, but it was heady advice in those days, and it served us well. It forced us to be fully aligned with our customers from the beginning.

Our "funding" came from serving our customers well. Now I'm not saying companies never need to raise cash; in fact, some companies, by nature of their market or business model, require it. My caution is that raising outside capital brings the risk of taking you out of alignment with your customers. Funded companies have to serve at least two masters: investors and customers. In my admittedly limited experience, too many entrepreneurs and early-stage companies I meet are chasing capital, when what they really need are satisfied customers.

If this sounds to you like the way things should work I'm glad you agree, but let me share a few recent experiences of the way things often work in the business world at large.

Fake It 'Til You Make It?

A friend and I recently met with a small software business whose CEO was trying to raise capital. We learned they already had a large number of customers, over fifty I believe, but their finances were still tight. We quickly discerned one problem—they were trying to be all things to all people. We counseled the CEO to speak to their fifty-plus customers, and to ask each one to define the key value they received from the software—the top three pain points it solves. "That's gold," we told him. "Once you learn from those customers you'll know where to focus. That could help you accelerate sales so you don't even need to raise funds—or it will put you in a much stronger position to raise and use the capital if needed." We met with them again a few times over the course of a few months. With each meeting, things were getting worse, but they still hadn't talked to their customers as we had suggested.

"We just need to find an investor," they moaned, "and that will solve everything." Finally, after we pressed them on it, they confessed that none of their customers was actually happy. Over fifty customers, and yet the company was unable to draw a good reference from a *single one of them*! It came out that in each case they had oversold the customer with a vision for what the software "could do," rather than what it actually did. The result was, for each new sale, they had to build a bunch of features that didn't exist, and for which they weren't getting paid. This, of course, left them continually behind in supporting all these half-finished solutions.

Then his words revealed the root of the problem: "You know the way it is, we have to make them think we're a big company," the CEO told me, "or they'll never buy from us." The stress of maintaining that charade was killing him and his team.

Always Be Closing?

Consider another example that hit a little closer to home: I was in a meeting when I noticed someone I didn't know peering through the glass door of our meeting room. When he saw I was busy, he waved, mouthed he'd be back, and left. Now this was rather unusual because our front door requires a fob to enter our office space, so after my meeting ended, I asked our team who the man was. They explained he was a salesman from a trade organization, and he'd snuck in the front door behind one of our employees. A little later, I retrieved my brown bag lunch from the kitchen and was at my desk clearing emails when the guy marched right into my office. (He'd snuck in the front door behind a well-meaning employee again.) I was literally in the middle of eating my sandwich as he set his notebook on my desk, cozied up next to me, and launched into his pitch.

"You got time?" he asked, clearly intending to proceed no matter my answer.

"No," I responded, but not wanting to be a total jerk, I said rather firmly, "You have three minutes. Max!" Like a giddy pony, he was off to the races, telling me all the reasons we just had to be members of his organization. Most of it had nothing to do with us. He could see I wasn't biting on his pitch but he continued anyway.

"You *have* to join! Look at this! There are *huge* discounts on FedEx freight. How can you pass that up?" he insisted. At that point he didn't realize it, but he was trying to sell ice to Eskimos. (We're a *software* company. We ship absolutely nothing!) Yet he persisted. At this point, he was way over his three-minute grace period so I cut him off.

"Hey look, I'm in the middle of five things and you came in here unannounced. If you have something on paper, I'll look at it later, but no promises."

"No," he replied, "I don't have anything. What more could you need to look at to understand what an amazing deal this is? C'mon, I'll even give you a discount if you commit right now." I told him his time was up, it was time to leave. He spied my business cards on the corner of my desk, so he grabbed one on the way out (without asking permission, of course). Not five minutes later, he sent me a text from the parking lot. "My apologies," he began. Not that he had barged in twice mind you, and deceptively— uninvited and unannounced—tried to strong-arm me into a sale that had absolutely no relevance to our organization. No, his apology was that he wasn't able to convince me how valuable membership in his organization would be, and he'd be happy to come right back inside with the application since he knew I regretted not acting on his discount.

Sales for Me, Not You

I suspect you know where I'm going with the two stories above. From a spiritual lens, both examples are clear illustrations of kingdom business practices. The software company CEO was following established sales guidance like, "Look bigger than you are," and, "If the customer asks, the answer is always 'Yes!'" and "Fake it until you make it." He had decided he had to shape every customer's perception, so his company became a chameleon that changed into whatever the customer wanted or needed it to be. He wanted to raise money so he could be even more things to even more customers, hoping that would finally bring them sustained profitability. In this case, more money would only have made things worse because his model was totally unsustainable. Not to mention highly deceptive...

The trade organization salesman, likewise, had been following accepted sales procedures, like "Always be closing," and, "Do whatever it takes to make the sale." His shtick was based on pressure, manipulation, and deception—whatever it takes. While his pitch attempted to "demonstrate the value" we'd receive, the interaction couldn't have been further from that—it was completely about him making a sale. Which of course served only the salesman, not the customer!

In the kingdom, the key question in a transaction is "What's in it for me?" That was clearly the motivation behind the manipulative sales techniques in both examples above. If the point is to generate satisfied customers, as I mentioned at the start of this chapter, none of the practices followed in either example actually produced any!

As with managing our cash, we didn't have a checklist of Kingdom practices to consider in our early days as we first sought to generate revenue. We weren't even really sure exactly what we were selling. Again, it's interesting to look back on those days from a Kingdom perspective to understand why some things worked and what we could have done better.

God Knew Our Product before We Did

In the early days, we kind of stumbled upon our customers. We didn't know how to practice the "lean startup methodology" we use now, as it hadn't been formalized or published yet. We also didn't have the Kingdom language we now have. We were just trusting God's promise that He'd provide—if we would "seek first His Kingdom." And He did. To be honest, it didn't always look the way we expected.

On the success of our initial contracts, we developed a "slideware" solution pitch. That turned into a consulting pitch, which landed some contracts that got us into the Intelligence Community. In turn, this sustained us for long enough to develop some actual products, and opened opportunities to sell those products, which then forced us to build key security features into the very core of the product.

While we never imagined the Intelligence Community as a customer when we first started, we can now appreciate God's work in nudging us in that direction. Those security features originally built of necessity still persist as a moat around our product, and continue to drive our sales across disparate market segments to this day.

As we tried to figure out how to sell our products and services, we were trusting God's promise so we never engaged in high-pressure sales tactics.

> *We trusted God's promise that He'd provide if we would "seek first His Kingdom," and He did, though it didn't always look the way we expected.*

Similarly, we never sold vaporware (concepts still under design but claimed to be currently available). This didn't prevent us from talking about futures—the things our software "could do" based on its architecture—but we were always honest in explaining it didn't do that yet, and more importantly, it wouldn't unless someone was paying for it. As you'll see in Chapter 14, we wanted to "do stuff that matters," rather than just booking unsustainable revenue. This way, if we couldn't provide value and actually be a blessing to a customer, we didn't want to force that sale.

The so-called downside is this meant we grew a lot slower than we might have. That's no small risk as a technology firm, since there's always the threat of obsolescence—of the market passing you by. Even when we were anxious to grow more quickly, however, we never felt like we had to take on a bad customer just for the sake of increasing our revenue. I had learned earlier in my career how much a bad customer costs, not just financially, but in team morale. If a prospect didn't value our proposal, or tried to get us to do a whole lot of work free, we just walked away. (You'll recognize this relates to the contrast between honor and manipulation we discussed earlier in context of cash flow. We weren't going to be on either the giving *or* receiving end of manipulation!)

Is That Your Final Answer?

My friend, Vaughn, shares a powerful and directly relevant story in this regard. In the early days of his software company, when they desperately needed more revenue for their fledgling business, a very large defense contractor took note of their software and invited them into a project. After a couple of positive meetings, the contractor's program manager asked Vaughn to build a custom prototype to demonstrate the concept.

She assured Vaughn that success would mean his software would then be a critical part of their billion-dollar prime contract; this would require at least a 5,000-person license, and he'd have more business than he could handle as they embedded his software into other prime contracts they held too. Vaughn told the program manager he'd have a proposal back to her shortly. After an awkward silence, she looked at Vaughn and said, "I don't think you understand the way this works. This could be an enormous opportunity for you, and you need to do the work free of charge."

To Vaughn's CFO's dismay, Vaughn said, "Sorry, if you don't respect our team's work enough now to place value on it, you certainly won't later. You'll need to pay for the work you're asking us to do."

The program manager replied, "Well, let me go back and talk to my bosses and see what we want to do." She called Vaughn back a day or two later and said, "You are making the wrong decision; you are about to miss out on an enormous opportunity! Are you still taking the position you won't do the work free?" Vaughn reiterated they would not be doing the work free. Comically, like one of those game shows, she asked Vaughn, "Is this your final answer?" Vaughn had spent lots of time in prayer, and he knew he was standing on a biblical principle; the "worker is worthy of his wages" (Luke 10:7; 1 Timothy 5:18).

Emphatically he said, "Yes, that's definitely my final answer."

I knew exactly how Vaughn felt. When I wouldn't sign a deceptive agreement giving a kickback to the associates who approached me for Yakabod's first contract, I was sure that was it. I was deeply anguished at the missed opportunity, but totally at peace with the decision. Vaughn figured that was it too. As much as he needed the revenue from the immediate and subsequent opportunities, he'd taken the stand he knew he had to take, and was totally at peace.

To Vaughn's surprise, after he said no, the program manager immediately explained that her bosses wanted the work done, but had told her to push for the work free of charge on the promise of the future potential. They told her most small businesses would fall for that. Since Vaughn had said no, however, she could tell her bosses she had done her duty but that they would have to pay Vaughn's firm for the work.

Her bosses' direction was to put the contract in place, and Vaughn got paid to build the prototype. Ultimately, however, the large defense contractor never won the big billion-dollar contract they had dangled to manipulate Vaughn. If he'd have done the work free, it would have all been wasted. (Vaughn has also set his heart on building a Kingdom business, and has plenty more powerful stories like this. His book is coming soon—*Lessons from the Edge* by Vaughn Thurman—and when it does, you'd do well to read it!)

I hope you can appreciate just how counter-intuitive Vaughn's stand was to accepted business practices. You *never* turn down revenue, or opportunities for revenue, if you're operating at a kingdom level. Yet, operating from a Kingdom level, Vaughn ended up achieving the optimal outcome in the circumstances. Let's dig into the contrast between Kingdom and kingdom when it comes to revenue in a bit more detail…

WHEN YOU RULE REVENUE

10

In the worldly system of business, if cash is king, then revenue rules. In the Kingdom of Heaven, though, revenue doesn't rule you—you rule revenue. I hope Vaughn's example in the previous chapter effectively demonstrated that Kingdom business is just a totally different mindset than what's prevalent in much of corporate America. Let's explore some of the contrasts between way things are typically taught in business school and the way things work in Kingdom.

Provision Flows from Kingdom Purpose

In the worldly kingdom, everything starts from the sale. Of course, it's true that you don't have a business if you can't sell your product or services. Unfortunately, however, completing the transaction and making the sale often become the highest priorities; the things most valued by the organization. Any other "value" like the welfare of employees, the prosperity of the broader community, any higher purpose or mission of the organization, are often secondary to making the sale. In the kingdom, you do whatever you can do to generate revenue, and then secondarily, if you're "enlightened," you try to wrap some redeeming purpose around it.

It's just the opposite in Kingdom, where provision flows from purpose. God has specifically created and shaped you for a plan and purpose. (Plans to prosper you, and not to harm you, by the way.) If He calls you or your company's leaders to build or run a company, He's already made provision for that. There is no lack in His Kingdom. In fact, He promises that if you seek first His Kingdom, the rest of these things (referring to daily provision) will be provided as well. In the Kingdom then, the highest value in the context of revenue should be on understanding who God made you to be, and what He's purposed the company to be.

> *In the Kingdom, provision (revenue) flows from purpose.*

That Kingdom purpose almost certainly has something to do with being a blessing to others around you. It may be meeting unmet needs in your market or your community, maybe it's helping others to come into their purpose, or simply being a conduit of provision for your employees and their families, but it has something do with being a blessing. Figure out your purpose and actively partner with God to pursue it, and provision should flow from there. As we explored in previous chapters, God is certainly not short of cash. Neither is He limited in the ways He can deliver it to you.

There seems to be a growing awareness of this in culture at large, with the millennial generation more focused on careers with purpose, and government bodies even creating legal entities to enable "social-good" corporations. That's all a step in the right direction as far as I'm concerned. (They are, however, often missing the connection to the Father. It's good that they caught a socially beneficial mission, it would be better if they connected with His heart.)

Purpose Impacts Your Business Processes

Of course, knowing provision flows from purpose is no excuse to sit in your office waiting for revenue to fall from the sky. You need to be out engaging with prospects. Not just trying to sell them something, but learning how your products or services deliver real value—even a blessing—to them. It also means you are equipped to ask bigger questions concerning any potential transaction. Instead of asking, "What's in it for me?" you can ask, "What's in it for us?" meaning both parties in the transaction. This can be further extended to include the question, "What's in it for the community?" (Or at least some greater good.)

Likewise, if you are filling a legitimate market need flowing from your Kingdom purpose, you just need to be authentically you. You don't need to compete destructively, using tactics like building up your offering by tearing down your competitor's proposal. There shouldn't be any need for pressure, manipulation, or deception. A customer whose needs are met by your product or service should desire to select you. There should never be any need to pretend you're something you're not. If you are operating from your Kingdom purpose, you will "speak as one with authority," and prospects will resonate with that.

Note also, starting from purpose, with faith that God's provision will flow, means you can price your offer fairly. You don't need to gouge an unsuspecting prospect (who will eventually resent you once they figure it out.) Similarly, you don't need to lowball your pricing, either out of desperation or with a hidden agenda of raising prices later. If your solution offers real value, addressing a legitimate market need, customers will buy.

If there's not enough value after this, maybe it's a clue you need to refine your offerings, or pivot altogether. Perhaps you're not operating in your purpose after all. Maybe you have the right idea and the wrong implementation. Alternatively, it could simply be poor execution holding you back. In addition to having plans to prosper you your Father also knows what you need even before you ask Him. If sales aren't meeting your expectations, spend some time in prayerful conversation with Him and let Him lead you. That's the way things work in His Kingdom!

When you understand your calling in terms of God's plans and purposes for your company, generating revenue then typically becomes more of a marketing challenge than a sales challenge. It's more about understanding how to find the customers who will derive value from your product, rather than focusing on how to manipulate a prospect, who may not even be a good one, into buying. If these concepts all sound familiar, you may recognize this as an essential strategy in *The Lean Startup*[12] methodology. As far as I know, there was no deliberate "spiritual awareness" behind the formation of the methodology, but it's what we now use for our new product launches, because the concepts, at least the way we apply them, look more like Kingdom than kingdom!

Looking back, I'm not sure we ruled revenue in those early days, but it certainly wasn't ruling us. Even before we had Kingdom language to describe it, we understood fairly early that provision would flow from purpose rather than the other way around—so we approached sales from that perspective. (We knew we better seek first His Kingdom, because we recognized full well we couldn't possibly succeed without Him!)

> *We knew we'd better seek first His Kingdom, because we recognized we couldn't possibly succeed without Him.*

There are plenty more Kingdom contrasts to consider regarding revenue generation, of course, but some of those we uncovered through a series of painful circumstances. Consider, for example, the widely held notion that "the customer is always right."

The Customer Is Always Right—until They Aren't

There is of course some wisdom in the expression, "The customer is always right." In starting from the position the customer is always right you'll tend to think through things from their perspective, which is way better than seeing things from your perspective only. (It's hard to be a blessing if you're only thinking about yourself.) In the same way, it's good to go the extra mile to help someone, which sounds a lot like grace. As with many things, however, the Kingdom often holds principles in tension. For just as much as grace, selflessness, and service are part of the Kingdom, so are justice and honor. This means if a customer is taking advantage of, or worse, abusing your employees, well suddenly that customer is no longer right for your business. Operating as a Kingdom business may mean firing that customer for the sake of honoring and protecting your employees.

As an example, we did have one great customer we believed could position us for a breakthrough into a new level of scale in our market niche. Likewise, our solution greatly simplified their operations and allowed them to achieve a scale and breadth of collaboration previously unattainable, resulting in significant benefits to their mission. We were being a blessing, provision was flowing, and it was a great project until suddenly an unanticipated reorganization put new people in charge of the project. Just like that, they became a very difficult customer. The program should have been a flagship for our solution, but instead, the new program manager felt compelled to make things as difficult as possible for us.

First, he shrunk our budget by eighty percent, then he started requiring an inordinate amount of detailed justification for every few minutes of time we spent working on his project (on what had been a 6,500-plus hours per year contract). He'd then turn around and use our detailed accounting to accuse our employees by saying things like, "That should have only taken forty-five minutes, not an hour." Then we'd have to spend another hour at our expense to account for that expended hour in more detail.

119

If we told him it would take an hour, and we instead got it done in thirty minutes, he'd say he had never authorized the work. Then we'd have to spend another hour again at our own expense to re-create the email trail to prove he had in fact authorized it. You get the idea. You can imagine how quickly that demoralized our team.

We tried hard to work through it, trying to unearth any deeper issues and rebuild the trust we'd had with the previous team. We had made some mistakes, which we immediately fixed once we became aware, but nothing that would warrant the new program manager's level of obstinacy. When it finally became all too clear this would be the project's "new normal," no matter how hard we worked towards a more cooperative and productive relationship, we decided we'd have to fire the customer. We asked our team to bear with us a few more months, and to operate in "grace" while we honored the current contract. As soon as the customer tried to issue the extension for another year, however, I called a meeting with the program manager and his contracting officer.

The program manager was expecting to use the meeting to negotiate our price down further. Instead, I told him we would not accept a renewal of the contract under any terms. I made it clear there was no way we would subject our employees to his treatment any longer. The contract officer's eyes were as wide as saucers—he'd never experienced a contract being turned down in this way before. For us, it was a step of faith because we were in a season where we really needed the revenue, and everything else in our sales pipeline was blowing up in the most heartbreaking way possible. Still, we figured the way our people were treated was more important than cash from a contract with an abusive customer. We recognized that if we needed more work, we'd just have to broaden our business development efforts, while trusting God to provide in some

> *We figured the way our people were treated was more important than cash from a contract with an abusive customer.*

way He had already worked out but that we couldn't see yet.

It turned out to be the right choice, of course. In the end, we made it through the lean period just fine. More importantly, our people knew we were serious about "doing stuff that matters," and when we said we weren't a "billable body shop," we meant it. This of course helped to attract some more great people when it was time to hire again.

Playing Fair When Others Aren't

The situation above was rather unfair but it wasn't the worst one we've faced. Consider the circumstances in normal business where "the gloves come off." That is, the other party isn't playing fair, so worldly logic suggests you don't need to either. That's not the way things work in the Kingdom, though. We're accountable to "work as unto the Lord," regardless of what anyone else is doing, trusting in Him for righteous justice. This concept has real consequences when you're trying to win and sustain business in a competitive environment. Clarity on this Kingdom principle came through some even more trying circumstances.

In this case, a government organization had issued us a long-term contract to build their corporate knowledge-sharing solution. As is common in Federal contracting, the customer also had a SETA contract (Systems Engineering and Technical Assistance) in place with a well-known consulting firm. Now, the way SETA contracts legally work is that the consulting firm is supposed to provide independent vendor-agnostic support to the government entity across all their projects. As this function gives them access to proprietary technical and financial information from the projects they oversee as an agent of the government, SETA contractors are contractually excluded from providing a solution or performing the work on those projects on which they are providing oversight. In other words, they are supposed to be an "honest broker" for the government.

Well, in this case the consulting firm was anything but honest. They spent years trying to convince the government to ditch the fully-functioning solution based on our technology (and thus the government's contract with us), in favor of a solution built on top of a software giant's broad and generic off-the-shelf product. Now I'm not knocking the other product, but it couldn't technically meet the stringent security requirements for the project. It simply wouldn't work. No matter, the SETA contractor kept pushing.

Eventually, our government customer reorganized and the new guy overseeing our project bought the SETA's biased arguments. Part of it was our messaging—in hindsight, we just didn't differentiate our solution well enough. To be fair, though, the security requirements should have made the other product an absolute non-starter. The bottom line is that a big part of the new program manager's course of action was due to outright deception on the part of the SETA contractor.

It turns out in our particular market niche, companies were finding they could hire newly minted college grads, pay them $60,000 a year, and bill them out at $300 an hour or more as "experts" on the software giant's product. You've probably figured out where this is going. The SETA contractor was pushing the software giant's application in place of ours, because the SETA was actually proposing to provide the software integration team to build the replacement. All providing extremely attractive margins to the SETA contractor, of course.

Well, with all this as the backdrop, one day the new government guy called us into his conference room—with no warning to us—and with the SETA contractor at his side told us he was dropping our solution. Of course, he added that he needed us to help the SETA contractor transition our system to their solution. He even bragged about the award he would receive for "saving the government so much money." I guess it's an understatement to say that was a frustrating moment. We sat there knowing the consulting firm literally stole the contract from us by playing dirty pool (it was, after all, contractually illegal); that their proposal was deceptive at best, unable to meet key "show-stopper" requirements, using cost estimates that were visibly and obviously understated by an order of magnitude or more. It felt like the robbers brazenly stole our wallet, then convinced the police to send us to the ATM to draw more money for them.

Even so, we told the government guy that while we were very disappointed, we had always wanted the best for his mission. If that meant his organization needed to move away from our solution, we'd do whatever was required to extract their data out of our platform in the right form. We also assured him we'd do whatever necessary to ensure our system remained fully operational in the interim transition period.

I'd like to tell you I walked out of the conference room perfectly at peace, knowing we didn't need to compete destructively, that our provision would flow from purpose, and God had something better planned. Instead, I was mentally plotting how we'd put the dirty consulting firm out of business.

Once I had calmed down, though, and prayed it through, I instructed the team to take the "high road," just like we said we would.

While we took that high road, and put the consulting firm in a position to deliver the desired solution to the government, things unfolded just as we expected. The consulting firm quickly blew through their budget, then quite a bit more (vaporizing any potential cost saving). Even so, they still couldn't replicate even the basic functions of our platform (while offering no hope they ever could). In the middle of that, the government guy actually

> *I was mentally plotting how we'd put the dirty consulting firm out of business.*

did collect his performance award for the "major cost savings" he had supposedly "produced." Predictably, he immediately transferred out of the organization.

The customer kept our system on minimal life-support funding for nearly two years, while the SETA contractor continued to burn funding with no solution in sight. Finally, another re-organization brought some new people into the customer organization, resulting in yet another new program manager over our project. He looked at all of it and quickly realized the previous program manager had been swindled by the consulting firm. They finally cancelled the (still non-working) replacement effort and issued us a new contract to ramp things back up from where we had left off.

I am certain a good part of this was because we played fair even when the others didn't… and God honored our actions in the end.

Blessed to Be a Buyer?

As you can see, this journey hasn't necessarily been easy. Honestly, we often felt like the Israelites wandering around the desert for many years, but we did our best to seek God's Kingdom first, and He provided. We didn't always get everything we wanted, but we received way more than just the manna necessary for our survival. We seem to be well on the other side of all that now, and sales have been expanding rapidly over the last few years. On the Federal side of our business, where sales are driven by referrals in tandem with the growth and expansion of existing projects, both aspects have grown significantly over the last few years. We still haven't figured out how to effectively do inbound (or demand) generation in that business, but we also haven't needed to!

Meanwhile, with our commercial mid-market CISOBox product, our lead Andy has been following The Lean Startup methodology, with a discovery-based sales process. That's how we knew we had a viable product. He'd cold-call or email a CISO (Chief Information Security Officer), and say "Hey, we're considering launching a new product. This is absolutely not a sales call, but we would love to understand if you'd find such a product valuable. If so, what key features would you require?"

To our pleasant surprise, a large percentage would actually take the call.

Andy was true to his word—he didn't sell, didn't try to "convert," and didn't apply pressure; he simply asked the CISO what he'd love in a product, and told him openly where we were (early stage or pre-product). No "fake it 'til you make it," no "vaporware," no "always be closing," just asking people what they need. Andy was essentially asking how we could be a blessing to them without using this language.

Invariably the CISO would ask Andy how to buy our product. Andy would say, "Well, we're just in the early stages of launch, but when we get the first release of the product would you like me to call you to set up a demo?" And most agreed they would appreciate a call.

I do understand doing all the things I've described above means we haven't grown nearly as fast as we could have, or as external expectations would dictate. We've never made the Inc 500 list, or anybody else's high-flyer, hot-growth-company list for that matter. There certainly have been points where we had hoped to grow faster, but as I've tried to illustrate above, we've never had to pressure, manipulate, or deceive anyone to generate revenue. We've been able to build a healthy sustainable business that gives our employees a sense of purpose in a market overwhelmingly dominated by "billable body shop" contracts. Alongside that, we've always had enough work. To put it another way, this Kingdom stuff works—our provision has indeed flowed from our purpose.

Strolling Through the Valley of the Shadow of Death

I'd like to wrap up our experience of pursuing revenue from a Kingdom perspective with one more practical example. As I was finishing the first draft of this chapter, all our projections—even the most conservative ones—suggested we would still need to hire between four and six more people (after already hiring nine over the previous year). That's not much if you're IBM or a Silicon Valley firm that just landed your B round, but for our self-funded, thirty-five person operation it's a significant increase.

A few weeks later, every one of our customers was suddenly, inexplicably struggling with funding for our contracts. These weren't problems with our performance or execution—most of these customers were trying to *increase* the size of their contracts, not reduce them, when this hit. Even so, they were all, for different reasons, having trouble with funding, leaving us to wonder if we had actually hired a few people too many. I don't know what wakes you up at three in the morning, but this is the kind of thing that does it for me.

As I tried to make sense of this (as if anyone could make sense of it at 3:00 a.m.), I could literally feel the fear and anxiety trying to set in and take over, as though it were a tangible presence. At that point, thankfully, I was experienced enough to recognize which kingdom that nonsense was coming from. It was definitely not from the one I serve. It took conscious effort, but I just had to start praying. Right now, I could rattle off dozens of scriptures telling of God's promises to provide, but about the only one I could pull up in the fog of those early hours, with fear stubbornly seeking a foothold in my soul, was Psalm 23:1.

I just kept declaring "The Lord is my shepherd. I lack nothing." Mercifully, that eventually got me back to sleep. I came to work the next morning, created a new spreadsheet to help analyze all the current situations, put some "actual, probable, optimistic" numbers on it, and could see we may have a lean month or two coming but it's likely we'd be expanding again in a few months. More importantly, I also knew by then my spreadsheet doesn't supersede God's provision. He knows a way where there is no way, He's already provisioned all we need to accomplish His purposes so that's what we'd pursue. There's more to that story, of course, which we'll explore in a later chapter.

Meanwhile, since ruling revenue rather than it ruling you means trusting that provision flows from Kingdom purpose, and since Kingdom purpose flows from God-given identity... it's probably a good time to explore another key Kingdom concept: authenticity.

Summary—Revenue
Kingdom
- Since good works have already been prepared for you by God, you simply need to find those for whom you are able to provide value (or those to whom who you can be a blessing).

- There is no need to compete destructively.

  ○ Work as unto the Lord—take the high road even when others aren't.

- There is no need to take a bad customer.

kingdom
- Do whatever it takes to make the sale—pressure, manipulation, deception.

- Make your competitors look bad so you look good.

  ○ The "gloves are off"—anything is fair.

- Always be closing, any deal is a good deal "as long as their money is green."

Key Points
- Focus on selling to customers, rather than investors, where possible.

  ○ Be conscious of who you partner with—don't be unequally yoked.

- What are the practical implications on your sales process? (Make sure you comprehend these details.)

- Be willing to fire a bad customer.

- Provision flows from purpose—so you need to understand purpose.

SECTION 3.4: AUTHENTICITY

11

THE POWER OF AUTHENTIC CORE VALUES

In previous chapters I shared that provision flows from Kingdom purpose. In our case, even before we had Kingdom language to fully describe it, we just trusted in a general way that if we were doing what God called us to do, He'd provide all we needed to accomplish it. In time, we also came to understand that while provision flows from purpose, purpose in turn flows from identity. Let's explore the deeper issue of identity in a business context.

Identity? Or Perception of Identity?

What you've generally experienced in the business world is likely the opposite of what I've just described. That is, in many companies, the desired outcome drives identity. On the other hand, maybe it's just a perception of identity. We want to make the sale, we want to appear culturally relevant, now who do we have to be (or more likely, who do we have to make people believe we are) to achieve that?

As I'm sure you've encountered, some people spend a lot of energy to project a certain image; that is, to ensure others perceive them in a certain way. (There's a reason for the nickname "Fakebook.") Companies do the same thing, though, we just use more sophisticated words to describe it. Take "branding" for example, it is one form of marketing effort expended to influence the way customers and external stakeholders perceive the company. Likewise, many companies invest heavily in "corporate culture" initiatives intended to shape the way employees perceive the company. That's great if the perceptions in either case come from authentic experiences. It means the corresponding branding and culture initiatives are fruitful investments. I don't think I need to convince you, however, that corporate branding and culture initiatives are often built more on shaping perceptions than providing authentic experiences.

> *If provision flows from purpose, then purpose flows from identity.*

These initiatives end up being manipulative or deceptive because they project a picture of *who the company wants you to think they are,* instead of who the company really is. Why do companies do that? They generally do it to achieve some desired and often self-serving outcome, as opposed to pursuing some greater purpose.

This is another one of those concepts where Kingdom business takes a shift in mindset, because things just work differently in the Kingdom. In the Kingdom, provision flows from purpose, and purpose flows from identity. It follows then, that authenticity is a building block of the Kingdom. That is, being authentic to your organization's God-given identity and purpose should be a foundation for not just your branding or culture initiatives, but for *all* your business processes and operations.

I'm not sure we really understood this in our earliest days. We were more focused on proper behaviors back then. We were operating in a "servant" mindset—doing things for Him—which is task oriented and transactional in nature. We were intent on honoring God, and we focused on how our corporate actions and behaviors did or didn't accomplish this. That's not a bad motivation, it's just not the fullness of maturity in the Kingdom.

As we started the mental shift, however, from servant to friend, pursuing activities "with Him" not just "for Him," we really started to grasp the deeper concept of identity. We began to understand that our behaviors should flow from identity, from who He made us to be. Of course, sometimes we'd also realize our behaviors were lacking in that they were demonstrating the current gap between who He made us to be and who we actually were. So understanding and living from our true identity became far more important than simply modifying our behaviors. (For an example of this read Matthew 12:34b-35).

We also came to understand that if you're operating in the authenticity of a God-given identity and purpose, there's an authority you carry from that. Being an authority endowed from the spiritual realm, from the Kingdom, it carries greater weight than authority endowed by men. We came to understand it doesn't matter who anyone else says we are, be they a competitor, detractor, disgruntled ex-employee, whoever, or who someone like a customer or partner expects us to be, the real question was, "Who does God say we are?" Then, if we aren't who He says we are, what do we need to do to better align with what God expects of us?

This is why firing the bad customer in Chapter 10 was an easy choice. His words and actions conveyed we were "just greedy contractors," a mindset far too common in that market space. We knew it wasn't true. That simply wasn't our identity. We knew we didn't need to try to convince him of this just to salvage some revenue from the contract, especially when nothing would convince him otherwise. We knew God endowed our organization with a purpose, and from that authority, it became clear we should no longer "cast our pearls before swine." God would have other projects to provide for us, and those projects would come from customers to whom we could be a blessing. In fact, I think that's probably what most unsettled that hostile customer in our final meeting: he thought he had authority to do whatever he wanted to us. He mistakenly thought that because he controlled contract dollars we were captive to him. We clearly had greater authority (and peace) in the freedom that came from knowing our identity. It simply never occurred to him that we would actually walk away.

> *We had greater authority (and peace) in the freedom that came from knowing our identity.*

Authenticity—a Building Block of the Kingdom

Even before we had Kingdom language to describe it, somewhere in our growing understanding of the shift from "*for* Him" to "*with* Him" we somehow "got it" that authenticity was a building block of the Kingdom. Earlier we'd intuitively done some things, whether in our marketing, hiring, or product development, that were consistent with our identity, that felt natural and authentic. In fact, I guess I'd seen enough "fake" in my career before Yakabod that our very first tagline was "Real People. Real Software. Real Solutions." I know, I know, that's my silly engineer-guy attempt at a tagline, not a professional marketer's polished product, but people seemed to like it, and clearly, we had some intuitive sense we wouldn't do "fake" in those early days. Nevertheless, once we were able to fully grasp, articulate, and internalize the concept, recognizing it as a building block of the Kingdom, we were far more deliberate and intentional in our pursuit of authenticity throughout our business.

Consistent with my earlier disclaimers, I'll openly admit our contribution to Kingdom business isn't the revelation that authenticity matters. Even good secular business books recognize the importance of authenticity. (I'd heartily recommend *The Experience Economy*[13] by Gilmore and Pine. Even twenty years later, it's an immensely insightful business book that builds heavily on authenticity. Of course, another book I would recommend is their follow-on work published a half dozen years later, explicitly titled *Authenticity*.) Our breakthrough is that we actively pursued authenticity in *everything* we did—hiring, recruiting, marketing, office space, engineering practices, user experience, customer support, business model. In contrast to the secular approach, we evaluated and refined all these things not against who we wanted to be, but rather in light of who we understood God has made and purposed us to be.

As we continued to grow in our faith and understanding of Kingdom business, we also came to understand this all goes beyond identity—who God made us to be—it actually relates to *presence*, that is "Christ in me." The closer we are to Him, the more we understand who He made us to be. This means we should not only remain close to Him, we are meant to represent that little tiny aspect of Him within our areas of influence. Likewise, though, the closer we are to Him,

> *Operating out of God-given identity is good. "Leaking" His presence is better.*

the more we expose that "Christ in me," the tangible presence of His Holy Spirit, to our surroundings. In other words, understanding and striving to be who He made us to be is a great start. Being "leaky," or exposing people in our areas of influence to His very presence, is even better.

Interestingly, isn't that that the way Jesus unleashes us personally? To go into all the world, to carry His Kingdom, to represent Him well, but according to our God-given identity? Re-read the way He sent out the twelve (Matthew 10:1-42), and then the seventy (Luke 10:1-23), and you'll see He didn't micromanage them, He didn't tightly control the message. In fact, He gave them dangerously few instructions. He did give them a unifying purpose and mission, but it was expressed through their unique identities. Ultimately it conveyed His power and presence. I believe it's the same today in the context of your corporate identity. Your mission and purpose as an organization is to do the stuff He does, and in so doing, "proclaim the

Kingdom is at hand," but He doesn't expect us all to look the same while doing so. In fact, organizations were purposely created to each provide a unique expression of His glory or to convey some unique experience of the Kingdom.

I know we've veered from nice concrete business subjects like cash and revenue into deeper, hazier abstractions really quickly, so let's explore authenticity through a few more practical examples.

Appeasement—Decisions from the Outside In

As I started writing this chapter just prior to the Christmas of 2018 (yep, this book has taken me a while!), there was a fitting example in the headlines of how an organization caved to the pressure of public perception rather than their own internal values. A radio station in Cleveland (along with many others) banned the 1944 classic song, "Baby, It's Cold Outside" because within the current context of the #MeToo era the lyrics were accused of carrying an undertone of a date-rape scenario. Perhaps they do, I don't know—I can't say I've listened closely to the lyrics, but the song seems fairly tame in comparison to the station's normal rotation of modern pop and hip-hop songs that feature a far more lurid slate of sex, violence, drugs, and debauchery. Why did the station choose to ban the classic song but continue playing the way-more-raunchy modern songs? It was simply because some listeners complained about the former, not the latter.

Similarly, in May 2018, the University of Maryland suspended their head football coach after a lineman, who weighed in excess of 300 pounds, died from heat-related illness following his collapse during a spring practice. After an extensive four-month long independent investigation, the University concluded the head coach had done nothing wrong and reinstated him. A student protest followed, so the next day they fired the coach after all. Why? Again, they were worried about the "media optics."

Please note, I'm not making any statement on the corporate actions in the above two examples. They may have ultimately made the right decision in each case, I don't know. I just find it very interesting that each organization took headline-grabbing actions based not according to their own internal values, but rather in reaction to outside opinion. Further, the University and the radio station each had a desired course (reinstate the coach; and play the song like we've always done), but went the other way to appease a vocal subset of public opinion. Neither acted from who they were, but chose rather to project the image their detractors were hoping to see. The clear priority was managing perceptions rather than acting from their own values. We could debate whether they ultimately took the right action in each case, but I think there's little question as to whether their actions were authentic.

Another example is an incident that occurred after the 2019 March for Life. While a group of high school students from the Diocese of Covington was waiting for a bus, a student was caught between a group of protesters and a man who deliberately played a drum just inches from his face, clearly attempting to provoke the boy. The student stood his ground, only smiling at the man trying to intimidate him.

With only a cropped segment being played on loop in the mainstream media, the ensuing frenzy immediately found the boy guilty for his "smirk." This influenced the school's and the Diocese's decision to initially condemn their own students. Later both the school and Diocese backed down as more information was revealed when video clips of the entire incident were released. Various media outlets were sued by the student, and at the time of this writing, a major news network had just reached a settlement with the student for defaming him. One would expect a basic core value of the school board and its related Diocese would be to stand by their students, or at least presume their student's innocence until all the facts were known. Instead, they condemned their own student to appease public pressure. To illustrate the gravity of this inauthenticity, the boy's attorney has since successfully won landmark legal punitive compensation against multiple mainstream media outlets.

I won't even go further down the rabbit hole with the insanity of 2020's COVID outbreak, BLM/Antifa riots, and controversial election. Everyone has opinions, facts are secondary, with many hopping on the bandwagon trying to be "woke" on both sides of the aisle. It all rings out as very shallow, temporal, and inauthentic.

Authenticity—Decisions from the inside Out

In previous chapters, we showed how provision flows from purpose, and decisions related to your sales cycle are certainly one aspect of moving in authenticity. I hope the above examples show you, though, that authenticity goes far beyond sales and marketing.

Making decisions to manage other people's perceptions is a kingdom strategy; it's an "outside in" approach to manage who people perceive you to be. In contrast, decisions made from a Kingdom mindset are "inside out," that is, they flow from who you are.

Every person has a unique identity endowed by God, and since it's from God, it comes with a beautiful plan and a purpose. Distorting that identity under the sway of public opinion is not the way things work in God's Kingdom. In fact, numerous scriptures warn us not to make decisions through fear of what other people might say. One such scripture is found in Proverbs, which states: "Fearing people is a dangerous trap, but trusting the Lord means safety" (Proverbs 29:25).

Let's look at Jesus for a perfect illustration of this. Many times through scripture, we see He speaks on a topic and the people are amazed, because He "spoke as one with authority." Why is that? Well, he's the King of kings and Lord of lords. He knew who He was, and He spoke from that identity. The Pharisees had important religious titles and significant authority in man-made organizational structures that Jesus couldn't (didn't need to) claim. They'd been teaching the people for decades, yet when Jesus spoke, crowds immediately saw the contrast. His authenticity conveyed His true authority—a permanent, supreme, spiritual authority far beyond anything man-made. He was real, and as Lebron James says, "Real knows real."

I know I've been talking about personal identity, which may leave you wondering if God really cares about, or if any of this applies to, companies and corporate identity. Well, let's talk about nations first. He used His interactions with a nation (Israel) to show the whole world His character and ways. We also read about sheep nations and goat nations (Matthew 25:31–46,) and that Jesus actually receives the nations as His inheritance (Psalm 2:8.) Throughout the biblical narrative, certain nations are described as having specific attributes and characteristics, unique identities if you will. God clearly cares about the organizational construct designated as a nation, along with its purpose. Why wouldn't He also have a plan and purpose for companies, using them for His glory? After all, a corporate entity does mirror a nation in many aspects: providing necessary functions to society beyond the capabilities of individual actors, looking out for the well-being of its constituents or stakeholders, facilitating provision and economic resources to employees, and developing a specific culture.

As a practical example of pursuing authenticity at an organizational level, a non-profit board on which I serve was recently feeling the pressure to put out a statement related to the racial justice movement that exploded in response to the death of George Floyd during a police arrest. While board members all agreed that any "ism" (racism, sexism, ageism, etc.) was unacceptable to our organization, and our practice was to treat everyone, inside and outside the organization, with nothing less than dignity and respect, there were mixed feelings about putting out a statement, with members taking passionate stances both in favor and against. By recognizing the inauthenticity of public statements others rushed to publish, and by calling us into our own organizational identity as a non-political consortium, I was able to bring the team into unanimous agreement on the way forward.

We would walk before we talked (i.e. we'd focus on our actions before

139

making statements), acting only where our organization was relevant and our voice actually carried credibility and authority. This led to the formation of a task force to convene and listen to a diverse collection of community members so as to understand any barriers they faced getting into or advancing in the local tech community. This was done with the intent of listening before we actually proposed and/or implemented solutions. (That is, we would undertake the Discovery process referred to in Lean Startup methodology.) The organization is now engaged in the noble and just cause of racial equality (certainly a Kingdom concept) squarely centered on our area of influence and expertise, but with authenticity, authority, and free from political entanglement! All because we formulated our response from identity, rather than outside perception or pressure.

In any event, whether personally or corporately, there's no need to worry about the way others perceive you. Who cares what they say? The better question is, "What does God say?" Who has He purposed you to be? You just need to authentically be that.

This is where core values come in.

Why Core Values Matter

As shared earlier in Chapter 5, when we were wrestling with what it meant to build a company for God's glory, one of the first tools we discovered was core values. As things were coming together to get Yakabod started I read John Eldredge's book *Wild at Heart* and Jim Collins' *Good to Great* in the same time period. That wasn't unusual as I was a voracious reader during that season. Most of the books I read had a few good ideas buried in a lot of consultant-speak. (I could tell the author was just trying to build his resume for the speaker circuit.) The Collins and Eldredge books were different, they were just mind-blowing epiphanies to me. As unusual as the pairing might seem, each book totally shifted the way I looked at everything.

Among other things, Eldredge's work helped me understand my personal identity: the sense that the God of the universe had made me—specifically me—for a unique purpose; and I had freedom in being totally authentic to that purpose. Meanwhile, Collins' work, though I have no idea if he has a spiritual foundation, helped me understand the same for corporate identity: the sense that companies could actually be great in a broader context, and that greatness wasn't solely defined by their ability to produce profit. Together, those works really shaped the way I viewed Yakabod as I was starting it up. Now it took me probably another ten years to really process through what that meant for the workplace every day, but the seed had been planted.

Trying to bridge the gap from a mind-blowing read into everyday practice led to plenty of introspection of course. I spent much quiet internal work, wrestling with beliefs, philosophies, and strategies in light of what I was learning about God-given identity. While much of that was abstract, I discovered one very concrete implementation tool—the notion of defining Yakabod's core values. Which, of course, were closely related to *my* core values. I came to understand core values helped quantify "identity," maybe not exclusively or exhaustively, but enough to serve as a practical tool to express the foundation of who we are.

As a parent, I could see, as you probably do, how much more powerful it was to correct behaviors by calling my sons into their identity and purpose, rather than simply disciplining them for bad behavior, or trying to goad them into good behavior. Don't get me wrong, when they were three years old, it was "no means no" and it was about learning obedience and respecting authority. The more our sons matured, however, the more effective it became to call them into their identity than simply punishing them to drive certain behaviors. For example, our oldest son made a big mistake as a sixteen-year-old.

At his request, we trusted him to carry some adult-level responsibilities, which he betrayed. At the same time, he engaged in some activities reserved for adults he shouldn't have. We didn't punish him with a big list of painful consequences and a "that'll teach you." Instead, we gave him the privilege of paying for his own cell phone. ("If you think you're adult enough to do the stuff you did, then you're adult enough to take responsibility for your cell phone, with no help from us; and you're just going to have to figure it out.") It felt like punishment to him, but can you see the difference? While he didn't always show it around us, we knew our son had God-given leadership skills. So instead of punishment, we called him into his identity as a leader with an opportunity to carry some adult responsibilities. (If he wanted a phone, he'd have to take initiative to land and successfully hold a job, save some money, work through buying a phone without cosigners, pay a bill every month, monitor his own usage against data plan, etc.)

If we'd have just taken the phone and grounded him, he'd have been "good" for about a week and nothing would have been resolved. Instead, it was an important step in his personal development—from the inside out, not the outside in! I'm not saying he never made mistakes again, or that the turnaround was instant, but years later he encountered a friend in their mid-twenties who was still on their parents' cell phone plan, and it gave him a real sense of pride and accomplishment that he'd been paying for his own phone for years. (That was our goal as parents, after all, to equip him to stand on his own in adulthood.)

This is exactly what you are doing with core values for your organization! You are quantifying an aspect of your organization's identity so you can call your team into desired behaviors, making any necessary changes from the inside out. Not artificially inducing those behaviors with yet more rules in the employee handbook. Those rules just feel like punishments and constraints to the innovative and resourceful people you'd like to hire. Further, this call to core values is setting up your team to stand on their own, so you can scale.

I learned—probably from another Jim Collins book, *Built to Last*—that there is no one right set of core values, but all enduring great companies explicitly have a set. A *real set*. Not the kind that the executives defined on their recent golf retreat, bought posters for, then forgot about, but rather real values that truly shaped the company's culture. As I was learning, I wanted to build a great company, not a crappy, self-indulgent one that made some money for me, but didn't do anything for anyone else. I wanted to build a great company where employees loved working. A company with whom customers loved doing business, and the community felt blessed to have. (I was starting to understand purpose, even if I didn't yet fully understand identity.)

> *There is no one right set of core values, but all enduring great companies explicitly have a set. A real set.*

These aspirations, along with some additional introspection caused me to realize "passion" must be one of my personal core values, which in turn became one of our company core values. Fortunately, the timing of all this "identity" work allowed me to define Yakabod's values early, even at formation. I could then focus on staying authentic to these values.

I didn't realize it at the time, but I can see now how critical it was that I had these defined by the time my business partner Scott W and I merged our respective start-ups into the new Yakabod. He and I were able to agree on those core values, and the broader faith and worldview from which they were derived, before we even merged. In fact, had we not agreed, we wouldn't have merged. I know many companies that struggled (or even failed) because the founders ended up with very different expectations over time. Shared, defined, authentic core values can help to mitigate minor differences in expectation. Likewise, I came to understand the words we chose were only core values if *all* our decisions were consistent with them, not just the convenient ones.

Of course, the company was never going to be just Scott and me. The whole point was to build a team and scale the company. This meant we had to figure out what core values meant not just for us or for the company, but in terms of the people we hired. That's what we'll explore next.

Chapter Appendix: Yakabod's Core Values

I wanted to include list of Yakabod's core values as an example for your reference. Please note, however, these are *our* core values. There is no right set meaning these are likely not yours, at least not all of them. These are, however, authentically Yakabod's.

Passion

We didn't come here simply to do a job. We're pursuing a calling. There will be good days and tough days, but we're exactly where we want to be. We love our work because it taps into something deep in each of us and makes us each come alive.

Grace

We treat every person with respect, nurturing a culture where grace prevails. Each of us has unique talents, and every role in the organization receives equal regard. While God's design for us is perfect, we all make choices that aren't, so we're committed to creating an environment where accountability is expected but grace prevails and honor is extended.

Integrity

Truth is not relative. Ethics are not situational. Integrity is not optional. As a corporation, we strive to uphold these standards. As employees, we have the authority and responsibility to make the right choice, even when it's difficult.

Excellence

We do the very best we can do. Then we strive to do even better. Everything we build—solutions, operations, relationships—is built to last.

Consistency

We do what we say. Our actions are in keeping with our words. We're not perfect, but we strive at all times to "practice what we preach."

BUILDING YOUR TEAM FROM CORE VALUES

12

Defining and understanding your personal or organizational core values is one thing, building a company authentically expressing these core values is a different thing altogether. It will take several chapters to explore this in earnest, but in this chapter, I would like to start by looking at core values in the context of people.

With regard to people and the core values you wish to instill in a company or organization, there are two key aspects of this to consider. First, core values are key to your personnel decisions—who you're recruiting, hiring, and firing, or as Jim Collins would say, getting the right people on the bus.

The second aspect, to be addressed in parallel with building core values into the company, is culture. Culture is the way your employees experience your company. Since we're talking about Kingdom business, this means a culture authentic to your God-given identity, not a superficial expression meant to shape their perception. Team and culture are essentially inseparable, but to explain each properly we'll need to tackle them separately. We'll focus on teams in this chapter and address culture in the next.

> *Culture is the way your employees experience your company.*

Since this begins with an understanding of your own core values, you may be wondering just how it is that you figure that out. Let me share one example to get us started.

Introspection and Internet Cheese

Right around the time I was defining Yakabod's core values (which of course meant understanding mine), during the earliest days of the internet, "e-commerce" was still a novelty, and Amazon didn't sell much beyond books. (Ancient history, I know.)

During that time, I read an article in some magazine, maybe *Wine Spectator* or something, on the "Best Cheese in America." Maybe there was a top ten list, I can't remember all the details, but some place in Wisconsin was producing an aged cheddar, which the article declared was the hands-down best in America. I looked them up online (it wasn't a given that I'd find them back then), and sure enough, they had a primitive but functional online store. I bought some of the aforementioned cheddar; admittedly it was a little pricey for cheese, but hardly extravagant. It was also supposed to be the *best cheese in America!* That seemed an affordable indulgence worth experiencing, to see just how good it really was.

I can't remember how it came up, but I was talking to some friends at church and they just couldn't believe it. "You actually bought cheese from the internet?" they asked incredulously. They thought it was the craziest

146

thing. "You could go down to Safeway and buy a good block of Kraft cheddar for a few dollars." Literally ten years later, they'd still playfully joke with me about the internet cheese. Interestingly, this is one of the ways I came to understand excellence was one of my core values. If there's a "best"—within reason—I want to taste it, experience it, listen to it, see it, and study it. I want to celebrate its excellence! More importantly, I also want to produce the same excellence in the things I do—if I can. At my core, I resonate with expressions of excellence.

My friends were fine with "good enough" and to them excellence was actually negative—it felt more like extravagance. Of course, excellence and extravagance are actually different things. For example, I'd love to try a well-aged, top vintage, *Domaine Romanee-Conti La Tache.* Experts would generally acknowledge this chateau as a standard of excellence for the universe of wines, not just Burgundy wines, French wines, or red wines. I've never tasted it and it's extremely unlikely I ever will. For me, it would be beyond extravagant. Most likely, it would be for you too. (That *La Tache* is probably $5,000 a bottle, if not more.)

Personally, I'd much rather find the hidden gem, that overachieving small estate afforded nearly the same rating from Robert Parker, but which sells for thirty dollars instead. I'd appreciate the small producer's pursuit of excellence, "punching above their weight class" if you will, and I'd consider that thirty-dollar bottle a bargain worth acquiring. (In my mind, any fool could find a good bottle for $5,000. It takes some serious diligence to find excellence at thirty dollars!) Most of my friends, those who enjoy wine anyway, would consider that a worthy splurge as well.

My point is, those same friends who gave me grief about the internet cheese would consider even the standout thirty-dollar bottle of wine an absolute extravagance. Not because they can't afford it, but because they don't value it. It's a bit of a silly example, I know, but this is one of the ways I came to understand that excellence (versus extravagance) really matters to me—and it therefore had to be a key part of the culture of any company I helped shape. I'm sure you have similar clues in your own journey.

Proactive Beats Reactive

Recently, I've had the opportunity to mentor and counsel a number of early-stage entrepreneurs in our local community. It's made me realize I "got lucky," or more accurately, benefitted from a big dose of God's grace. I established Yakabod's core values in our earliest days, before we actually hired anyone. Largely because that's when I happened to read those mind-blowing books, not because I understood the rare opportunity I had. This is why I've been challenging these entrepreneurs I've been mentoring to define their core values *now*. I've explained to them it's just as important as cash flow. Having your core values defined allows you to hire against your values. In the fragile early days of a startup, every hire is critical; it only takes one bad hire to sink the ship.

That might sound extreme, but candidates who don't resonate with your core values (if those values are authentically part of your culture) won't enjoy working at your firm anyway. For example, if excellence is a corporate core value, and you find a candidate who's willing to declare something substandard "good enough" because it's Friday afternoon and happy hour beckons, then your team is going to be annoyed with that candidate, and the candidate isn't going to enjoy your culture either. Notice I'm not saying someone who knocked off early on Friday can't hold excellence as a core value. The difference is they'd take that breather, but then push back in on Saturday or Monday, rather than declaring the substandard thing "good enough."

> *If you start hiring people—but you don't understand your core values—you'll quickly lose your opportunity to define those values.*

In contrast, if you start hiring people—but you don't understand your core values—you'll quickly lose your opportunity to define those values. *You* can't change people's core values (*Jesus can*, but you can't). If you don't hire people who already resonate with your values it doesn't matter what the employee handbook or website says. The corporate culture will become a random amalgamation of the core values of the people you hire— which almost certainly won't line up with the ones you've stated. I'd like to say we knew how to do that early on. Turns out, we had to learn how to do this the hard way...

Recruiting, Hiring, and Firing from Core Values

Even though we had some missteps early on, we were serious about embedding our core values into our company culture. We hired by these values, fired by them, and referred to them in team meetings whenever we'd make some decision affecting our team. One benefit we realized early on is that our core values helped us gracefully navigate our "faith at work." Clearly the core values were derived from our own Christian faith—and I said so on the website—but employees have never had to share or agree with mine and Scott's faith to prosper at Yakabod. They just need to resonate with (and live out) the core values. They can believe our values were delivered by Martians, and there'd really be no issue, unless they objected to living them out.

That got us through the first half-dozen hires, but we quickly learned we needed to go deeper. With grace being a core value, and my patient temperament, I was far too willing to give people the benefit of the doubt in the early days. Sometimes we weren't good (okay, it was mostly me that wasn't good) at discerning whether a candidate really resonated with a specific core value, or if they were just telling us what they thought we wanted to hear. For example, we had one guy early on who was passionate about technology. That was good, because passion is one of our core values. We always pay our hires well, naturally, but we also want people who are willing to do stuff in their area of expertise even if they are *not* being paid to do so. To this day, most of our software team love writing code so much,

149

they have little personal projects they do at home, but this guy was a little too passionate.

We were all working from our homes in those days, then we'd meet at Scott's farmhouse to sync up. When the guy started consistently missing deadlines, we discovered he was actually running another company from his house. Unacceptably, he was billing the time he spent working on the side projects to us. He got an A on passion, but an F on integrity—which is also one of our core values. We had to fire him. He was really indignant when we first confronted him. Surprisingly, he wasn't embarrassed about fraudulently billing us, his ire was based on the fact that we caught him. In fact, he was so angry, when Scott and I called him into the office a few days later to fire him, we had a plan all worked out—you go low, I'll go high—because we thought it possible he'd have a weapon with him.

We had pretty strong motivation after this crazy incident to rework our initial phone screenings to give us a better read on candidates upfront. That also caused us to design a full day interview process to dig in even deeper with candidates. We devoted a whole interview segment—ninety minutes or so—to understanding the candidate's core values, even if they couldn't necessarily articulate them as such. Other segments were devoted to specific job skills and attributes, but we ensured we were analyzing those responses in light of core values as well. In other words the desire to be excellent is necessary, but having the skills to do so is equally important. In time, our recruiting and hiring processes got much better in terms of hiring against our core values and building a team who authentically resonated with them.

Scaling Core Values beyond Founders

We also realized it wasn't enough to just talk about our core values with the team when making big decisions—we had to model them consistently within the company's mundane, everyday activities as well, and hold ourselves accountable to everything this encompassed. For example, if we're constantly preaching excellence to the team, but our coffee sucks because we're trying to save a few dollars on that budget item, people would quickly recognize the hypocrisy and we'd have a problem. Likewise, if we say grace is a core value, but then we treat the UPS driver or cleaning guy with less respect than we treat the visiting customer executive, we'd have a similar problem. That's the progression of authenticity—being consistent with your core values, derived from your God-given identity, in *all* your actions.

It takes a while to build an operational rhythm and consistency with your core values. Earlier in our corporate lifecycle, whenever we were faced with an issue, we'd have to consciously ask, "How do we evaluate this in light of our core values?" By this point, though, I can say we don't really have to think too hard about it. Our core values are simply a natural part of our corporate culture. Basing decisions and actions on them has essentially become second nature. We've developed a "muscle memory" with our core values, a lot like a professional basketball player who's spent so much time making that three-point shot in practice it just happens naturally under the pressure of the game. In other words, we've been intentional over long periods of acting from core values, rather than operating under conventional business practices. That's the beauty of it—if they're really your core values, they're just an expression of who you are. If that's the same as who God made you to be, it doesn't take work.

While there's no work in just being who you are personally, there *is* a discipline to implementing the core values for your organization, of course. It starts with having the humility to observe, learn, and refine. To willingly admit to a gap or inconsistency—where your culture or business process is not reflecting your core value—and then make the necessary changes so the gaps are closed, and your values are clearly reflected. It may sometimes be inconvenient, but it's not difficult. Chances are, that specific problem was bothering you anyway. You and your team will be much happier once you resolve it, and probably wonder why you waited so long. It simply requires focus and intentionality until you develop the "muscle memory."

It's Just Who We Are

Let me share an example illustrating the link between core values and identity. We were in the middle of upgrading an existing customer to the latest on-premises version of our software when they sent us the most encouraging note. In it, they remarked, "There are a great number of companies, and we could easily name 20 of them, who could totally take lessons from Yakabod on their customer service. I'm not just 'saying' that. I work with other people who aren't in <my department> and who do not have any idea of what Yakabod does for <our organization>, but they've noticed too that Yakabod is very responsive."

That's a direct quote, and we really appreciated their kind words, but the interesting thing is we really weren't doing anything "remarkable" or "extraordinary." Brands like Zappos are intentional about "extraordinary" customer service, so in light of that, they devote disproportionate resources and maintain obsessive focus towards achieving that "extraordinary" customer service. We don't. That positive interaction our customer experienced happened organically for two reasons. First, Michael, Carole, Andy, Dan, anybody who interacted with that specific customer wasn't consciously thinking, *Well I had better go the extra mile to make sure they have an awesome experience.* None of our employees had any specific customer service training. No, our employees were just being who they naturally are, treating the customer like they would want to be treated in return. Which is just one expression of our core value "grace," where we do our best to treat everyone as someone loved by God.

Equally important, we have a culture encouraging our employees to live that out. This is not true in all corporate cultures. In some cultures, whether stated implicitly or explicitly, the higher value would be placed on revenue or margin. It's not that these financial measures are not important for us, they are, but they aren't core values. We act from our core values, sometimes in pursuit of revenue or margin. We don't produce revenue or margin in spite of core values. Practically, this means, Carole didn't have to

152

think, *Well, this customer issue is going to take more time, but since I can't upsell them, I better stop wasting my time with them.* There was no internal conflict: that's not Carole's personality, nor is it our culture.

I shared the contents of the note, and my take on it, with the team at one of our regular corporate sync meetings to encourage them. I told them that the customer's encouraging note was one little data point of validation that we hired the right people and that our culture authentically expresses core values.

But there's even more going on here from a Kingdom perspective, which is why I also asked the team if anyone was surprised by the feedback? Like, did anyone have any doubt this is just "who we are" as a company? (It was a mid-COVID lockdown Zoom call so I could see a lot of their heads nodding in agreement as they got it. Yes, of course, this is who we are, this is just us being us!)

Can you see, this little thing is exactly what I referenced in the parenting example with our son earlier? I wasn't giving the team a rah-rah, I was calling them into and reinforcing our corporate identity. All our employees have some internal resonance with our core value grace, they know that aspect of their personality has the freedom to shine in our culture. We treat customers well because that's who we are, both personally and corporately, not because the corporation has prescribed certain procedures or behaviors to our customer service interactions. In some cases this may not even be the employee's highest personal core value.

As in many tech companies, we have plenty of introverts, many of whom don't like to interact with people they don't really know. If they're working here, it's because we saw something in them that resonated with our core value "grace." In the example I just shared, I'm actively calling, even equipping them, to confidently express that part of themselves in their workday because "that's who we are." Now it's not going to work if we've hired a narcissist who feels superior to our customers, right? If we made the mistake of hiring that individual, we'd eventually have to fire them, because me calling the team into corporate identity is not going to change the narcissist's behavior. This reflects all the more reason it's important to hire against your core values so the right people are on the bus!

Some Business Benefits of Core Values

We've spent a bit of time discussing core values already, and since it's a "softer" topic than cash or revenue, you might wonder if there's any real business benefit to defining and implementing your core values. I can assure you there is, but let me start with three specific benefits we've experienced in light of what we've covered so far in this book, and I'll keep sharing more as we go.

Core values help with stewardship: I would suggest core values tie back into the stewardship discussion in Chapter 8, since provision flows from purpose, and purpose flows from identity. Understanding your identity by quantifying your core values will help in your pursuit of good stewardship. As noted earlier, you can simply ask God before making every significant purchase or investment: "What do you think Lord? Is this a wise use of our cash? Is this aligned with Your purposes?" If you're like me, though, sometimes, maybe even most of the time, it feels like you aren't necessarily hearing anything back on the specific topic you're praying about. In that case, if you have gratitude in your heart, rather than entitlement, and you're moving from identity and purpose, then you're probably moving in the right direction with your spending decision. In other words, if excellence is one of your core values, go ahead and buy some of that internet cheese for the team break room, you'll get no shame or guilt from me!

You don't need to control the message: We recently realized another benefit of these embedded core values. It takes the pressure off the founders to "control the message" outside our walls. We're not into that anyway, but early in the company's history I'd have felt more pressure to personally represent the authentic Yakabod brand externally. So, when the County

Office of Economic Development recently approached Jonathan—one of our executives—to appear as an ambassador of the company and the region for a PBS segment they were filming, Jonathan initially danced around it and suggested maybe they should ask me. Now I've never been on PBS, but I get to speak at plenty of events; it's not as if I felt like I'd be missing out. I was fine that it was Jonathan's turn. In fact, it was probably better.

It was a great demonstration of the freedom core values can bring to the organization. Earlier in my career, I'd have felt compelled to work with Jonathan on talking points, making sure we represented the brand the right way. Not to manipulate the way people perceive us, but rather to make sure we're conveying accurately who we are. But with core values deeply embedded in our culture, I didn't have to do any of that. I have no concerns with Jonathan representing us. He is "us" after all. He was free to be himself in the interview, and I could have full confidence he'd authentically represent "us." Which of course, he did.

You don't need to control behaviors either: As I touched on earlier, defining core values streamlines your employee policies and procedures handbook. You don't have to build an ever-expanding list of rules, policies, and procedures to define or control behaviors. With Integrity as one of our core values, employees know it's not just about the company doing the right thing, it's that employees are each empowered to do the right thing without having to seek pre-approval from the company. If, for example, a customer were to ever put an employee in a compromising position—maybe requesting they work unpaid hours or miscode the hours to another project—our employee is free to make the right decision.

They don't have to call back to HQ, don't need to fret that they're between a rock and a hard place, worry that if they don't comply with the faulty customer request they may cost us revenue, or that we'll punish them for that. Nor do they have to comb through the employee manual, which couldn't possibly address every questionable scenario. Our core value is integrity, not revenue. Revenue's important, but it's not a core value. The employee can make the right decision, which would be obvious in this case, fully confident we're a hundred percent behind them.

We've been focused on the composition of your team being a key element of building your company on core values, but as I mentioned at the start of the chapter, there's a second inseparable element you must address to be successful—your culture. This is the way your employees experience and express your company's values, so let's explore that...

BUILDING CULTURE FROM CORE VALUES

I know there's plenty of discussion in the business press about "company culture" and its importance. I agree with this, but people define "culture" in a number of different ways. Much of it looks nothing like what I just described in the previous chapter. Many companies trying to "create a positive culture" will buy the ping-pong table, hold the happy hour, or provide free vegan snacks—and those may be good things—but they're all rather superficial expressions of culture. I believe real culture—the kind that's sustainable and authentic, that ties into Kingdom—actually stems from your core values. Culture is your organization living out

> *Culture is living out your core values.* **Kingdom** *culture is living out core values that reflect your God-given purpose and identity.*

your core values in the reality of every day. *Kingdom* culture comes from living out core values that are consistent with who God called, created, and purposed your organization to be.

Authenticity in Culture

People who have visited our offices or joined us for a function know we have great coffee, a custom-roasted YakaBlend, and we make our own Yakawines with grapes from high-end Napa Valley vineyards. You'd consider these products to represent our culture in a way, but they are simply expressions of two of our core values, excellence and passion, and are representative of our creative, entrepreneurial spirit. (If we couldn't make great wine with the assistance of a skilled winemaker, or great coffee with a respected local roaster, we wouldn't do it.) Likewise, we recently bought the team a OneWheel. Many people would consider it an expression of our corporate culture, which in some ways it is, but for us it's not about how "hip and urban" we are, it's just a natural extension of the personalities on our team.

A few of our guys have a passion for skateboarding. Those who do skateboard are passionate about the OneWheel, and a few other non-skateboarders have started using it too, in the journey of exploring something new and eventually mastering it. That's authentic to our culture, derived from living out our core values every day—specifically our expressions of excellence, passion, and consistency. (If you've ever tried to ride one, you'd understand that an environment of grace from your teammates is pretty handy too!)

Another way to look at it is that the core values you choose will be the lowest common denominator for your team. It doesn't mean everyone's the same, or has the same interests inside or outside the office. Not at all. Likewise, there's nothing in our core values unique to race, gender, political orientation, religious affiliation, ethnicity, age, etc. Our team has personalities, interests, and backgrounds all over the map, but at the core, we share these values. Not everyone is a skateboarder or a OneWheeler.

I'm certainly not. Even though I do snowboard, which might be roughly analogous, I figured out pretty quickly it would not end well if I kept trying to ride that OneWheel. But there is something about an adventurous, entrepreneurial spirit that comes out in pursuit of excellence, the kind of thing that would attract someone to master a OneWheel, and that's common to our entire team.

Another example of authenticity in our culture comes from our Christmas and holiday events. I've been in organizations where they rented a fancy hotel and threw a big shindig in the ballroom. After experiencing several of those, as an employee I found myself dreading them. It was a nice gesture, but the events often felt forced, inauthentic, and awkward, not to mention fraught with excessive drinking, sexual innuendo (and/

> *The core values you choose will be the lowest common denominator for your team.*

or harassment), and other compromising situations. We tried a family-oriented variation of the big Christmas party once or twice in the early days; not the big hotel, but a local restaurant's event space. The team appreciated it, of course, but we all realized it just didn't fit us. Most of our team didn't need another obligation to work into their hectic family holiday schedule. Plus we'd have trouble booking even some off night, like a Tuesday, and still have to greatly overpay for rather underwhelming catering. One year while we were sorting through options, one of our guys made the offhand comment that we had enough culinary talent on our team to cook up a meal far better than most of the options we were looking at. Turns out he was right.

One of the side benefits of having a team of people who share the core values of excellence and passion, is that those who like to cook are really good at it. Many of us like to cook, so we decided to just throw a potluck lunch after one of our December corporate sync meetings. The food was so good, and the event was such a hit, that we now have a wall in our office with this crazy line of electrical outlets, each tied to their own breaker. Any electrician would shake his head and wonder what that was all about (in fact ours did shake his head when he first saw the specs). Quite simply, it's for all the crockpots.

We also have a massive commercial fridge so there's plenty of space for leftovers. The whole approach to our annual holiday potluck and reasoning behind it is an authentic expression of our culture. Part of the way employees (and anyone lucky enough to be visiting us that day) experience our company, a tangible expression of who we are. To the point where for many of our team it's one of the highlights of the year. (Now, so you don't think we're cheapskates, we do a post-holiday party in February or March when high quality catering, facilities, and employees are far more available, and often the whole family is included. One year it may feature a mobile brick oven and our Yakawines; another year we might bring in our favorite caterer to a local craft brewery or distillery.)

Here again, I'm not suggesting your culture should look like ours, or that ours is the "right way." It just needs to be authentic to you. I have one friend, a founder and CEO, who does ski trips for his team. He positions his company as a collection of hard-chargers, and hires mostly younger, single people. They can pull off the logistics of a ski trip, and it's a natural reflection of who they are. We're mostly families, so it would never work for us to take our team out to Colorado for a week. Just start with your core values, and your culture will naturally build from there.

> *Buying the ping-pong table or vegan snacks isn't "building culture," unless there's something in your core values that means it is.*

I hope you see too, there's an intentionality involved here. Buying a ping-pong table or furnishing the break room with vegan snacks isn't "building culture," unless there's something in your core values that means it is.

160

Keeping Core Values Real as You Scale

During our recent expansion I began thinking about core values again. They're instinctual to our core team; so instinctual in fact, I'll often challenge candidates facing an all-day interview to ask every interviewer the same questions about culture and values to see if they get the same answers. I do this because I'm very confident they will. And they usually do. With all the new hires we've brought on board recently, however, I've been wondering if I need to be more deliberate in this area; to ensure the core values are really embedded throughout the layers of our organization as we scale more quickly.

New hires certainly know the core values, as they were hired against resonating with them after all. They *do* see the core values consistently modeled—they look at a beautiful metal sign reflecting their image back at them every time they get a cup of coffee. Our core values also come up naturally in our corporate meetings—but I've been wondering if I need to hold a special session with them, or just take any extra steps to make sure the values don't fade as we scale.

In the midst of wondering all this, I was recently encouraged when Scott came out of a tech team meeting all excited because one of our mid-level managers had worked through a technical issue with a recent hire by invoking core values. In other words, this is how we know the core values are really part of our culture, even as we scale—when we see the next levels of leadership actively instilling and managing by them without our prompting.

This is the payoff for an intentionality and discipline in building culture on your core values. There comes a day where the professional athlete's "muscle memory," developed over countless mundane practice repetitions, pays off as he pulls up, under tremendous pressure, to attempt the game winner at the buzzer. Similarly, that intentionality in building core values pays off in interactions you could never script or anticipate. It's what happened for us in the situation in Chapter 12 where the customer sent the encouraging note. It's what happened when our next level leader was mentoring his team with core values. It's what happens when someone who's not typically the "voice of your brand" has interactions that end up representing your brand better than you could have ever imagined. I'm encouraged that at this point our culture can and will scale without dilution, as long as we keep our eye on core values.

Not Just for Founders

Given my push to define your core values at company inception, you might be leading a company or team you didn't start and wonder what use all this talk about core values is to you. While it's true it's most efficient to define them at the organization's inception, and intentionally recruit, hire and fire against those values, it doesn't mean you can't instill core values if you no longer have that luxury.

If you're a new leader in an organization where the core values are already established, the first question should probably be: are they real? Are people really making decisions based on them? The posters on the wall may describe one set of core values, but you may observe different values in play in practice. A famous example of this is Enron's case, where one of the core values on the website was "integrity" but the actual value in practice was "whatever it takes." It's not limited to high profile cases, though, and you've probably observed similar discrepancies at companies in your own business network.

If the values aren't real, then establishing new core values—whether the actual ones currently in play or aspirational ones towards which you're driving—will be a process. This will take diligence, time, and a process of attrition. It won't happen overnight and you will undoubtedly lose some people, but the people who remain will reflect those core values—*if* you handle the process properly. Again, this is the process Jim Collins describes in his book *Good to Great* as "getting the right people on the bus and in the right seats." Core values are your tool for doing so. There's really no use, in my opinion, of attempting any "culture" initiatives until you know the core values upon which you'll build that culture.

As a practical example, I serve in a local non-profit, techfrederick. As we grew from a loose coalition of local tech companies to a formal 501c3 non-profit, we realized we needed a set of core values. We went beyond the small board to the broader advisory board, a dozen members or so, and asked for everyone's input. Some great phrases and concepts came back in response, probably a dozen different candidates for our set of core values. After looking at the consolidated list, though, it struck me that they were mostly aspirational. They were all good things, but the question was, are those things who we really are? One of the candidate values was "Impact through Innovation." That's a great thing that would play well on our website and it might well have been a core value of some of the member companies, but it wasn't really who our organization is. Our non-profit gathers, supports, and empowers innovators, but doesn't drive innovation itself.

As I started thinking through all the decisions we'd made over the preceding few years, actions we'd taken and discussions around things, a different list began to emerge. There were maybe nine or ten principles that had really driven our decision making, and those principles really represented aspects of four or five core values. For example, one member drove home the point from our earliest meetings that we shouldn't host networking events where the tech folk were just "meat" for vendors (like insurance agents, etc.)

In our experience, this had plagued other networking groups and we all agreed we weren't going to do that, so we'd been consciously using that in our decision making all along. I've never seen a core values poster for "not meat for vendors," and suspect you haven't either. It's not some bland generic platitude that works on a poster, but it really is us. In a list with nine or ten of these principles, it became apparent "not meat for vendors" and several others were all just different expressions of a core value which we initially named Honor, but with feedback and discussion, revised to Respect. Similarly, we condensed the full list of principles to four or five core values.

Now I was an early entrant in the organization but not the founder, and was only one of several key players. We'd already been operational in one form or another for many years, so unlike Yakabod, the candidate list of five core values didn't represent my *personal* core values, at least not the five highest ones. The list probably didn't represent any single advisory board member's highest values. When we all got together, however, and put our personalities into the mix with a collaborative and cooperative spirit in play—with each of us driven by our own core values—these trends emerged in our collective decision making and actions. This is the way we worked harmoniously together as an organization, so it was something we could distill down to a real set of core values.

Once I shared with the advisory board the three bullets under Respect, including "not meat for vendors," there was instant resonance and agreement. Yep, that's who we are. Not aspirational, and not hope-to-be, we're already that, and we're confident in it. By codifying these things—the consistent and natural ways we were already implementing together, rather than the aspirational values we would hopefully attain—it became much easier to refer to them in our decision making as we scale the organization. We were only a dozen or so people, so we were still small enough to define and build on the core values without any attrition. I understand it's an entirely different challenge if you're trying to implement core values in a long established 5,000-person organization. That's going to be a much longer process, both in discovery and implementation, and may include more emphasis on aspirational values. My point is, though, you don't have to be the founder to do something about core values.

Not Just for Executives

Perhaps you see the benefit of implementing real and appropriate core values in your workplace but you're not the CEO or leader of the organization, you're a leader in the middle or lower tiers of a larger organization. Core values are still relevant to you. If the larger organization has real core values, you should be actively aligning your team with them. If the organization doesn't have a list of core values, you can still help define and implement them for your own team, and enjoy all the benefits described herein. You may well find your team enjoys an even greater influence within the broader organization because of your success in implementing real core values at your level of the organization. This concept goes back to the notion of bringing the Kingdom into whatever space you occupy, wherever you may be. This Kingdom vision doesn't rely on the size of your sphere of influence—it relies on how you emulate Jesus and how you focus on bringing His presence into your environment. Part of the way you do this is through seeking His purpose and identity for the team you lead, which becomes codified in part through your core values.

This all sounds like common sense, there's nothing terribly sophisticated here, but it's anything but common in the business community at large. As an example, I recently read a relevant case study[14], in which a company, after undergoing a merger, realized the behaviors present in their company were not aligned with the culture they imagined they had. Since they understood culture is a powerful perk and motivator, the company decided to do a "culture audit" to better understand where things had gone wrong. They didn't believe in "core values," probably as a backlash to seeing fake ones in play, but did prescribe "behaviors" that were expected in the new organization. Changes were implemented, but about a year later they realized the gap between desired behaviors and actual behaviors was still present. More adjustments were made, and while things in general did seem to improve, the same nagging issues continued cropping up. After two well-intentioned attempts to create a harmonious corporate culture, it seems they're headed for a third, fourth, or even a fifth culture audit, continually adding new "mantras" until they can no longer keep them all straight.

Ironically, the case study never came to this conclusion, but it's pretty obvious what happened. The organization tried to build their culture by shaping behaviors. That's like religion—you put a bunch of rules in place prescribing how people are supposed to act to "manage their sins," but it never works. Not in a church, not in a business. This is because behaviors flow out of what's already in your heart, out of the core values from which you naturally, even subconsciously act, whether you've taken the time to codify and understand them or not.

> *Building culture by shaping behaviors doesn't work. That's like religion. Instead, focus on identity. Behaviors flow from who you are.*

If the organization in the case study understood authentic core values, they could use those as the foundation of expected behaviors and call people into that corporate identity. "This is who we are." They would then recruit, hire, and fire based on those values until the bus was filled with people who already resonated with their core values. These employees would then, with some cultural reinforcement, exhibit proper behavior naturally! Likewise, many of those currently employed with the organization who didn't resonate with those core values would self-select "off the bus." They'd get the message that "this is who we are" is not who I am, and it's time to polish up my resume. It seems neither the organization under study nor the case-study authors ever thought about the make-up of their employees! They just kept adding more religion…

Of course, making the transition they desired was going to take time one way or the other. Resetting the people on the bus through turnover and attrition would likely have been successful, but does not play out overnight. If nothing else, their story serves to drive home my point about how much more efficient it is to define your core values in your earliest days rather than trying to superimpose them at a later stage.

Not Just for Leaders, Either

I recognize these last two chapters on building team and culture with authentic core values have been largely aimed at company founders, entrepreneurs, and executives. For better or worse, all my experience with core values comes from that context. You might feel that if you're working as an employee or manager in someone else's firm you don't have much influence over the company's core values. That's only partially true.

You'd still gain much from understanding your personal core values in light of who God made you to be. By understanding your identity in Christ you'll have more clarity on what you're bringing to the organization—what purpose does God have for you there? Since, as a Jesus follower, it's critical to the integrity of your life-path to "seek first the Kingdom," that's a much better question than "What do I get from the company?" It's also a good way to be led into the right decision when choosing a place to work. The mentality of "What do I get out of it?" may lead to a rash decision, as opposed to a mindset of "What am I bringing?" The difference is choosing to make an investment as opposed to looking for a payout. Likewise, understanding your personal core values may give you clarity during difficult periods where you're sorting through whether it's time to stay at your job or time to look for a new one.

Assuming you've taken that step, you're now in position to have some influence on your team's core values. Maybe you can start the discussion by asking your boss, "Do we have core values?" She might snicker, because she knows the posters on the wall don't mean anything. She may, however, list some real values that guide her decision making. In either case, you can almost certainly call your team into them. I'll refer you once again to my friend Jim the janitor in Chapter 2. Jim didn't talk about core values. He wasn't even thinking about them. Jim just set his heart on worshipping Jesus with his work. By doing this, in just a few short months he totally shifted the atmosphere of his workplace. I'm sure that at this point you can see, whether Jim, another team member, or a supervisor—someone who *was* thinking about core values—absolutely had a window of opportunity to quantify the newly positive aspects of the culture they were experiencing. They could now codify and institutionalize those aspects through a real set of core values.

Bringing the Kingdom to Everyone—Not Just to Believers

At this point we've spent a lot of time on core values, understanding the God-given purpose and identity of your organization, and building people and culture to authentically reflect this. I started by asserting that authenticity is actually a building block of the Kingdom, "at work as in Heaven," but I know from personal experience some of my evangelical friends will remain unconvinced. They will consider all this as a waste of time, since the priority of believers is "witnessing" and "saving souls," and this Kingdom-business-core-values stuff isn't getting anyone saved. That's where I'd beg to differ... in fact, I insist on presenting an alternative viewpoint!

As it turns out, core values are not only a building block for Kingdom practices—they are a great way to further propagate Kingdom culture, especially with pre-believers. At Yakabod, we established early on that our core values come from our faith—our Christian worldview—but employees don't necessarily have to agree with our worldview. Anyone who resonates with the values would agree on their "goodness," regardless of their spiritual convictions. Who doesn't think integrity is essential, or that excellence isn't desirable? Who doesn't want to experience grace in their daily work-life? We've simply taken a Kingdom concept and expressed it in normal, workplace language, not church talk, and then built culture around that concept. Using this process we've created a culture which, through its core values, looks more like God's Kingdom than the kingdom of this world. A culture through which people can experience God's goodness. You might remember that our good Father makes it "rain on both the righteous and unrighteous," and that ultimately His goodness is designed to lead to repentance. Core values aren't the only tool in this context, but they sure are an important one!

For a more concrete example, let's refer back to the events of summer 2020, with the nation's focus on racial justice following the horrendous manner in which George Floyd was killed. CEOs and marketing departments, large and small, all over the nation and right here in my personal business network, were feeling a pressure to address the explosive events. The Lord nudged me on the morning of one of our corporate sync meetings, impressing upon me that I needed to address the issue. Not necessarily externally, but certainly with the team. A big controversial topic like this, fraught with politics and emotions all around, I could have easily taken a week to prepare for the ten minutes I'd spend with the team on it. I didn't have that luxury, though. The Lord was nudging me now.

So, with way too little preparation, I told our team how lots of CEOs were feeling pressure to address the issues, but it wasn't as easy as they might think. I made clear our stance that the cause of racial equality is just, noble and proper, but too many were trying to hijack the just cause for political gain with "virtue signaling" and tangential issues, and we weren't going to get entangled in any of that nonsense. I told our team we didn't feel any pressure to address the issue externally or make public statements, and we would be far more focused on our walk not our talk. So internally, our approach to racial justice would be the same one we've had for twenty years, and we'd approach it from the context of our core value, "grace." I asked the team to bear with me, because with something complicated like this I just had no other way to process it except from my faith.

Accordingly, I understood, and our core value grace defined, that *every* person is loved by God and we treat them as such. That no "ism" was acceptable: racism, ageism, sexism, or any other. I told them we would treat every person in our ecosystem with respect and dignity, whether it be a visiting dignitary or a random UPS guy. I reinforced that they weren't accountable for *why* they exhibited proper behavior, in other words, they didn't have to see the input as an issue of faith, but they were absolutely accountable for output behavior, and anything less than dignity and respect to everyone in our ecosystem was unacceptable. I also reiterated that if any of our team knew of any systemic or even one-time issues in our culture and practices counter to that, they were encouraged to bring it to our attention and we'd fix it. I was too engaged in my unprepared presentation to observe the team's body language in much detail, but I did notice several private Zoom chats from individuals thanking me for addressing the topic and expressing gratitude for our culture.

As the meeting ended, I sat down with a sigh of relief, grateful for the Lord's grace to carry me through an emotionally charged topic. I'd barely had a moment to decompress, when one of the guys walked over to my office. Stammering a little at my doorway he admitted it would be an awkward and vulnerable conversation for him to have, but he'd like to chat. I walked him to a more private space and told him to just speak his heart, not sure what I'd hear. To my surprise, he just wanted to tell me how grateful he was for our "inclusive" atmosphere. (Now I would never use that word to describe our culture due to all the political baggage around it, but I knew exactly what he meant. He felt fully accepted as part of a "family.") The backstory is even more important: he's a self-proclaimed atheist/agnostic, which he reaffirmed in the conversation.

Turns out, he had gone to a church earlier in life, but when he could no longer attend due to his intellectual dissonance, he watched his social fabric disappear. I didn't dig into it, it was clearly a deep wound, and not an issue for that moment. His point was, in spite of me using my unavoidably Jesus-centered faith language to talk through a hard problem, and him being an atheist, he totally resonated with my message. In fact, it had touched him deeply, deep enough to bring some tears, with gratitude for being part of a family in which he personally *felt* the grace we were talking about. To put it another way, he experienced a little taste of the goodness of God, a little taste of the superior ways of the Kingdom.

What's next for him? I don't know, that's up to my Lord and our employee, but I would suggest our employee is several steps closer to healing from that "church" wound, and perhaps even seeking out the Father whose Kingdom he is gratefully experiencing in some small measure every day.

Is that "witnessing?" Well, I've spent plenty of time earlier in my faith journey, as the frontman for a Christian rock band, unashamedly sharing the gospel in very public, secular places. Fireman's carnivals, street festivals, malls, public schools, medical facilities, and a whole lot more. I had at least one pastor tell me the presentations I gave in those places were among the most powerful presentations of the Gospel he'd ever heard. It wasn't wrong, what I was doing. In fact, I believe God was pleased with us for our courage to honor Him in those settings rather than worry about what people might think. But do you know who actually listened to all those so-called "powerful" presentations? Believers. Churchgoers. Essentially, I was preaching to the choir.

What about the people who actually needed to hear the message in those public places? Most of them kept walking. You could never accuse me of being ashamed of the Gospel and my relationship with the Lord, but even though many of my evangelical friends would label it as such, I can see now what I was doing back then wasn't "witnessing." At least not effective witnessing. Ironically, I still don't actually do much of it. The authenticity of our corporate culture largely does it for me. Far more powerfully than my words ever could. (If the Lord says speak to them, I do. He knows far better than I do when it's the proper moment for that.)

There are plenty of benefits to embedding core values into your culture, values derived from your God-given identity and purpose, but this may well be the biggest one: you are imitating the Kingdom by making it "rain on both the righteous and the unrighteous," demonstrating the goodness of our loving Father to people who may never enter your church, read your tract, or listen to your message. I wish I'd learned this twenty years earlier!

So far, we've explored authenticity through core values, people, and

171

culture. There's plenty more to authenticity, though. In the next chapter, we'll look at authenticity in your business model.

DO STUFF THAT MATTERS

W e've been talking about authenticity in the context of personal and corporate identity, core values, employees, and culture. Perhaps the relationship between these things and authenticity is fairly obvious, so let's look at another aspect of authenticity that might not be so obvious—your business model.

If your organization is a business, and not a club, unless you have a solid business model that generates real income to pay your employees and sustain your business, you won't have much team or culture to worry about. In the worldly kingdom, you design (and expect) your business model to bring in greater revenues than the costs required to produce them. Anything generating revenue is therefore good in this model.

In the Kingdom, though, the business model should flow from your corporate mission and purpose, which flows from your corporate identity, which will have something to do with helping your community look more like His Kingdom. The Lord's bountiful provision equips you to accomplish this.

Life as a Billable Body

I couldn't have expressed it in those terms when we first started, but Yakabod's business model is certainly a direct reflection of our core values. It wasn't anything I learned in business school since I didn't go to business school. Instead, I had to learn from observing the companies I worked at earlier in my career. In the years before I started Yakabod I learned plenty about what I didn't want to do.

I know it's not a good strategy to build a company in reaction to what you're against. For example, consider my response if someone were to ask: "What services does your company offer?"

If I said, "Well, here's a list of things we *don't* do," it would be considered a strange reply. Even so, I had seen enough of the "billable body shops" in the federal contracting market to understand I *didn't* want to build one of those. The kind of place where people were just commodities to be leveraged for the profit of the company. I was on the wrong end of that equation as an employee in some of those firms. My friend John—one of the best systems engineers I know—once said about the company at which we were both working, that management "tossed people around like a sack of potatoes." I'm not sure what his potato-sack-tossing experience was... but it always struck me that he was dead-on with the analogy.

Most of the jobs required a security clearance, so the widespread joke went something like this: "Should we hire such and such a candidate?"

To which the standard reply was, "Well, does he have a pulse and a clearance?" invariably followed by a snicker and a final comment, "If so, then good enough. Hired."

I spent plenty of time employed in those types of companies, having been promised exciting, innovative, groundbreaking work to do—when I was really just hired to clock billable hours. I'd usually end up developing piles of engineering documentation that I knew would sit on some shelf, and even worse, for which the customer had already acknowledged they would never actually use in practice. That's the tech-world equivalent of digging a ditch one day, and filling it back in the next. No problem though—the company's real concern was that I charged every last one of the billable hours available.

In our ongoing discussion of the contrast between the way things work in the Kingdom of Heaven versus the kingdom of this world, I think you already know where the above examples fall. It sure never felt like "at work as in Heaven" to me.

Doing Stuff That Matters (DSTM)

I knew if I had the opportunity to start a company it wouldn't be run like a body shop based on this dubious model. I didn't want to be a billable body, I wanted to do stuff that actually mattered. So I wanted to ensure the same for our future employees, knowing that would impact the types of projects we'd pursue. This wouldn't mean some people (including me) would never have to do the occasional less-exciting peripheral work that just had to be done. In general, though, I envisioned the company being built on a purpose, and everyone would understand how their role was connected to

> *I didn't want to be a billable body, I wanted to do stuff that actually mattered.*

that greater purpose. In light of all this, I'm not sure why it took us so long to settle on a tagline. We went through three or four that took us part of the way there, but never quite captured who we were and what we did. Perhaps we were trying too hard to make our tagline comprehensively describe everything in our "value proposition?"

Finally, about seven or eight years in, something clicked and our tagline ever since has been: *Do Stuff That Matters®*. We loved it because it worked in multiple dimensions. It described our culture; we were no billable body shop, and our employees would have the dignity of doing work that mattered. It also described our software: helping customers eliminate the manual drudgery from their underserved business processes, so they could focus on their mission and priorities instead. Finally, it even captured the essence of corporate stewardship, which we eventually would understand we were being called to. Our tagline showed we weren't only building a company to produce a profit, but to help prosper a community.

Similarly, it's why our business model was focused from the beginning on building a solutions company (selling software plus services) rather than a pure services company. This allows us to build and capture economic value from something beyond our employees' billable hours, as well as tying the services work to something constructive. We didn't get there in one step of course. I often counsel startups that sometimes you just have to do what it takes to keep the lights on long enough for everything to take hold. We had to do the same, by taking some pure consulting (billable hours) work in our early days. I'm not saying you never need to do one-off things for the sake of generating revenue. The difference is motivation. Is the revenue a bridge that brings you one step closer to the real goal? Is it revenue that keeps the lights on long enough for your model to come to fruition, or at least past the break-even point? Or is it just money—the only goal being to make money and you made some?

Even in those early days when our revenue was tied purely to consulting hours, before we had any software product to sell, we were building a solutions company and those billable hours were generally related to designing and architecting solutions. To this day, a good portion of our revenue comes from the services we provide to customize and integrate our software, but throughout all our business operations we look entirely different to a "services" company. What I'm saying is, authenticity in your business model goes far beyond the source of the revenue.

This means the way we pursue business looks entirely different to the body shops in our market. They often start by partnering with established companies to fill open slots on existing contracts, then graduate to being a prime contractor, pursuing big competitive proposals. This means their business model typically comes down to providing qualified resumes at cheaper prices. It's not about the skill or dignity of the employee, but rather the checklist their resume satisfies. One common strategy for a prime contractor pursuing a re-compete of an existing contract is to submit a proposal that assumes they'll simply hire some large portion of the incumbent's employees at a reduced rate (in terms of salary, benefits, or both.) Building a successful business in this realm comes down to recruiting and resume writing. You can build a large company relatively quickly this way, but it also means the notion that people are little more than commodities—to be tossed around like sacks of potatoes—is baked right into your business model!

Our business model, built around "Do Stuff That Matters," led us to pursue prime or directed subcontracts based on the solution we deliver, not resumes that check certain boxes. This means we can charge realistic rates and focus on getting productive work done, not just billing hours. We don't hire people just to fill a slot on a contract; we hire people to help build our organization. There's a lot more nuance to all this than matters for this context. I know I'm talking about this from one narrow industry example, but the point is, authenticity has direct bearing on our business model, and you can see that when you contrast it with others in our general marketspace. Since our business model is *authentic* to who we are and who we hire, it's caused us to grow much slower than we would have as a "body shop." In return, though, we're far more profitable (three to four times so in a good year), have far better employee retention, and no one on our team feels like they're digging a ditch and filling it back in again.

> *We don't hire people just to fill a slot on a contract; we hire people to help build our organization.*

DSTM—Even When It Hurts

During the last economic downturn, the one before the COVID-19 shutdowns, our resolve to stay authentic to our tagline and business model was tested. You may not remember "sequestration" and "the fiscal cliff," related to the Federal Government shutting down in a political battle over the budget. I can assure you, if you were working for a federal contractor, you definitely remember. Some of my friends who spent years, even decades, building very successful firms, literally watched the clock tick down on their corporate survival. They faced cash flow crises as the government suddenly stopped work on all their contracts, and stopped paying their bills while they played their political games. One friend literally had about four hours left before his company—the one he'd poured his heart and soul into for over a decade—would evaporate. As soon as the crisis was over and he re-stabilized operations, he sold his company. He just didn't have it in him to go through that torment again.

This concept of "doing stuff that matters" is a Kingdom value: you were created by God with a plan and a purpose. That makes you valuable. This stands in direct contrast to a worldly kingdom, which only values your revenue potential as a billable body in a services company (or a disposable body in a manufacturing company). In the kingdom, if you're on the bench you're not producing value. Obviously you can't be foolish in this regard, but the Kingdom values people beyond just the numbers. Revenue per employee is important; it tells us something about our efficiency and value proposition, but it's not more important than people. You don't treat the janitor or receptionist as worthless just to maximize those efficiency and value ratios. Maybe if you valued their roles it would help you increase those ratios. Especially since your receptionist or the appearance of your space influences the first impression many people form about your company.

During the shutdown, however, most companies in the market—and certainly all the "body shops"—simply furloughed any non-billable employees to preserve cash. As an employee in one of those companies, if

178

you couldn't bill your time to a contract, you couldn't collect your paycheck. Fortunately, we had enough cash reserves and were adept enough at forecasting to know we could last about four-to-six weeks before we'd have to start the furlough process to buy more time for our corporate survival. Meanwhile, we'd been wanting to release a new derivative product, and we didn't know how we'd find the development cycles to do it. So once sequestration hit, instead of sending people home (illustrating the "you're only valuable to us if you're billable" philosophy), we put our entire team to work on developing and launching the new product.

This sent a powerful message to the team: it said, "We'll cover you for as long as we can. We're in this together, and let's make sure we're doing stuff that matters!" The government shutdown lasted about three weeks—just long enough for us to get version 1.0 of the product released!

People Aren't Commodities

I hope the contrast between Kingdom business and kingdom business in the example above is apparent. Body shops follow a business model that reflect the kingdom of this world, where people are just commodities. I'm just speaking from the market we're in, but I'm sure you've seen examples in other industries, whether in manufacturing, insurance, finance, medical, or any other sector. In most industries, there are business models built on treating employees like commodities, and the exception are cases where people are highly valued.

No matter how much they claim people are their most valuable asset, we've all seen far too many companies where the company does only what's best for a privileged few, causing the ambitious at lower levels to do what's best for themselves. You've almost certainly heard the guiding philosophy in that context: "You need to get what's yours." Most likely you've also experienced some of the ugly corporate politics and ladder climbing this kingdom mindset fosters. You've probably also experienced the corollary, where your value to the company is determined only by what you've produced. (What have you done for me lately?)

Again, this stands in stark contrast to God's Kingdom. Your value is determined by your heavenly Father, and He says you are worth the life of His Son. This makes you literally priceless! In His Kingdom you are blessed so you can be a blessing to others. Following this pattern, a Kingdom-leaning company would consider not just what's best for the company or shareholders, but what's best for the whole employee team, its customers, and the community at large. It would value you in a broader context for who you are, not just what you produced yesterday.

This doesn't automatically mean everyone will be a fit for our company. Instead, for those who are it's our job to assist each one to work according to their strengths and God-given gifts. We keep them aligned and working together towards a common goal. In other words, it's our job to apply the Kingdom principle of recognizing we are one body consisting of many parts.

These Kingdom concepts also don't alleviate an employee's responsibility to contribute to, or produce value for the whole. Instead, production becomes a natural extension of "who they are," not a permanent "prove it," hung out there to shame them into ongoing performance. Furthermore, if we do it correctly, team members hold each other accountable even more than management is required to. Grace as a core value allows for natural ebbs and tides in productivity, within some boundaries.

Grace in Action: One Body, Many Parts

This brings us back to our tagline of *Do Stuff That Matters*, a concept that is really an extension of one of our core values, namely *grace*. Well, the other core values all play a part in DSTM, but grace is probably the biggest contributor in that it explicitly recognizes the dignity of our employees and the role they play, no matter where they are in the organization chart.

The two kingdoms are clearly juxtaposed—in this worldly kingdom, some roles are "more important" than others. I've worked in tech services companies where the line of business staff (i.e. the engineers) were valued, but support personnel, like accounting staff, were not. The crime of it is the latter were even shamed into working as much unpaid overtime as everyone else. I've worked in other organizations where it was just the opposite (where the "bean counters" held sway), and I've worked in organizations where some roles—like the janitor or receptionist—were ignored or even treated condescendingly. I'm sure you've seen the same in your career.

In God's Kingdom, however, every role matters. It's "one body, many parts" and the head is not more important than the legs or the elbow. This does not mean there aren't different types of roles, with different levels of responsibility and authority, but it does mean there is no "social hierarchy" attached to those roles. In Kingdom business culture there are no little people. The concept is summed up by the words of Jesus: "'You know that the rulers of the Gentiles lord it over them, and their high officials exercise authority over them. Not so with you'" (Matthew 20:25-26a, NIV).

This plays out in daily operations with everyone being treated like a valued, contributing member of the team. Unless, of course, they aren't contributing, in which case they should be counseled and mentored back into good standing or released to find a more suitable opportunity.

One practical habit we've taken up is the "one-minute story." It wasn't our idea; we got it from some business author—probably Verne Harnish[15]. At the beginning of our corporate "all hands" meetings held once every few weeks, we pass around a timer. Everyone has one minute to tell a story— something going on with the individual, their family, or whatever—a quick story that helps us to get to know them a little better. It might be about some celebratory thing, like a wedding in the family; it might be some tough thing, like a family member with cancer, or even something adventurous, such as the snowboarding trip they just took.

As we've grown, we've had to start drawing cards, so we hear somewhere between ten and twelve stories at each meeting as we can no longer accommodate everyone at every meeting. You might think we're wasting the fifteen minutes, which is pretty expensive when you add up the overhead hit we take on that many people. I can tell you, though, this exercise has more than paid for itself over the years. New hires initially feel a little awkward when they have to come up with a story, but they quickly fall into the rhythm, and as the team has grown it's kept everyone connected, like one big family. People no longer refer to "that guy in the department over there"—his personal story is part of our corporate story and we all see him as a person, not as a function. It also "humanizes" everyone in that it keeps people at different levels of responsibility in the organization from looking down (or up) on people because of their role; instead they're just real, relatable, approachable people.

Vendors Are People Too

Kingdom business culture extends beyond your employee team and into your whole ecosystem. In our case, we've never had to tell Carole or Amber, who normally open the door for visitors, to offer the UPS guy a cup of coffee. They just do it because that's our culture. Now our UPS guy will often stop by for a cup of coffee even when he has no packages to deliver. And we're glad he does!

It's really quite simple to express appreciation for people whose work you value, as we did with the construction guys who worked on our new office. The rest of our team wasn't in the space every day during construction, but I was. I could see all their hard work, and just how much they cared about realizing our vision for the office, going the extra mile and doing things the right way. I had recently attended a grand opening where the company's CEO spent the entire time talking about how great his company was. (Ironically, they laid off a bunch of people shortly after.) It felt so kingdom.

So, instead, at our grand opening celebration, we intentionally skipped the Yakabod hype, and focused on *authentically* honoring all the roles normally invisible at such an event—Jason the electrician, Mark the carpenter, Roger the project superintendent, and more. All the people without whom we wouldn't have a stunning showplace of a new office. Note also the emphasis on honoring them authentically. It was easy to honor them in a heartfelt way because that's the way we actually felt, that they had for that season, become extended family and were worthy of honor.

Similarly, our friend Tim, who has his own cleaning company, does a superb job of keeping our offices clean, but he rarely sees most of our team because he's often working after normal business hours. On the occasions when other staff members do see him, they treat him just like part of the team. Not because we told them to, and definitely not in any patronizing sort of way, but rather because valuing people is just part of our culture. We normally give everyone "downtown gift cards" at Christmas, which are good at most local downtown stores. This is a win for both our employees and our downtown businesses (our ecosystem!) We, of course, gave one to Tim as well, because even though he's a contractor with his own firm, he *is* part of our team after all these years of faithfully serving us.

Tim pulled me aside last spring (I hadn't overlapped with him for a while), and he kept thanking me, over and over again, for the previous year's gift card, saying how much it meant to him and his wife each year. I appreciated how grateful he was, but I could tell from his moist eyes he felt way more than simple gratitude. It wasn't about the money either. It broke my heart to realize he felt such gratitude because he is simply not treated as a valuable team member by his other clients very often. At Yakabod, Tim knows both he and his role matter. I'm not saying giving him a gift card along with the rest of the team is some praise-worthy thing or that we deserve any extra credit. We're just doing what we ought to do, yet it blows me away how uncommon this basic level of grace is in corporate America.

Leaders Still Required

Please don't be confused about my emphasis on valuing all people and the dignity of their roles. To be clear, I'm not talking about some amorphous, flat, one-dimensional organization with no leadership. Naturally, some people need to lead, and the more an organization scales, the more leaders you'll need.

The question is how those leaders lead. We've all experienced companies where a leadership position often equates to some sense of greater self-importance. You're in charge, and it's all about you. Do whatever it takes to climb the ladder, and the higher you go the more you deserve. (Remember the example in Chapter 7? "We're all in this together. Except for me.") Sometimes in backlash to that, you'll see a totally flat, egalitarian structure (where the people with authority and responsibilities should be leading, but they are absconding instead).

Both of these extremes flow from the wrong kingdom. In the Kingdom, leaders are more like fathers and mothers,

> *In the Kingdom, leaders are more like fathers and mothers, "not like the Gentiles who lord it over people."*

"not like the Gentiles who lord it over people" (Matthew 20:25). They hold their team accountable, but they're also raising team members up to prosper, in greater roles if so equipped. (This book is long enough already, but that's probably worth a few chapters in and of itself...)

Please don't confuse this with corporate socialism either. Different people take on different risks, and make different contributions to the organization. Some of those contributions should certainly be rewarded with a better financial return. For example, in the parable of the talents, and the parable of minas, we see that success in all roles is not rewarded equally, and not all contributions are compensated the same—but *they all receive the same dignity.*

I hope by now I've shown you how your business model has a direct relationship with authenticity. It doesn't matter how hard you work at building culture, finding the right employees or saying the right things—if it's not actually baked into your business model, authenticity won't happen. For us, that means a business model explicitly, intentionally, and sacrificially built to *Do Stuff That Matters,* as a natural consequence of our core value *grace*. That grace conveys a certain dignity on each individual in our ecosystem, which shapes the way not only employees, but also vendors, customers, and community members,

> *If it's not baked into your business model, authenticity won't happen.*

experience our company. Grace, however, also carries some unique ramifications on our operations that our other core values don't. This is worth a deeper dive, which is where we'll head next...

RAMIFICATIONS OF GRACE AS A CORE VALUE

In the previous chapter, I shared how our core values influence our business model, and why, and in the interest of authenticity your core values should impact your business too. In our case, this was mostly focused on grace because grace is the unique core value in our set. You've probably seen excellence or integrity as core values, maybe even passion or consistency, but it's unlikely you've seen grace as a core value on someone's website. It's the one value recruits or potential partners immediately pick up when they look at our website. While all our core values play a part in driving our business model, grace probably has the biggest impact in driving us towards DSTM, even in our earliest days. This is because we wanted our employees to never feel they were just digging a ditch only to fill it back in. As a result, our intentional pursuit of authenticity comes with some real-world ramifications on our business operations, especially in light of this unique core value, grace. Up to this point I've largely been describing it from the company's perspective, but let's look it from a different angle, namely what it means for the way an employee experiences our company.

Something that makes dignity easy to understand is there exists inherent dignity within any role, regardless of how society perceives that role. Imagine life without garbage collectors? You should be thanking God every day that you don't have to drive to the city dump with your weekly stash of garbage—wouldn't that get old really quickly? The dignity of these folks is they do what many won't, and with a great attitude. (I'm of the mindset they should be paid handsomely for it too.) The guys I pass on my walk into work certain mornings are almost always smiling. I don't think I have to convince you, though, that a good portion of society would consider that role as having a lower social status than others. It's not that way in the Kingdom, of course.

Ultimately then, we should see beyond the perceived social status of a person's job description, but there's another aspect of dignity I'd like to focus on in this chapter—the dignity of *you* as a person. Not your role, but your personhood; the fact that you were created by a God who makes no mistakes. In that vein, we like to say everyone has the potential to be an A-player *somewhere*. Not everyone lives up to that potential. Likewise, not everyone has the ability to be an A-player at Yakabod (or at your company, either) so we do our best to find those who have both the ability and drive to be A-players in our environment, then we treat them accordingly.

> ### You were created by a God who makes no mistakes.

The Dignity of You

Do you remember the example from Chapter 7, where the company kicked back my mentor's expense report over one can of Coke? He was running a hundred-million-dollar division of the company at the time. (Yet they couldn't see to trust him with one Coke!) In practice, he was quite trustworthy, one of the most integrity-filled leaders I've known. You can imagine what happened for the company to implement this narrow mindset: one person, somewhere in this big company, was cheating the company on their expense reports, so the accounting department implemented a whole host of new rules and checks. Forget all the administrative overhead that would be wasted across the company—cheating on an expense report would never happen again! Except, it would have been far more effective to just fire the person who was doing the cheating, and focus on hiring people they *could* actually trust. If the company continues to employ people they *can't* trust, it's simply a matter of time before someone else figures out how to game their new system too.

My mentor probably handled it better than I would have—he just shook his head and moved on, but if I'd have received that pushback over one can of Coke, and had to go through the hassle of resubmitting an expense report, I can't imagine my motivation or productivity level would have been very good the rest of that day. Even perhaps the next. (For my Jesus-following friends, this is the exact opposite of Matt 6:26, 30. You might be far more valuable to your Father than the comparisons, but in that company, they feel you're not even worth a can of Coke!)

It's silly policies like this that caused us to take a more "grace-filled" approach based on the "dignity of you." It's exactly why we have no policy against our employees using the fax machine, the printer, or the copier for personal use. As our employee, when you need to fax something to the IRS (because who else would actually take a fax anymore?), then go ahead and use the company's fax machine. That's one less hassle or distraction in the way of you getting real work done. If you start faxing spam to strangers from our machine, well then we're definitely going to address that with you, but we won't put some sweeping policy in place that prevents your teammates from using it.

Another practical example of how we apply this Kingdom mindset is evident in our computing infrastructure. We're a software company full of developers so most of them have or want their own laptop and computer anyway, which also plays seamlessly into our core value of *passion*. Rather than providing a company computer, we give them a stipend upon hiring so they can buy a new laptop. In addition to the stipend, we offer employees an annual benefit called Personal Development Supplement which they can spend on refreshing their hardware, software, or both. If they don't need a laptop they can spend the PDS on anything related to personal development: gym membership, new snowboard, guitar lessons, or whatever else helps them grow in their personal development.

This means we don't have to worry about what you're downloading onto corporate machines. You want to download your music library? No issue—it's your laptop. Checking your personal email account? Organizing your kid's soccer calendar on lunch break? No issue with any of that—it's *your* laptop. We trust you're a professional and you'll get your work done. Naturally, we understand the cyber implications of this and we put our efforts into minimizing those risks rather than maintaining or locking down a set of corporate workstations.

These are small examples, but they're a direct result of our core value, grace, which causes us to treat all the people in our network, employee or not, with a certain dignity. I hope you're starting to see that it's not only about "being nice" to people at a personal level, it has real consequences for the way we operate corporately.

Everyone Has the Potential to Be an A-Player Somewhere

This "dignity of you" naturally extends beyond our employees and into our hiring processes. A few years back, we interviewed a candidate who was really strong in many ways. She was definitely an A-player in a specific work environment, we just weren't sure she was going to be an A-player for us. There were one or two functional skills she still needed that we weren't sure she could pick up, so we just had a candid conversation with her during the hiring process: "We'd like to move forward, but here's where we see some potential issues. If you can overcome those, you'll prosper here. If not, it's not going to work out. Do you want to give it a go?"

She was confident she'd overcome those issues and accepted the position. A few months in, it became apparent she was struggling with the skill-set she lacked. The way forward was simple. We put a more focused plan and some milestones in place related to the necessary skill-set, which came as no surprise to her. She showed no indignation, and there was nothing awkward about the progression of our plan. A few months later we had to let her go and there was no loss of dignity on her part or ours. She was a great person; she just wasn't able to prosper in our environment. Likewise, she saw Yakabod as a great place to work, just not one for which she could use her skills—so much so she continued to refer candidates to us, even after we let her go.

I heard a pastor give a great message illustrating how this dignity concept works in the Kingdom. The message explored the fact that Jesus appointed Judas as the treasurer. Now remember we're talking about *Jesus!* Do you think He didn't know Judas was a thief? Of course He knew. He was calling Judas to a greater identity… *The world knows you're a thief, but I know what you were created to be. And I say you're the treasurer.*

Of course, we have to believe God's grace was available for Judas to become an excellent and honest treasurer, but that part we have to manage personally. You know how the story ends. Judas wasn't able to get past his selfish ambitions, so he failed. (Incidentally, we're not Jesus, so if, when we're interviewing you, we find out you're actively engaged in being a thief, we're not going to hire you. Unless, of course, He tells us to.)

Bureaucracy Is Just Religion at Work

The point is, Jesus' default position with Judas—and thus our default position with the people we hire—is to trust them, and treat them like professionals. We're not hiring "bodies" after all, we're hiring new parts for our one body. If they start taking advantage of our trust, then we need to reel them back in. In some cases, we may even have to fire them. (Just as Jesus let Judas bear the consequences of his actions.) What we simply *refuse* to do is put in a bunch of rules that punish everyone else. This shortsighted method too closely resembles the traditions men insert into religion, which is precisely how the kingdom of this world attempts to counterfeit God's grace—with manmade legalistic religion. Most corporations do the same thing. You'd call it bureaucracy in that context, but it's ultimately the same thing. It's a whole bunch of rules aimed at managing "sin" (or poor behavior) so you or the company, respectively, look "good."

> *Bureaucracy is just religion in the workplace—a whole bunch of rules aimed at managing "sin."*

Jesus offers us grace instead. He empowers you to represent His Kingdom well. For example, if you forget all the rules, but you simply love the Lord your God with all your heart, all your soul, all your strength, and with all your mind; and you love your neighbor as yourself (Luke 10:27), everything else will work out. Translating this into our corporate context, if you live out our core values in your daily work-life, you'll do well.

The Perfect Chief Recruiting Officer

A big part of the reason this all works is because God is an awesome Chief Recruiting Officer! He knew your candidates—and potential candidates—before they were in their mother's womb, after all. (Jeremiah 1:5).

Now that doesn't absolve us of responsibility in the hiring process, so over the years we've learned how to progressively increase the diligence we apply. At this point, after a few phone-screenings to narrow the pipeline, we invest a full day interviewing top candidates. That naturally yields plenty of data for us, but also gives the candidate a good glimpse of what it would be like to work with us. After that process it's sometimes just obvious, and we can make a decision based on our instincts and experience.

Even so, no matter how obvious the decision seems, it's important that we keep asking God about the candidates throughout the process. He knows who fits, and who doesn't; who'd be a blessing to our team and customers, and who would be blessed by being here. Every once in a while, through gathering all our interview data, and then praying through it, He'll lead us into a decision that runs entirely counter to our natural instincts.

We have one guy on our team who set off some major caution flags in the all-day interview. Our concern brought us to the point where we'd normally pass on such a candidate, but after prayer, it became clear we should hire him anyway. We did and it's worked out well; he's been a strong contributor in a few different roles for a long period.

In another instance, we really loved an executive when we first started talking to him, but we just didn't have any obvious fit for him. He was lacking a few key credentials that would normally be necessary for a few different roles he might otherwise fill. Natural instinct would have said it was too much of a stretch to hire him, no matter how much we liked him. Yet once again after prayer, we felt the urging to move ahead and he's been a key player in our recent expansion.

Thankfully, this principle has worked the other way too. We were just starting up when I was first introduced to Emma. She was at the very peak of her career (with all the subsequent demands on her time) but I asked her to be on Yakabod's board, knowing I was punching way above our weight class. As she was driving to my next meeting with her, prepared to graciously decline my request, she prayed over her decision and felt God prompting her to accept a position on our board anyway. She did—and she's been with us ever since.

Of course, asking God about candidates already in our pipeline is great, and that seems to be where we are now—with a good, organic pipeline. We have also, however, been through stretches where we've had to really focus our prayers on finding suitable candidates in the first place. It turns out God knows exactly who we need even when we have no idea how to find them. We went through about a seven-year period where we were in a constant state of needing to hire with no suitable candidates to be found, no matter how much energy we devoted to building a pipeline. Then somehow and quite unexpectedly, an ideal candidate would show up out of the blue, just as it became critical to fill the position.

When a Promotion Is a Demotion

Another benefit to this Kingdom approach around "the dignity of you" emerged recently, and it was one I hadn't previously recognized. John, one of our senior developers, was given an opportunity to take a position at his previous company that would essentially be a promotion. John turned it down. He realized the position would require him to do more program management activities while writing a lot less code. In addition to this drawback, he knew that while the position earned more pay it was also less valued by that company since it was the first position to be cut when a project or contract ended. This would leave him searching for a new job, with diminished tech skills to boot.

To our benefit, John knew he wouldn't have the same concern with us. He'd been through the sequestration episode I described in the previous chapter, so he knew we valued all our people and all their roles. When we asked John to take on expanded responsibilities—as a VP leading our whole development team—he jumped in with none of the fears he experienced in his previous company. This is so great for us because John has turned into a star performer in his new role; even better than we'd have imagined!

A Dignity Program Beats a Diversity Program

Given the discussion above, you might think we have a pretty sophisticated diversity program. Actually, we don't. Here again, grace has real ramifications on the way we operate. While considering this issue, we realized most diversity programs are built on a specific formula. This didn't make sense to us as it forces you to assess a person's value to the organization based on those superficialities around which you are trying to diversify— the fruit of this process is very evident in our society. Furthermore, this superficial process seems to add another attribute upon which you should diversify just about every other week. In other words, the formula needed to pull off the ideal politically correct mix is rapidly becoming increasingly complicated, as suddenly one narrowly defined group or another now feels underrepresented or even victimized. This literally is the oldest trick in the book; Satan set up Eve to think she was a victim, and that somehow God was holding out on her.

Please don't misunderstand my point—I'm not making light of some very real, historic, systemic abuses and oppression in the workplace specifically, or in society more generally. Likewise, I appreciate the fact that bringing people from a variety of backgrounds and cultural experiences into an organization will certainly help make it stronger. Within that context, a diversity program is definitely

> *Despite the improvements diversity may bring to the broken tribal system, both are ultimately inferior kingdom solutions.*

much better than a broken tribal system that only hires people who look like the current members of the tribe. What I am saying is despite the improvements diversity may bring to the broken tribal system, both are ultimately inferior kingdom solutions.

Things work differently in God's Kingdom, and scripture presents this truth in plain detail: "There is neither Jew nor Gentile, neither slave nor free, nor is there male and female, for you are all one in Christ Jesus" (Galatians 3:28, NIV). This tells us there certainly is a superior way. When Martin Luther King Jr. was dreaming of a day when people would be judged by the content of their character, and not the color of their skin, he wasn't dreaming of a diversity program. He was dreaming of the Kingdom! (His dream is readily extended to any other "diversity" attributes, like gender, ethnicity, etc.)

This is why Yakabod has a simple *dignity* program. Since our core value grace says that every person is deeply loved by God, we're compelled to treat them with the respect that status affords. We're not worried about your "diversity attribute," which has no bearing on whether you'll be an A-player with us. We also understand we will sometimes have to put more effort into finding candidates outside our current employees' default "tribes," but that's entirely different to a program that qualifies candidates solely on superficial diversity attributes in an attempt to hit some arbitrary formula.

Check Out Our Special Diversity Bikes…

Allow me to show you how silly this diversity notion has become. We recently completed an application with an organization that certifies "bike friendly workplaces," which we are. We have many cyclists, across the spectrum: recreational and commuter, century riders, mountain bikers, self-supported tourers, enduro-riders (my business partner Scott has three times now ridden the elite 200 mile in a single-day LOTOJA race!), gravel grinders, and more.

Corporately, we installed some bike racks, equipped a specially secured bike storage room with video monitoring, bought some loaner "townie" bikes for the team, and even a fat bike for winter lunch runs. A number of us regularly commute to work via bike, so we have a shower in the office to accommodate that. Many of us ride the annual *Tour de Frederick,* in which the company participates by sponsoring both employees and the event itself. I could go on, but I think you'd agree by now that biking is authentically part of our culture. So much so that we're actually getting requests from various organizations to feature us in case studies for bike-friendly workplaces. Recently I was even invited to be the featured speaker at a webinar on the topic hosted by an office in the State Department of Transportation. I don't know what other companies are doing—we're not bike activists—we're just doing what we do, but some outside organizations that focus on biker-friendly workplaces seem to think we're fairly advanced in this regard.

In spite of that, the certifying non-profit couldn't put us above their bronze level. Now that's not an issue for us. We don't do what we do to get the "biker friendly" window decal, we're just doing things that are authentically us. The only reason we even applied was because someone in our city government asked businesses like ours to apply so they could position the city as a bike friendly community (which we supported, because it is).

So while it's no big deal to us, it does strike me as rather ironic that we could only muster a "bronze." If that were true, why would we be getting calls to do webinars and case studies? You'd think they'd want the "gold" level firms, wouldn't you? I can only speculate, but it seems likely that our "shortcomings" in the certifier's eyes don't lie in our biker friendliness, but in our (lack of) political correctness. The certifier's application form asked a bunch of questions on what we were doing to ensure "inclusiveness" for people of color, LGBTQ, and other "diversity classes" in our bike program.

We must have failed that part, because I had no idea how to answer such a question. What does being LGBTQ have to do with our bikes? The same goes for being a person of color or any other "diversity attribute"—how would we make our bikes any more inclusive? Our whole team is welcome to our bikes, racks, *Tour de Frederick* ride, etc. We did make sure to buy unisex bikes in a full range of sizes, so anyone, short to tall, could safely and comfortably operate them. The last time I checked, as long as you can reach the pedals the bikes really don't care who's riding them! Neither then, do we. How do we possibly make it more "inclusive" without descending into pandering to a kingdom mindset to gratify a non-existent need?

Obviously, this all has nothing to do with biking. The certifying non-profit is trying to show how "progressive" they are, when in fact all they're doing is encouraging us to judge people based on superficialities for the sake of generating some meaningless metrics. We'd rather elevate above that and just treat everyone in contact with our firm as someone who God loves. As would, I'm sure, our bikes.

Challenges with Grace as a Core Value

I think you get the point by now, I've probably hammered on that one. Kingdom treats people as having an inherent dignity, and that's far superior to the kingdom approaches. It's only fair, though, that I also share some of the challenges we've encountered implementing this approach in the real world. These are almost certainly due to our personal shortcomings, rather than any weakness in the overall approach, but we've sometimes struggled to hit the right balance.

Often during the recruiting process, we'll attract a candidate who becomes enamored with us after seeing our website listing grace as a core value. Unfortunately, in their head they sometimes translate grace to mean "work-life balance." And yes, we certainly are about keeping things in proper context. If you're working fifty hours a week, every week, then there's something systemically wrong we need to fix. Typically, however, when we have a candidate talking about work-life balance, what they really mean is, "I expect you to keep giving me that paycheck, but just about everything is a bigger priority to me than the company."

Unfortunately, our experience has been that self-identifying Christians are often the worst offenders in this regard. They seem to forget one crucial aspect of grace—it comes with accountability. Another hiring difficulty we encounter is, "You should hire me because I'm a Christian—that's my biggest qualification." We learned the hard way to dig deeper into these code words during our hiring processes.

> *People sometimes forget grace comes with accountability.*

198

We have a similar challenge even with some employees who've otherwise proven to be A-players. As one of our executives noted, Yakabod is the most forgiving place he's ever worked in his lengthy career. He's right, and in light of the discussion above that's what we want to be. Unfortunately, because of this we tend to bear the brunt of every working couple's scheduling challenges. For example, if the cable guy is coming at noon (which may end up being 4:00 p.m.—you know the way it works), it's our employee who stays home to wait for him. Every time. Similarly, when the kids get sick, it's always *our* employee who stays home with them. Every time! Perhaps it's because we have a flex-time policy for exactly those situations.

With some couples, the spouse *never* takes a turn, because the spouse's company makes it really painful for her (or him) to take those hours off. The more people we have as we scale, the more likely it is that someone's missing a meeting or conversation in which they should be engaged, because our employee stayed home instead of the spouse. I don't know what we could do differently to improve this situation. We *want* our employees to have that freedom in which we treat them like professionals, trust they'll get their work done, and allow them to manage around the complexities of daily life. For the most part it works, but it sure would be nice if our company wasn't taking the hit *every* time.

Sometimes, on a case-by-case basis, we have to pull an employee aside and tell them they've pushed things to the point of taking advantage of the policy. Typically, they bring things back into balance. Now if they aren't getting their work done, that's a different issue, and we need to have a different talk to make sure they prioritize getting their work done, and denote the consequences if they don't.

We had one extreme example a few years back. Our guy was always late to customer meetings, and it was starting to become embarrassing. He covered his tracks so well, however, we realized too late that he often wasn't showing up to our customer's site at all in spite of the hours logged on his timecard. We realized this only when it hit the project crisis point with the customer he was supposed to be serving.

Boy, that meeting really sucked! It was possibly the worst meeting I've ever been in, as I was blindsided when the customer blasted me because our guy—who I trusted—*wasn't even showing up.* Of course, the customer was right in their indignation. Who can blame them for being upset? We confronted our guy the moment we came out of the meeting, and started doing some investigation. (Interestingly, God actually revealed some of our employee's deception to me in a dream.) It turns out our guy was using the time he was supposed to be using to work with the customer, to work for his church. Incredibly, he wasn't sure why we were so angry. This was another case of mistaking grace for "work-life balance." We obviously had to part ways with him.

That's the worst example we've experienced. Most cases are far more mild and manageable, but candidly, I'm not sure we really have it dialed in yet. I guess if we're going to err on the side of rigidity, we'd rather that happen during our hiring process. If we're going to err on the side of flexibility, we'd rather it be in dealing with our employees.

Even so, in my opinion, this grace approach is far more preferable to a bunch of bureaucratic regulations that bind up our great employees. Thank God He doesn't expect us to follow rigid laws, but instead seeks a personal relationship with us, valuing us as people created in His image. This is what we want to model, in that we strive to authentically be who God purposed us to be as an organization, while recognizing the "dignity of you." One body, many parts.

I've shared many examples of what we do, but please don't treat any of this as a formula—like that's what you should do. Instead, look at your own corporate culture, hiring practices, workplace policies, and ask, "Is this the way things work in the Kingdom of Heaven?" and "Is this authentic to who

God made and purposed us to be?" If not, I hope you have learned by now, that your next step is as simple as asking God how to change it...

Many chapters ago, as we started our deep dive into authenticity, we said our contribution at Yakabod is not the revelation or insight that authenticity matters. That's already well documented in the business press. Rather, our contribution is that once we really "got it," we pursued authenticity in absolutely *everything* we do, not based on who we hope to be, or hope to make you think we are, but rather who our Father made us to be. We've talked about a whole range of topics—core values, people, culture, business model, and more—but we haven't quite fully covered authenticity yet. There's one more aspect I'd like to address, and it kind of feels like saving the best for last to me. Because of the nuance, and unexpected blessing it brought us, this may well represent our finest moment in pursuit of authenticity. We call it, simply, Home Court Advantage...

> *Despite the challenges, grace is far preferable to bureaucratic regulations that bind up great employees.*

HOME COURT ADVANTAGE

If your organization is going to be authentic, you need to be authentic in all you do. It may surprise you to learn, this even means your office space. Fortunately, with regard to this, we received some sage advice from a friend before we even understood it.

Prevailing, but Not Necessarily Wisdom

Like many small firms that contract with the Federal Government, our early survival hung on a few large contracts. Admittedly, these contracts were only large within our corporate scope of business, but if we lost one, we were in trouble. The situation was even more precarious, as they were all with one specific government agency. The prevailing wisdom within that industry is to locate your office as close to that agency's campus as possible or they wouldn't travel to meetings at your facility. Since that agency represented all our business at that point, a location nearby would seem especially important in our case.

Similarly, according to the prevailing wisdom, your office shouldn't be any nicer than the government customer's facility, or they would falsely assume you were getting rich off their contracts, which would lead to them micromanaging your contract in response. This set the bar pretty low, because the government spaces—at least at that agency we worked with— weren't exactly inspiring. Every time I worked in one of those offices I felt suffocated. I couldn't imagine trying to recruit a team of high performers expecting them to put up with such poor conditions.

When I sought startup advice from a CEO in the commercial dot-com space, he suggested I view our office as a marketing expense rather than a facility expense. His company had beautiful office space so it wasn't hard to see he was right; you really wanted to be in his space. My friend unfortunately forgot a key piece of the equation though. He moved from one beautiful space to another bigger, more beautiful space as dot-com fever took hold, but in doing so, he over-leveraged. When the market crashed, it cost him his company. In spite of that, I could see the wisdom in his counsel if I just implemented his advice within the bounds of fiscal responsibility.

My own experiments confirmed his wisdom. Our first step out of the spare bedrooms and into a physical office was in the form of an "executive office suite" just down the road from our customer. It gave us a generic room within the suite, big enough for two or three desks, and a fixed phone number and answering service (way back when landlines mattered). It also gave us access to a shared conference room, which was a big deal for meetings. This enabled us to look like a real company instead of an arbitrary assembly of consultants—or so we thought. This move was still problematic because the location near our customer made it expensive, while the transient nature of the space made it dull and lifeless. We had a developer or two in that office most days, but it felt so "plastic" to me that unless I had to be there, I'd just set up in some coffee shop nearby.

Discovering Beautiful Historic Downtown Frederick

As we grew and I started looking for a more permanent office home, balancing cost with livability, we stumbled onto the town of Frederick. I'd seen the strip malls and suburbs at the edge of town, but I had never been aware of the beautiful and historic downtown area just a mile or so off the interstate. It felt instantly right. Back then I couldn't articulate "authenticity," or what that looked like for us, at least not in the way I can now. I knew enough, however, to understand we couldn't just set up in some industrial cul-de-sac, spending at least eight hours a day in a one-story flex-space of windowless office cells and an array of Dilbert cubes, and then expect to differentiate us or our software from the hundreds of "body shop" government contractors in our market space.

I loved the charm of the old buildings, the vibrancy of the downtown environment, and the ability to just leave your car parked and walk to grab some lunch or take care of a few errands. It matched the experience we had envisioned for our employees and our customers. Discovering Frederick caused me to look at some other small historic town centers, but none of them had the same vibe, being either too sparse or too touristy. It didn't hurt that this beautiful, historic downtown office space in Frederick was about halfway between my house and my business partner Scott's house, and that it was a fairly low-stress commute. With some research, we discovered it would be an easy commute for all our team, because no matter where they lived, they would be traveling against traffic on their trip to the office. So we happily settled on beautiful historic downtown Frederick as our new home—or BHDF as we geekily called it.

We quickly found a great little office on the third floor of a turn-of-the-last-century building right on the main corner of town. The building had been derelict just a decade before, so seeing the promise in the empty third floor took some real vision. It did, however, afford us a blank (if oddly shaped) shell, with plenty of historic elements to incorporate into our renovation. We worked with the landlord's architect to create a beautiful space that included restored hardwood floors, exposed brick walls, plenty of glass to bring in the daylight, and a productivity-enhancing open-floor plan. We also included some compelling "getaway" spaces like our library, and the executive conference room overlooking the town's main square.

Before very long, we moved into our new home. Many locals wanted to view the space, as they had fond memories of it being a department store when they were growing up in town. (The historic elevator still had the chair the "driver" sat in to shuttle customers between floors during the department-store heyday!) Of those who did view our new space, we were honored that many told us it was the coolest office in Frederick. Of course our friends at other government contracting companies thought we were nuts, because we were an hour away from our customer agency's main campus. Following the standard protocol of prevailing wisdom, however, just made no sense. The absolute cheapest, lowest-end, Motel 6-class space near the agency expected a rental payment of twenty-five dollars per square foot in those days. Even though we felt as if we were taking a big, scary, step of faith to accept a five-year lease at our early stage, we were still paying less than twenty dollars per square foot. For the coolest office in Frederick! Not to mention it was a place we loved being every day, and a place in which our employees loved working. Needless to say, we were comfortable with our decision.

Like a Field Trip!

Once we were settled we invited our customers to come visit for quarterly reviews of our new product features—the items they'd automatically receive with our next product release. At first they were hesitant since we were all the way out in Frederick. Typically, however, there were one or two people on the customer team who lived much closer to Frederick than to their agency's campus, and they'd convince their colleagues to come out for the day. Of course, government workers didn't want to leave their building, walk across five football fields of parking lot to their car, then drive ten minutes across the parkway to sit in a meeting for an hour at a contractor facility that was just as lifeless as their own… only to return to a thirty-minute search for a parking space. It was different when they came to visit us. It felt like a field trip! As it turns out, the conventional wisdom ignored some key realities.

Sure, it was an hour-long drive for the customer to come visit us, but by the time they had walked from the parking deck to our front door, they'd already walked past several cafes and shops, with the charming historic architecture almost always having its effect, as they thought, *I really must bring my spouse back here for a date night*. Once they had entered our space it would feel totally different when compared to their daily office experience—more like they were hanging out in a Starbucks with some friends. In fact, that was part of the experience—we served them real coffee, not the awful mess hall swill they were given at other places. We also brought in excellent food from one of our great, nearby cafes. If they'd make a comment about "rich contractors," I'd explain with a chuckle that we were paying less per square foot than the lifeless spaces they were used to visiting closer to their campus.

> *The conventional wisdom had ignored some key realities. Customers loved to visit us, because it felt like a field trip!*

This soon proved the prevailing wisdom to be wrong. If we could convince the customer to come out for that first visit, they'd start requesting to come visit at least once a quarter. Before long, our team began referring to this as our "Home Court Advantage." If the meeting was at our place, it seemed nearly guaranteed to be a good, productive, collaborative session! This experience was recently reinforced when a customer came out for a meeting, bringing some new players, with some different agendas, and it seemed likely their new office politics would result in a hostile meeting. There may have been a few tense minutes, but only a few.

Scott and I marveled at how smoothly the atmosphere shifted, and how it ended up being a great meeting. We hadn't thought about it for a while, but as we reminisced about our Home Court Advantage prevailing again, we realized we couldn't think of a single bad meeting we had *ever* experienced in our office. We have had some tough meetings in *other* spaces, like the customer's office or another contractor's facility, and I've written about a few of those in other chapters. In our own office space, however, we literally have never had a bad meeting. Not one.

There's more at work behind Home Court Advantage than just our nice office and great coffee, of course, and we'll dig into that shortly. First, though, you may well be wondering what this story has to do with the Kingdom.

Your Slides Say One Thing—but the Office Says Another

As I hinted at above, your space has to do with authenticity. Authenticity is being true to who God made us to be and consistently expressing this truth, even in the design of our office home. When you walk into our office, the physical space provides you with an authentic experience of who we are before we've even said a word.

As we've addressed in context of culture, people, core values, and other topics in previous chapters, I believe authenticity is also a key building block in a Kingdom approach to marketing. I've been talking about marketing in terms of the brand impression gained from our office space, but the same applies to any impression we leave on those outside our organization.

> *Authenticity even means your office space...*

There's nothing inherently wrong with marketing as a practice, of course, but perhaps at this point in the book, if you're thinking from the grid perspective of kingdom versus Kingdom, it's easy to see how the "prevailing wisdom" related to office space in our industry was based on a kingdom mindset. It's a big enough step for many people to recognize that your office is actually a marketing statement, as my dot-com CEO friend had. "Prevailing wisdom" missed that part. Yet even those who do realize it are sending conflicting messages. They choose the office based on conveying a specific message to the customer: "We're close by and we didn't spend much." What they're really demonstrating though is: "We're a commodity, and our greatest value is just being "next door."

Meanwhile, these same companies will share many PowerPoint presentations in their generic conference room proclaiming how innovative, different, or impressive they are. It's totally inauthentic, because what you experience when you visit them is not at all what the PowerPoint purports the space to be.

Likewise, these companies are telling their candidates, "You want to work here because we're totally different to all those other body shops," or they're saying, and this is my favorite, "Our people are our most valuable asset." Yet this is totally counter to the employee's everyday experience with the company, starting with the office they sit in every day.

This is simply the way marketing works in the kingdom—it's based on attempting to shape someone's *perception* of your brand, company, or product, rather than allowing them to experience the way it actually is. This at best is disingenuous; at worst, manipulative, deceptive, and even fraudulent.

With a Kingdom approach you don't need to *shape* anyone's perception; you simply need to be authentically who God created and purposed you to be! Because God says that's good—it was His idea. This is where my CEO friend, while probably not a believer, actually caught hold of a Kingdom principle (yes, it happens all the time—Matthew 5:45). His space clearly and authentically reflected who he was, and what his company valued.

Again, I couldn't articulate this in terms of authenticity back then, but we knew we couldn't create a fake portrayal of our company image. Simply stated, if we didn't want to hang out in the office every day, why would our customers or employees want to? We had (and have) no intention of manipulating anyone's perception, and neither did we (nor do we) hope to make someone think of us in a certain way. We simply focused on crafting a space that reflects who we are and what we value. More importantly, we created a place we generally love spending time in every day.

You're Only as Authentic as Your Coffee

This cultural ethos flows through everything at Yakabod. Excellence is one of our core values, and it is reflected within a beautiful, handcrafted metal sculpture—portraying excellence in its own right—on the wall of our current lobby. Just past the lobby displaying this exquisite metal sign is our coffee station. As previously mentioned, if we served inferior coffee we'd be miserable, but even more to the point, you'd receive an instant glimpse into how inauthentic we would be in claiming excellence as a core value. We're never going to serve you McDonald's coffee here—that's just not who we are or how we treat our employees or customers. (Maybe you like McDonald's coffee, and if so, I'm sorry. Perhaps we can help you resolve this.)

Instead of serving bad or mediocre coffee, we found a respected local roaster, one who was already roasting custom blends for an accomplished celebrity chef, and worked with her to create our YakaBlend. We've been brewing it for years and oddly enough, because we've had a bunch of new people in our office for meetings recently, I've had at least half a dozen people over the last few weeks tell me we have the best coffee in Frederick. Maybe you disagree that you're only as authentic as your coffee, and that's okay. "Good enough" may work perfectly and this may be your approach only for coffee, and that's also fine. I'm just saying, as trivial as this is, I know plenty of organizations that would literally be willing to act as though they agree with whatever you offer them: "Oh, you love McDonald's coffee... oh for sure, we do too." At least while you're in their office. Then as soon as you leave the office, they forget they ever said it. (Pandering is just about the polar opposite of authenticity.) Now since another core value is grace, we just might make the effort to have some McDonald's coffee on hand for you when you visit, since we know it's your favorite. We won't be drinking it, though. That's not us, and we don't need to pretend.

A Kingdom approach to excellence goes beyond just the coffee we serve. When we host an event or corporate function, we serve our own Yakawines, and they're the real deal too. Winemaker Dave has the grapes shipped in fresh from Napa Valley immediately following harvest. You'll find the same grapes in bottles that retail for sixty to a hundred dollars, and we produce our wine for a small fraction of that. Dave is UC-Davis-trained, and has won plenty of awards for his winemaking skills. So when we sent some home with the caterer's serving team in appreciation for their awesome work at a big event, they were still talking about how good the wines were when they came back a year later.

Excellence is part of catering too, even if we're just serving sandwiches at the meeting. When we order sandwiches they're from one of our top-quality local cafes, and include some combination of handmade, farm-to-table, organic, local, and healthy produce being brought into the mix. Regarding presentation, everything is usually plated on some beautiful handmade clay or industrial galvanized serving platters.

Our core value of excellence is not just in play when we cater, or serve wine and coffee—the bedrock of our excellence is our hospitality. We've always approached things this way because it just felt natural, reflecting who we are. Now, please understand that we're not snobs; we won't complain if we come to your place for a meeting and you're serving build-your-own-PB&Js and pass-around-the-Costco-bag-of-chips for the working lunch meeting. I'm being honest.

> *Authenticity is not the poster on the wall. It's intentionally aligning all the little details with your core values, identity and purpose.*

I've slept in the dirt for two weeks on backcountry treks; believe me, I'm perfectly comfortable with anything you might serve at your place. That doesn't mean I'll like your coffee, but I'll drink it without complaint or judgments on your character or values. It just doesn't matter to you. That's fine. I'm simply assuring you that when you come to our place, you'll experience an authentic experience of what we value; and hospitality is one of those things.

If I haven't hammered it home enough yet—authenticity is not about the poster on the wall. It's all these hundred little details where you are absolutely intentional in ensuring they aren't inconsistent with your core values, your identity, and your purpose. It's not work to be authentically you, but it does take intentionality. In my opinion, that's the gap for most people between authenticity and their current reality. They probably know that little thing "isn't quite right," but don't bother to do anything about it. They feel it just doesn't matter, when in fact it conveys a message to everyone around your organization what's actually important to you.

> *For most people, the gap between authenticity and reality is simply intentionality. They know that little thing "isn't quite right," but don't bother fixing it.*

Help Yourself. We're Glad You're Here

We've only recently come to realize, while we were just being authentic and our sense of hospitality simply followed our natural inclination, it's actually an expression of our core value, *grace*. For our practices, we define this value as reflecting a fundamental standard: every person is deeply loved by God, so we'll serve them with the same love and respect that His example demonstrates. Extending hospitality is part of this mindset.

People sometimes catch that wonderful coffeehouse aroma while walking up the stairs to our office space. I'm sure the UPS guy figured out we have great coffee even before he entered our lobby. Now he knows for sure, because as I have previously mentioned, Carol or Amber offered him some on one of his early delivery runs here. Again, they did it not because

I ever told them to, or even thought about it. Rather, as employees here, they resonate with the concept of grace, and hospitality is one way they just naturally express it. The fact that he'll stop by for a cup, even when he doesn't have any packages to deliver to us, reflects on our hospitality. We love it that people—at least, most people—love to be here. That's all part of our Home Court Advantage. Not because we set out to make you like us or manipulate you into thinking about us in a certain way. Rather, it's because we're expressing that little sliver of God's image He instilled within us, which is in itself attractive... at least to the people we're supposed to reach.

While excellence and grace are core values that reflect the focus of who we are and what we hope to achieve, these things may sound silly to you, and that's fine. Just do you, and focus on being who you are. If you're building the organization, project, or team that God purposed you to build, and you just do you, then it will likely be attractive to those He intends you to reach.[16]

You Be You

Let me provide a practical example using a friend we have who also owns a tech company. He really wanted to own the building he works from so he bought an old garage with rolling overhead doors in an industrial park. There's a large lobby and lounge area right out front where he can hold meetups, tech events, training sessions, and the like. It has a concrete bar, open space to mill about, and a cool sliding glass wall to partition off or open up the conference room. His employees are drinking coffee made from K-Cup pods, but on warm, breezy days, he can roll the garage door up, let the sunshine in, and they can write code while they're swinging in a hammock.

There are lots of electronics and vibrant colors everywhere, and his space is far more hip and big-city-urban than ours is, but this is a direct reflection of his customer base. He spends a lot more time in DC, among the VC-funded startup scene. He also does work with professional sports leagues and teams. He and I talked early in his process of purchasing the space, and I know he was deliberate in making his space reflect who they are as a company. It authentically does just that. My friend's team loves their office, and feel like they have the hippest office around. Which they probably do. A few of our guys were there for some training, though, and after drinking K-Cups for a few days, they opined on how happy they were (relieved almost) to be back in our office, in our restored and repurposed factory setting. The point is that his team is happiest being who they are, and ours feels the same way.

We have another friend who owns a workflow software company. Their value proposition is all about delivering productivity gains, automation, and cost-efficiencies to manual business processes. In keeping with their value proposition, their office is a bit more spartan than ours. The owner doesn't care a lick about his coffee. He's in more of an office-park setting, with lots of (aargh!) Dilbert cubes. I personally couldn't work in that space, at least not at this stage of my career, but it authentically reflects his company values and brand promise. He treats his employees like family, and they have plenty of free parking right in front of the office.

I can't quite quantify why, or point to any specific design elements in his space, but there's just this feeling of *integrity* there, and I'm sure his employees feel it. He tends to travel to customer sites in far-flung locations, more often than they travel to him. He does big user conference-type events, but holds those offsite, not in his office. This makes it very different when compared to our scenario, but again, it's all very authentic.

The Era of Personalization and Your Faith

What I'm talking about above—that you should be you and if that's aligned with your God-given identity, there's something attractive, even purposeful to it—is all part of a broader trend we can even observe in our society at large. Business author Seth Godin has been writing about this for years. In the old days of the broadcast era, you could run a TV ad selling toothpaste, and as long as it was a decent ad you could quantify the return in sales proportionate to the frequency in which you broadcast the message across the limited available channels. For my Jesus-following friends, "witnessing" worked the same way: the Billy Graham Crusade could rent a stadium, broadcast to drive attendance, and expect to see some results. Interestingly, many (most?) churches are still running on this broadcast era model, expecting to use some "invite cards" to draw people in to their church setting to hear a message. This marketing strategy was appropriate for a specific time and season—a little like the era of John the Baptist when you could tell people they must repent, and they would!

In this modern era, in the days of internet, hyper-personalization, *Amazon Prime,* etc., this strategy is for all intents and purposes, completely obsolete. Brands have to go out and meet people where they are, because people self-identify and therefore seek others with a similar mindset before joining a community. You don't *sell* by broadcasting a message, you do things like content marketing and community building to attract those who have interest in your products!

As it relates to the Church, believers are called to do the same. We need to go where people are, because our programs aren't bringing more non-believers into church, they're usually just pulling in believers from some other church. We're playing Christian musical-chairs and wondering why the Church isn't growing, much less having any influence in our world. Jesus gave His Church the gifts of different disciplines, like apostles, prophets, evangelists, pastors, and teachers (Ephesians 4:11-12). He also gave us the responsibility to equip God's people to do His work and build up the Church—to equip the saints for works of service.

This idea is similar to when Jesus sent out the twelve, and then the seventy. He equipped them for service, then he sent them *out*! They would demonstrate the power of God's Kingdom, demonstrate the Father's love and grace, and declare the Kingdom of God is at hand. They didn't pass out a tract or an invite card, and expect people to come to the church building. They went out and met people where they were. *In our day, this includes ministering to people at work—demonstrating "at work as in Heaven"— because this is where people are most of their day.*

This is our relationship goal at Yakabod for our employees, and for our relationship with the broader community. It is also yet another reason our space has to authentically represent us. We may never draw our employees, vendors, partners, or customers into a church, but they sure will come to our office. There is something very attractive about the Kingdom, and God has designed that part of it we represent to be attractive to the people we're supposed to reach.

Authenticity Everywhere

I know I've been talking about authenticity as a Kingdom building block for marketing in the context of our office, but I hope you understand this authenticity extends to all of our marketing. Our website, while we update it in fits and starts, also generally reflects who we are. At least it's not trying to position us in a manner that is not authentically us. "Prevailing wisdom" would have us appear as large as possible, but we don't care if, while reading our website, you realize Yakabod consists of only thirty-five people. We're not trying to pretend we're a company consisting of 350 or 3,500 people. You will be able to tell we're not comprised of three people either.

I hope you also see by now, that beyond marketing, authenticity matters in everything, and that even means your office or workplace. The space tells people a whole lot about who you are no matter what your words say. For us, our office space has turned into our Home Court Advantage. But if I let you think that was only because we were intentionally authentic in every last bit of the design, flow, and function of the space I wouldn't be giving you the full picture. It turns out in our case, there's more. Something we couldn't do ourselves, couldn't specify, couldn't design, couldn't make happen, but which gives us a totally "unfair" advantage…

AN "UNFAIR" ADVANTAGE

U nderstanding our office is a marketing medium, and then deliberately designing it to be authentically us, definitely helped to create a Home Court Advantage in our first office. We were able to leverage this advantage exponentially in our new office, but this is only part of the story because really, we have an outright "unfair" advantage in our office, no matter the location.

This unfair advantage is *God's presence.*

I think there is a similar effect going on in our office in the way we as individuals, once we were saved, began to carry the presence of the Lord through the indwelling of the Holy Spirit. I'm not making a deep theological statement, I'm not even saying I understand it. Clearly, though, since the principals of the company, those with natural authority over this entity, have consciously chosen to submit and devote our organization to the Lord, to welcome Him here in prayer, to put His name on the side of the building—there's something about doing this—God has graced our office with a manifest sense of His presence.

So Present You Can Feel It

There have been very few places I've been where you could feel God's presence in the atmosphere. I'm not talking about a place I'm in all the time, where I consciously go to personally meet with God, like a church I regularly attend or a space where I pray regularly at home. I'm talking about an experience of showing up someplace as a visitor, and being overwhelmed with the sudden awareness of a sacredness to the space, where I could sense the holiness, where there was just a thick, tangible, extraordinary feeling of God's presence lingering in the place. I've experienced it in a few places where men and women of God had contended in prayer for years and years. Mind you, I didn't go seeking an experience of the presence of God (not that I'd ever want to avoid it), I was just going to see some historical site.

> *Our Home Court Advantage comes from authenticity, but our "Unfair" Advantage comes from God's presence!*

An example of this is when I visited one of the stone churches along the Blue Ridge Parkway in southern Virginia that was at the center of a move of God in a century past (described in the book *The Man Who Moved a Mountain*[17]), I got hit with that experience of God's presence I just described. I didn't go there looking for it, but it sure found me! Likewise, I felt it another time while visiting the prayer room of St. Francis of Assisi in Santuario La Verna, built into a stunning mountain gorge in Tuscany, Italy. I've been a few other places where I walked in as a visitor, and was pleasantly confronted with that tangible experience of the Lord's presence "dwelling" in the place.

In the same way but to a lesser degree, not nearly as thick or tangible, not always so obvious, but nonetheless present, you can feel something different in the atmosphere here in our office too. This experience manifests here in our office as something you would likely describe as "peace." Our office is marked by a supernatural atmosphere of peace. This is an absolutely "unfair" advantage we have.

Now again, I'm not making a theological statement. I'm just sharing what we and others experience. It makes sense. Most days—the days we're here in the office—we invite God into our workplace through prayer, welcoming Him into everything we're doing. The result, as my spiritually discerning friend Victor pointed out, turns our floor-space into "sacred ground." There's a certain "natural" element to the office—in the authenticity, the excellence of design, and the beautiful materials and craftsmanship, which all contribute to our home-court advantage of course. Ultimately, though, the biggest component of it is supernatural. It's God's manifest presence felt almost tangibly in our building, which often feels very much like peace. (Among other things, Jesus is the Prince of Peace, after all!) The contrast of "peace" with the conventional atmosphere present in many businesses is immediately apparent to anyone who walks into our office. That's because in many places, it's the *stress* that is quite palpable.

The Proposal Factory

Early in my career I worked in the office of a federal contractor, which I now recognize as a "billable body shop." There was always a certain bravado in the office, built on guilt and shame, which suggested the only *real* workers were the ones putting in ten-to-twelve-hour days without additional compensation. This kicked into high gear during proposal season, when a subset of the team would be consumed for months on end with crafting a multi-volume proposal to respond to a large, competitive government procurement.

Due to the nature of the work, the office had certain security requirements, including the provision that two people had to be present to work in the secure area. Since I was the young guy back then, I was appointed to show up at 5:00 a.m., as this was when one of the key proposal writers started.

I'd get there at 4:58 a.m. and the key proposal writer would be lying on the couch in the lobby, grumbling about how it was practically afternoon already. Then a different guy would be grumbling when I wanted to leave at 7:00 p.m. because "Kids these days have no work ethic." This gives you a sense of the atmosphere, which would continue for a whole year. A team would be bunkered down in a "war room," agonizing over and debating every word in the page-limited documents, spinning in circles on every rumor or innuendo regarding what the customer might be thinking, or the competition might be doing, twelve hours a day at least, and often more. For endless months this would continue. I remember one guy who actually had a family with small kids, would leave after a twelve-hour day, so we'd all shame him (including me, because I didn't get it back then). That was just the culture. I probably don't need to tell you the everyday experience did not feel like "peace."

Just One More Thing…

You can imagine the extreme level of stress the team lived under, day after day. You also wouldn't really recognize just how much stress you were under until you got away. One particularly taxing proposal went on for well over a year, and when we finally submitted the proposal I flew out on a trip to California the next day, just to clear my head and get out from under the stress. I had to change planes in Chicago, and went through that underground connection between terminals back when they had New Age chime music, neon lights, and everything else that was going on around the turn of this century.

I was walking through there thinking, *Wow, this is kind of cheesy, but it seems to be working—I can actually feel myself starting to decompress. I guess it's difficult to understand just how much stress I've been under until now… now that I'm starting to move away from it.* I let out a big sigh, mentally moving ahead into a week or two of total decompression, when I heard someone yelling my name. It was totally out of context, but I snapped out of my almost-relaxed state enough to recognize it was one of the executives from my company (what are the odds?) on the moving walkway going the other way. He was headed back to the office from somewhere, and honestly started barking action items at me; stuff he expected to have on his desk that very night when he got back to the office. By the time I was able to issue a weak protest that I was finally on vacation after a year of twelve-hour days, he was out of sight, fully expecting I was about to jump into action, getting eight hours of work done in the next four hours—on the plane.

I worked in another firm, with a similar high-stress culture, where one of the technicians was known to be a heavy pot smoker, decades before it became "medicinal" or a hot political topic. As a result, he was a little slow on the uptake, but this also rendered him a bit impervious to all the stress. Once in a while, however, the chaos would become so thick that even he'd become aware of it, at which point he'd turn wide-eyed to one of his coworkers, and focus just long enough to declare, "Dudes, we need to move our desks out into the sunshine…"

You probably have your own experiences with such high stress environments, and unfortunately, that was the norm in almost every office I worked, or closely observed before starting Yakabod. I think you know which kingdom *that* stuff is coming from.

It Just *Feels* Different

That's why—with an atmosphere marked by the Kingdom value of peace instead of kingdom-centric stress, anxiety, guilt, chaos and more—it immediately feels different to anyone who walks into our office. My Jesus-follower friends will often say something like, "You can feel the presence of God here." And they're exactly right. I mentioned my friend Victor earlier in this chapter who made reference to our office space resembling "sacred ground." This made me think of the burning bush that Moses approached, which was just a normal, ordinary bush… until God's presence arrived. It was God's presence that suddenly turned it into something remarkable, something which caused Moses to have to investigate. He's done the same for our office.

It's not only "religious folk" who feel something tangibly different in the office. It happens all the time, and I find it interesting, the way different people describe it. One of my favorite comments came from a visiting pair of Scott W's friends, who are New Age potters. "There's just such a different spirit in here," they said. (They were more right than they knew. It sure was different. Holy even.) Their spiritual radar was up, but they didn't know Who it was; they just knew the space felt different from what they typically experienced.

If you think that sounds unusual, I'd encourage you to refer to Luke 10, and notice how Jesus describes peace as a tangible presence; something the 72 can give away or take back again. Similarly, that peace is tangible in our office.

The Kindness of God Leads to Repentance

I've only recently come to understand what a powerful witnessing tool the simple experience of peace in our office truly is. I told my story in Section One, explaining how once I had made my decision to commit my life to Jesus, I grew up in my faith in an evangelical setting. In this environment, great importance was placed on sharing one's faith—which naturally I believe is important—but in that setting it was taken to an extreme, and led to what I can only term as "confrontational evangelism." It didn't matter if I was thumping people over the head with my Bible—whether they were ready for it or not, or whether I saw results or not—because I felt I had to be doing it.

I'm unashamed of my faith, and after all God has done for me I have no problem boldly declaring His name, sharing His gospel, or testifying to what He's done for me. When words were the only tool I had, God honored my words, but as I matured, I came to understand that actions are often far more powerful than words. In many situations, I could simply allow my actions to do the talking.

It took me at least another half-dozen years to understand God's presence is more powerful still. Carrying His presence and being open to Him is sufficient, so I can "do what I see my Father doing, and say what I hear my Father saying." I now recognize that sometimes I just need to let God's goodness shine through—no speech is necessary—and His goodness will indeed lead to repentance (see Romans 2:4).

There's *Healing* in His Presence

This is a clear indication the peace experienced by people who visit Yakabod is actually what evangelicals would call a "witnessing tool." It's attractive and it invites a conversation about the God whose peace is present. For most people His peace is very attractive. For at least one woman, that manifest peace of God present in our office has been life changing. I shared a post about her story some time back on Facebook:

> We just got awesome news! There's a woman who takes care of the plants in our office. About 18 months ago, she was diagnosed with a brain tumor, and it spread throughout her chest. Doctors gave her 5% survival rate—said she'd be dead in a year. A few of us have been praying for her ever since. Not as faithfully as we should. But often. She had to drop all her other clients. But she kept us—because she just felt peace when she was here.
>
> Today we learned that the latest MRI showed the cancer in her chest is gone. Like totally gone. She was still having some nausea, swelling in the brain. So they did brain surgery last week—to discover there was no more brain tumor either, just some scar tissue from the last surgery they needed to clean up.

She wanted nothing more than to be around long enough to raise her daughter. Now she will be. Her mom just told me "I've got goosebumps all over thinking about it—somebody's listening to your prayers." Somebody indeed. And I love how good He is...

Of course, there's even more to this story, and Kim has kindly given permission to use her name and share her story. Kim became so ill she had to quit working with all her other clients, but she felt such peace in our office she couldn't stop visiting. It finally reached a point where she couldn't drive here anymore so she asked her mother to drive her. That was a big deal in itself, because her relationship with her mother had been strained until then. Sure enough, this started the process of healing their relationship. Kim sadly became so ill she couldn't even get out of the car to come into the office, so her mother would come in to take care of the plants. Still, Kim insisted on joining her mom on the drive.

Kim would then sit in the car down on the street, so she could at least be near the office. Again, we didn't pray as faithfully as we should have, but we did pray; maybe once a week or so. In one of those prayer sessions, I sensed God telling me to stop asking for her to be healed, and instead declare that she *is* healed, because He had already taken care of it. The next several times we prayed for Kim I did just as I was instructed, declaring something simple like, "Thank you Lord that you've healed Kim, in the mighty name of Jesus."

> *Facing cancer with a 5% survival rate, Kim was drawn to the peace of God's presence she felt. Not at a church, but in the office. Then He healed her!*

A few months later, I was able to post the message above. Kim felt the peace of God's presence—not in a church or in some Pentecostal healing service—all she needed was to be within the vicinity of our office. She clung to the inner knowledge she sensed about feeling God's presence, and

God completely healed her! Now as God often does, He turned Kim's story into an even better witnessing tool. Here's the next post:

It gets better.

> Last week I shared the story of a woman with brain cancer that had spread through her chest, was told she had a 5% survival rate, and less than a year to live. A few of us prayed. To the doctors' astonishment—the cancer in her chest is gone. They're waiting on biopsy results, but it appears the cancer in her brain is gone as well.
>
> A friend saw that post and messaged me saying, "This is perfect timing. My mother has this growth on her jaw, they're not sure what it is, but it's very aggressive, it's probably cancer, she's got a biopsy next week, and things don't look good. I don't usually ask for stuff like this—but I asked some people to pray, would you mind praying too?"
>
> I said, "Of course. Now you know there's nothing special about my prayers—but there's something real special about the One I'm praying to. He'd love to talk to you about all this, but I'm happy to add my voice to yours."
>
> I saw the same friend at a business function last night. "How's mom?" I asked.
>
> "It's the craziest thing," she said. "Total reversal. Mom went in for her biopsy, and the big lump was gone, there were just a few little bumps. Mom said the hair on her arms stood up, the surgeon told her he couldn't figure out what happened, but told her there's basically nothing there to biopsy anymore."
>
> Draw your own conclusions. I think my buddy Jesus is up to something... :-)

Of course, the supernatural peace of God is not limited to a physical place, but I love how He took what happened here, and "broadcast" the display of His goodness at our office to someone we've never met!

225

Never a Bad Meeting

As you can see, our Home Court Advantage doesn't fully hinge on our nice office, and neither is it found exclusively within the foundation of authenticity driving our office design. Mostly, it's just the supernatural power of God emanating from our individual relationships with Him. It may not be as overt a miracle, sign, or wonder as seeing someone inexplicably healed, but the fact that we've never had a bad meeting here, is almost certainly due to His supernatural grace, mercy, and favor.

We've spent a lot of time on authenticity, probably a few too many chapters for you to remember it all, so you'll find a quick summary of the highlights at the end of this chapter. Through all this, I hope I've challenged you and encouraged you to reflect on your God-given identity. Not just yours, but also your organization's identity, and that you'd then think and pray through how you can be authentically that. In *everything* you do. I hope you understand that as much as He's given you dignity (and He has!), and as much as He's given your organization purpose (and He has!)... it's not ultimately about you. It's about Jesus. That in all this, He's simply calling you to reflect that tiny little sliver of His glory that you (personally and corporately) were created to share with a world that desperately needs to know Him.

The whole Earth *will* be filled with the knowledge of the glory of the Lord. His Kingdom *will* come, and His will *will* be done, on Earth as in Heaven. Are you ready to play your part?

I don't know about you, but that's what I'm hungry for. Even more so as He mentors me in how to expand this truth beyond our company and into the community on any given Tuesday. This is where we're headed in the next chapter.

Summary – Authenticity

Kingdom

- Intentionally be who God purposed us to be.

- All roles and all people are significant—one body, many parts.

    ° Dignity is endowed by your Creator.

    ° Dignity program to ensure everyone is treated with respect and honor.

- Core values guide decisions.

- Culture comes from living out core values.

- Scale by hiring people who already resonate with core values.

- Authenticity (and core values) drive business model.

    ° Provision flows from corporate and individual purpose.

- Home Court Advantage: God's presence brings peace.

kingdom

- Manage perceptions to shape who people think we are.

- Roles convey social or political status.

    ° Dignity is based on your performance.

    ° Diversity program to produce a certain "mix" based on superficial, arbitrary formulas.

- Opinion polls and perception guide decisions.

- Culture is aimed at shaping employee perception.

- Hire first, try to figure out core values or shape culture later.

- Anything to make a buck.

  ○ People are just a commodity.

- Office feels like the world: chaos, stress, anxiety, shame, fear, guilt, etc.

Key Points

- The underlying Kingdom principle—greater purpose versus "It's all about me." Looking at people as who God made them to be, as opposed to what can they do for us. Am I looking outward at how to benefit people or a greater good, or only looking inward at how to benefit myself and the company?

- Figure out how the role a staff member fulfills is aligned within the company, how they're valuable as a member of the team, and how that role helps the company prosper.

- Diversity is better than no diversity, and sometimes you have to work harder to find people who don't look like the tribe already employed, but as soon as you start putting formulas on it you're reducing that person to that formula. They may not be the best engineer, but they're the best engineer within a certain diversity attribute. As Martin Luther King Jr. proposed—a man should be regarded by his character instead of the color of his skin (or regarded by any other God-given attribute).

- Every person is loved by God, and that's the way we treat you.

SECTION 3.5: KINGDOM CULTURE

NOT IN MY TOWN

I don't know about you, but it seems as soon as I settle in on being comfortable with the way I'm approaching things, God places me in circumstances that call me to a higher perspective. In my quest to make Sunday matter on Tuesday, I was beginning to settle into the idea that when faced with a difficult or significant decision at Yakabod, we'd lead with the question "Is this the way things work in His Kingdom," and then seeking to prayerfully partner with my Father to figure it out. After all, the goal

> *This wasn't God's desire for only our company, but rather for our whole community.*

was to continually refine our little company so it would look a little more like His Kingdom than the wrong one.

God was about to teach me, however, that this wasn't His desire for *only* our company, but rather for our whole community. As I mentioned in the last chapter, God began leading me to think about how a business can bring the goodness of His Kingdom to a whole community. Recently, He taught me a powerful lesson in this regard, by encouraging me to take a stand even before I quite knew how to articulate what I was standing on...

Time for a New Home

We loved our offices on Frederick's *Square Corner.* The building is the perfect testament to a beautiful, historic, downtown district, right at the main intersection of the business area. After our Spirit-led move into the location, and God's subsequent presence affecting many lives in that location, it was time to move on. We had been there for a dozen or so years but had to move, not because our lease was up, nor because the landlord wanted us out, or even because we didn't still love it there; we'd simply outgrown the space.

When we began looking at potential spaces we settled on two simple criteria: A) we wanted to remain in the downtown area, so the new space had to be within walking distance of the current office; and B) it had to be an upgrade to what we had. Since the space we were leaving was 4,200 square feet, we figured we should look for somewhere between 8,000 and 10,000 square feet. We figured with an efficient layout, that size space would allow us to easily double our headcount, which might then serve us through four, or even five times growth in top-line revenue.

The problem we encountered, however, is we were looking in beautiful, historic, downtown Frederick—not *Manhattan.* There are only so many office spaces with the square footage we required, and even fewer were available for sale or lease. Fewer still were available on one floor, which is what we really desired.

Understanding the challenge we faced, we assembled a top-notch team to help us. We partnered with a well-regarded, highly experienced real estate investment group in case we needed to buy a building. They connected us with a local buy-side realtor who knew every building in town, including those that *could* be available for lease or sale, but weren't yet. He in turn connected us with an equally seasoned real estate lawyer. The city's *Office of Economic Development* offered to help in any way they could, and with this great team we started exploring all the opportunities.

A Swing and a Miss

We quickly settled on one building as our favorite. It had been empty for forty years, but we just loved it. It had the potential to be a beautiful building, and was situated in a prime location. We also had a strong vision for how we'd use the space, a key part of which was how the space would serve the community as well. Highly motivated, we made a premium offer to acquire it. In fact, our team told us our offer—if accepted—would be the highest paid figure per square foot for office space in the history of our downtown area. We'd have gladly paid it for the flagship office that would have resulted.

The seller refused our offer. We tried to figure out what the problem was to see if we could negotiate, but all we learned was there was a reason the building was still vacant after all those years!

We were disappointed of course, but had a few other viable options. The best two alternatives weren't for sale, but rather had leasable space that could be move-in ready within six-to-twelve months. Options beyond those either required major renovation, or would have a few years or more lead-time before we could move in. We didn't have a few years. We weren't sure we had twelve months before we outgrew our space so we pressed in on the two near-term options.

The first option just felt like us. We felt it as soon as we walked into the space. It was an empty shell, really—9,000 square feet on the top floor of an old mill building, that was in the early stages of restoration. It was situated right along the linear park on the creek, and we were immediately able to envision it as our home. In fact, ten years earlier I had been walking along that section of creek with my wife, long before the linear park was done, long before my family moved to Frederick, and long before the building was under any sort of renovation. I looked at the run down, derelict, old mill complex and said to my wife, "What a cool building! That really needs to be a tech company." I never dreamed that ten years later *we* would be the tech company looking to lease it!

A couple of potential issues existed, however—it was a few blocks away from our then-current office, on the other side of a busy commuter street, so it felt just a little disconnected from all the activity downtown, and I wasn't sure how the team would take this. They had become awfully used to having a slew of great lunch spots just a few steps from our front door. The bigger issue was, the owner—headquartered in Washington DC, not a local firm—had a reputation around town for being very difficult to deal with. If the rumor mill was even half-right, I wasn't sure I could trust the DC firm.

The second option was just a few blocks north on the main street. More importantly, it had recently been bought by a local investment group. They were not only well regarded in the community and had a strong track record in developing properties "the right way," but I also counted the principals as friends. They too had around 9,000 square feet available on the top floor of their historic building. We had a solid vision for how we'd use it, and I knew when we crafted the layout for the space my friends would make that space the best version of itself it could possibly be. The only challenge was that some fire code issues would force us to segment the layout in a way that made it feel like two co-located offices, rather than one big open office.

Although neither situation felt ideal, both were viable and the clock was ticking. Things were getting crowded and unproductive in our current space, and we still needed to hire another three or four people to jam in there. After much prayer, Scott and I still weren't sensing any definitive direction. We decided to take our leadership team on a tour of the two spaces to share the working vision for each space, and get their feedback and insights.

The team unanimously preferred the first option. They had no issue with the location, which alleviated that concern. Of course, I also knew they weren't the ones who'd have to deal with the notorious landlord!

We Win, You Lose

After more prayer, we decided to press ahead with the first option. We approached it like we always do: we told the developer we were win-win type partners. We told them we'd be happy to just give them their premium asking price without negotiation because we knew that was important to them, but we were expecting them to provide our premium finish-level on the build-out because excellence was important to us. They agreed in concept, but sure enough, things quickly turned difficult. While working through the first step in the process—a "letter of intent" (LOI), they started arguing over all sorts of inconsequential details. Not the finish-level we were specifying, to their credit, but things like lobby hours, parking spaces, bike storage, and space heaters—silly things with easy solutions.

I knew better than to work it through our lawyers, so I'd just call the developer each time we hit some onerous language in their next draft of the LOI. I'd say, "We're flexible, we can approach this a half dozen different ways, this is what's important to us, tell me what's important to you, and let's figure out something that works for both of us." Way too much wrangling and painful discussion would follow, over what I expected to be a simple solution, and then their next draft of the LOI would come back with some new onerous provision.

We were pretty deep into the process by then, and had spent a few months trying to get something worked out. It was at the point where I was just dreading any interaction I had to have with them, and when I did, I'd typically go out for a long bike ride shortly afterwards, just trying to blow off steam. I'd spend the whole ride—often fifty or sixty miles—rehashing it all with God, asking Him to help me figure out why these guys angered me so much. I could understand the obvious stuff, but was there some deeper thing I was reacting to? This negotiation was just too difficult, and it didn't make sense.

We finally got an LOI we could kind-of, sort-of live with, which left a lot of issues open to be resolved in the next step—the lease, but by that point I was already more than ready to walk away. I told our realtor the developer had about one chance to make the lease less painful than the LOI, and if not, we were done.

Predictably, their first draft of the lease came back with crazy stuff all through it. There was one provision that essentially said if Hurricane Agnes came through and blew the building down on the second day of our lease, we were obligated to pay uninterrupted rent for the ten-year duration. In return, their only obligation was to give it their best attempt to get the building operational again... at some point... when they felt like it. But if they didn't, "Oh well!" There were a dozen provisions more egregious than that. It was so bad I didn't even see anything to negotiate.

Our lawyer convinced me to give him one phone call before we just walked away. He called the developer's lawyer and said, "C'mon man, you aren't serious with this, are you?" Their lawyer spent an hour telling ours how much smarter he was than us, why those provisions were right, why we were just wrong, how dozens of clients supposedly signed up to those same provisions with no problem, and that we were just being difficult.

I couldn't see it at the time, but it was clear later that this developer's negotiation strategy was pretty simple. For most people, certainly those we consider our friends, if there's 100% on the table, maybe this time we're fine with 40% and we'll let you have 60%, knowing next time it'll be the other way, and in the end everything will all work out fine. That's what happens when two parties deal with each other in good faith. In contrast, this developer's strategy was to claim the full 100% *every time,* and make you fight really hard to get 20%, figuring you'd feel happy you won something, even while they still got most of it. It didn't matter how minor or inconsequential the provision under negotiation; they were intent on seeing that they won big while you lost big.

Not on My Watch

Our lawyer had made his one call to no avail, and I was done. I went out for another long bike ride, praying through and rehashing it all with God when it suddenly hit me: I couldn't be the guy who said it was okay to do business in our town that way. Frederick is not perfect—that's not what I'm saying. But one of the really beautiful things about our town is the sense of community. People live and work in Frederick because they love being here. It's not simply convenience, like many bedroom communities or developments. People build their lives in Frederick because they genuinely love Frederick. So business in our town, at least among local businesses, is normally based on trust, collaboration, and good faith, with honest and fair dealing. Frederick embodies what you'd expect to see in a (big) small town with a strong sense of community; where people know each other, understand the impact of their dealings with each other, and have a desire to see the whole community prosper.

It hit me that if I signed a lease under the developer's ridiculous terms, they'd turn right around and use that to strong-arm the next tenant, saying, "We don't know why you won't sign this, Yakabod did."

By the time I had completed the bike ride my resolve was firmly cemented. We were done. Totally done. We weren't going to be party to doing business that way. That wasn't happening in my town; at least not on my watch. I wasn't sure what we were going to do, as we really didn't have a good Plan B. At this point, anything else we pursued would have a move-in date at least a year away, or more likely two to four years. In light of this, our lawyer and realtor tried to convince me to let things blow over for a week and try again. Instead, I called the developer personally and told him we were done. I said we were the easiest people around to do business with, but they made everything arduous and we simply didn't do business the way he was trying to do business.

To no one's shock, the developer was convinced this was just a negotiating ploy on our part. After a week he called, trying to restart discussions. I told him, "Absolutely not!" He kept calling each week after that because he knew we didn't have any other options at hand. I even kept hearing around town that (according to the developer) we were still going to be moving ahead. (Yep, that's another feature of a small town—the rumor mill.) Friends, even close ones, told me I needed to be pragmatic, and that we couldn't always stand on principle—that I was being a little dramatic with my "wasn't going to be the guy" thing. They said nobody would care about any precedent a year from now, and that most of those egregious provisions wouldn't ever affect us on a daily basis, but growing ever more crowded in our current office would. I told them all I clearly understood the consequences, but I also knew God could drop three new buildings into downtown Frederick tomorrow. Of course, I wasn't counting on Him actually doing that, but I did trust He had a good solution for us that He'd reveal in time. I knew God had a way even where I could see no way.

I felt I'd much rather take my chances with God than the developer, and I really was at peace with our decision. In any event, it was no negotiating ploy. We were truly done, so we got busy exploring alternatives and stuck with our same two essentials—close enough to walk, and it had to be an upgrade. We did broaden some of our evaluation criteria, though, like maybe we could make things work on two floors instead of one. Little did I anticipate what the Lord had in store...

A PROVERB COMES TO LIFE

There's a proverb in the Bible—specifically, Proverbs 16:7—that says, "When a man's ways are pleasing to the Lord, He makes even his enemies to be at peace with him." I wasn't consciously thinking about that verse in the context of the developer's hostile, self-serving negotiations—that scripture has been hanging on the note board by my desk for most of the two decades we've been in business. It's just one of those scriptures I took to heart in our early days, trusting that if I focused on my relationship with the Lord, He'd take care of the other stuff I'd

> *When a man's ways are pleasing to the Lord, He makes even his enemies to be at peace with him.*

otherwise worry too much about. Little did I know, I was about to experience the practical reality of the proverb…

About four weeks after we walked away (and four weekly calls from the developer), Paul, a more senior executive from the developer's office sent me a voicemail. We had met Paul very early in the process before he left the negotiations in the other executive's hands. Paul explained he thought our lease was a done deal, and was really surprised when things blew up. I was getting a little tired of dealing with the ongoing calls from this developer, but Paul asked if we could meet so he could learn what went wrong. I called him back and told him if we ever lose a proposal or customer, I appreciate it when they give us candid feedback from which we can learn, so I was willing to give him a similar fifteen-minute debrief—as long as that was his true intent. I made it clear that if it was a thinly veiled attempt to re-open discussions he was wasting his time. Given all that had transpired, I was not looking forward to the meeting.

When the appointed time came Paul didn't show, and although I thought it ironic, I honestly was a bit relieved, thinking, *Now I can really wash my hands of these guys.* I was actually out looking at other buildings with our realtor when my business partner called and told me Paul was in our lobby, and asked whether I had forgotten about the meeting. "No," I replied, "he was supposed to be there over an hour ago. I'm in the middle of another meeting. Tell him it'll be at least an hour until I'm back in the office." I figured he'd be long gone by the time I finally finished my meetings.

Putting It to Rest

I was surprised to see Paul still sitting in our lobby when I returned a few hours later. He apologized profusely and explained that while he was sitting in our lobby with nothing else to do, he went back to his voicemails and realized he *had* indeed messed up the time. I felt bad for the guy; he had to have been pretty bored sitting in our lobby for a few hours, but it showed me he really had come in a spirit of humility, wanting to learn.

Maybe in light of how things happened, it ended up being a pleasant conversation, even though I had to be very frank. I told Paul that his company had simply made the process too difficult, and gave some examples of the silly stuff they made so difficult in the LOI. I explained how they approached every provision with the intent that they win big and we lose big, no matter how inconsequential the provision. Then I explained how the lease was even worse. I used the Hurricane Agnes provision to drive the point home. I pointed out how all of that was further exacerbated by me having to pay billable hours at a handsome rate to my lawyer—for the sake of listening to his lawyer's long-winded condescension.

Paul took it all in, and said, "You're right, I wouldn't sign that lease either."

Finally, I told him I wasn't going to be the guy who made it acceptable to do business in our town that way; "Maybe that style works in DC, but it doesn't work here in Frederick," I said honestly. I told him that we love our town and care about the whole community, which was why I was never going to "just live with it," only to have them use us as precedent to strong-arm the next tenant into signing the same egregious provisions. The conversation wasn't pointed or confrontational, it was all very relaxed, but very candid.

To Paul's credit, after hearing me out, he offered a sincere and humble apology. He said their firm had grown too quickly, didn't have all the right infrastructure in place, and he clearly had a lot to fix. As promised, he didn't try to re-open discussions, and offered no pitch, he simply said the door was still open if we ever changed our mind. I was glad we had the conversation, but had zero intention of ever restarting discussions. We were done with that option.

We continued with our exploration of alternatives, but about three weeks later I discovered that Paul had removed their DC lawyer from all of the firm's Frederick projects, hiring a local lawyer instead. Likewise, on another project in town, which had been through similar grief, he totally reset the process, throwing out the old lease and starting over with simplified terms to get rid of all the contentious provisions.

One More Try?

Following much prayer about the alternative options, a few weeks later I felt a nudge from the Holy Spirit to reopen negotiations on the old mill building again. Paul's space was still our best option by far; it just fit us so well, and we had such a great vision for it.

I called Paul and said I'd give him one chance to make things simple. I told him this wasn't a negotiating ploy either, that he didn't have to agree with everything we said, and we were still in the win-win business, but the process had to be simple and marked by good faith. He promised I'd have the exact opposite experience I'd had negotiating with his company in our prior attempt. True to his word, he called his entire team together to meet me in the space—his leasing agent, his new lawyer, the architect, the site manager, the construction supervisor—every team leader who would be involved in our extensive custom build-out. In the span of an hour, he went down the entire list of provisions that had earlier been contentious, and in each case we came to a reasonable solution that worked well for both parties, and that his whole team was comfortable delivering.

That solved the lease language, and Paul's new Frederick-based lawyer worked everything from that discussion into a far more reasonable lease document. We had a pretty tightly defined specification we'd worked out with their architect, but I knew that no documents can capture everything. I understood there would be countless details to work through during the build-out, especially since it was renovation rather than new construction, and that we'd have to carry that same collaborative, good-faith spirit through to the end for it to succeed.

I was pleased with these first steps at a restart; they were more fruitful than I had expected. Of course, we still had leverage because I hadn't signed the lease yet. I knew once we did, we'd have absolutely *no* leverage. I still wondered if we could trust them. If we signed, we would have to, but after all that had gone before, I wasn't sure I was ready to make that commitment on the basis of one good meeting.

Sometimes You Know It before You Understand It

These thoughts led to another long bike ride. If nothing else, this ordeal kept me in decent shape, and talking to God even more than usual, at least for a brief period! As before, I played the whole scenario before the Lord in prayer, asking Him if we should move ahead, because I was still not sure that we could trust them. In that moment, I heard Him telling me, as if with a smile on His face, "Now *that's* the way you bring the Kingdom to the community." I knew instantly He was

> *I heard the Lord telling me, with a smile on His face, "Now that's the way you bring the Kingdom to the community."*

talking about the stand I took, refusing to be "that guy." I hadn't seen it before, but this thing in Frederick—this way of doing business, this willingness to do what's best for the community rather than oneself, borne out of a love for the community, is actually a building block of the Kingdom!

Frederick is certainly not perfect, there are plenty of attributes that look nothing like the Kingdom, but my refusal to be bullied into a bad deal had far bigger implications than our lease or the next guy. I was holding onto an established Kingdom value in our town where a kingdom value was trying to gain a foothold to supplant it! But only when it was evident that I was serious about taking that stand, did God help me articulate it. With that understanding, I felt a release... like this battle was over and we were fine moving ahead with the lease.

So we did.

More like the Kingdom

Jesus followers will be aware that God makes it rain on both the righteous and the unrighteous. In keeping with this concept, He told the Israelites to embrace their life in Babylon so it would go well with them and they would prosper. This is just one little example of the way it happens; how God uses you, as a believer with an awareness of His Kingdom, to bless the whole community—even those who don't know Him and don't even care to know Him. When we did sign the lease, it was a great witness to our lawyer. He saw our willingness to walk away from the deal as real integrity, since the action we took put us at risk of facing great personal financial consequence. I never really thought of it that way until he said it.

We ended up having a great relationship with the developer's team and the construction team through the entire build-out, which took around eight months to complete. I was in the space just about every day, meeting with them, and there was plenty of give and take. I continued to look for ways to help them streamline their costs and schedule without compromising the level of quality we needed. They in turn made sure to bring us into the hundred little decisions that had to be made every day, no games, no shortcuts, just a sincere desire to ensure the result truly captured our vision.

As you might have gained from previous chapters, the vision was rather extensive and fairly intricate. We were intentional about all the little details in the design—the form, fit, function, and finish for *everything*. We had plenty of time to learn how we'd use the space from our experience with the previous office: we understood the importance of authenticity, and we'd long since recognized the effects of Home Court Advantage. This meant the space required a whole lot of custom work, from repurposing an "unusable" freight elevator space into our featured coffee bar, to preserving as many of the original elements of the old building, and working in reclaimed materials from other parts of the old mill complex.

We were also diligent with specifying every little fixture and tile selection and paint color. There's not a single generic, builder grade component to be found in the space, except perhaps the electric range in our kitchen. (Believe me, if we could have figured out the fire code challenges, it would have been a commercial gas range instead!) The point is, this was not a simple matter of throwing up some framing and slapping on some drywall. Yet the construction team—the landlord's team—more than rose to the occasion, and really acted like our partner through the process, which is all we wanted from the start.

If you're at all creative you'll understand this—you record the song, or you paint the picture, and it's pretty good. Your friends rave over it, but you know it's not quite that vision you have in your head; it just doesn't capture the fullness of your idea. Anybody creative has had this experience. I can honestly say this office build-out turned out to be one of those rare creative projects I've been involved with that actually captured the vision! Where that thing we had in our head is *exactly* what you experience when you walk into our space. A big part of that was the construction team—including the developers' own site manager—being fully engaged in the vision and working in close partnership with us. Indeed, the whole way through, it just felt like they all knew how special the result would be, and were proud to be part of it. The construction has been complete for a few years now, but they'll still stop by occasionally for a cup of coffee, or bring along potential clients by to show it off as a reference.

Even though the newness has worn off after a few years, I can still say our home is stunningly beautiful, definitely an upgrade from our previous office—and truly, authentically us. On first seeing it, one friend from a local tech company, said, "Wow, this really does represent who you are and how you see the world." (I hope she meant that as a compliment!) I know everyone's own baby is the most beautiful child ever, so you have good reason to view my statements as hyperbole, but I'd encourage you to check out the virtual tour and pictures on our website for yourself at www.yakabod. com/headquarters. Perhaps it's not to your personal taste, but I hope you'll at least see that I'm not exaggerating the quality of the workmanship and the diligence of the design. (More recently, we did get named as one of

Maryland's Coolest Spaces for 2020, even though we never submitted an application. So there are at least a few other people who think our baby is beautiful.)

We love to throw a good party too, so of course we had a Grand Opening celebration. We skipped the ribbon cutting and didn't really talk about us. Instead, as I shared in a previous chapter, we felt it was important to share the space with the community, and to explicitly honor the hard workers who'd helped us realize the vision. Of course, we acknowledged Paul for being a man of his word, and for making things smooth and simple.

It was quite a grand event; we engaged Minda—a top-notch regional caterer, and her team hit it out of the park! We invited a broad mix from the local business community, city and county government, and longtime friends of the company, serving them some of our Yakawine and local craft brews. One of our dear friends even flew in from Austin.

People were talking about that party for *weeks*. This may seem like a college-kid thing to mention, except that several days later the city's Director of Economic Development shared his feelings with me: "You don't realize how important that was for the city, and what an encouragement that was to the whole community." The city had been making infrastructure investments for thirty years, especially in the linear park and creek that runs just behind our building. Unbeknownst to me, they'd justified those expenditures on the hope they would one day attract more tech companies along with the higher-paying jobs that companies like ours provide. Seeing us in the space was a fulfillment of their decades-long planning and investments!

On her first glimpse of the finished space, another friend from the county's Office of Economic Development, said slowly, with a contented sigh, "Wow. Now this is who Frederick wants to be..." That's when it all started to make sense as to why we were supposed to be in this office; why there had been so much opposition, and how important it was we partnered with God to push through it!

When I consider Yakabod and where we are, the word "destiny" comes to mind, but it sure feels like there's something "prophetic" going on for our city as well. This has me intrigued to see what cool thing God does next. Yakabod continues to provide for our exquisite laboratory setting so we can keep exploring the challenges of bringing the Kingdom into our everyday workplace life and to our community, and it seems God is still writing that story…

BUILDING KINGDOM CULTURE

From a corporate standpoint, the events of the previous two chapters ("Not in my Town" and "A Proverb Comes to Life") felt like the start of a new era, with God positioning us for the next step towards our corporate destiny. Personally, it also marked a big shift in my understanding of my own call, and my leadership approach. Through those circumstances, the Lord helped me to see all the nuance better; not only in how this applied to specific business processes, but in the very fabric of our culture and even the community. It took the theoretical motto I'd recently adopted— that things work differently in the Kingdom—and turned it into a real and practical experience.

And So He Prospered?

As we were basking in the glory of our new office, settling in towards the end of 2018 and early 2019, business began to explode. All our contracts were growing. We'd hired half a dozen people, and our most conservative projections had us hiring half a dozen more. These were the projections based on what customers were cautiously telling us, not the even bigger growth they were hinting at. I honestly wasn't sure where we were going to find the people, but it felt like we were on cruise control to another record year.

Then suddenly, by mid-February, every one of the contracts blew up, and I mean every last bit of it was totally out of our control. Now if we'd delivered some really bad software or somehow screwed up, we'd fix it. We'd understand we were reaping what we were sowing, and figure out how to improve our product quality or business model, but that wasn't the issue. The issue with one customer was a sudden reorganization, which brought in a leader who was hostile to all external contractors (not just to us). Another customer suddenly hit budget issues. A third became concerned we were moving too fast, and throttled our pace so we wouldn't get too far ahead of their other projects (you can't make this stuff up—who gets penalized for performing *too* well?). Down the line it went, cut, cut, cut. Suddenly, I wondered if we had hired half a dozen staff members too many.

In retrospect, maybe I was getting some insight into how King Hezekiah must have felt after seeking to work wholeheartedly with God. One verse describing his life ends with the words, "He sought his God and worked wholeheartedly. And so he prospered" (2 Chronicles 31:21). *The very next verse* says, "After all that Hezekiah had so faithfully done, Sennacherib king of Assyria came and invaded Judah. He laid siege to the fortified cities…" 2 Chronicles 32:1. What? And so he *prospered*?

For about a week, panic tried to gain a foothold in me every day and most of the night. I sure felt like we were under siege. I knew which kingdom this was coming from, but it was a real battle not to give in to it. Right now, as you're reading this, I could probably rattle off twenty different scriptures that talk about God's faithful provision, but one night when I was having trouble sleeping under the weight of it all, the only thing I could recall was Psalm 23. I was totally blank, except for that. So I just declared over and over: "The Lord is my shepherd, so I lack nothing. *Nothing.* I lack absolutely nothing." Finally, peace gained the upper hand and I was able to fall asleep.

A Silver Lining?

I and everyone at Yakabod pressed forward, perhaps not in full confidence, but at least in some semblance of faith. Our conservative style of management helped greatly—we had built up a substantial war chest (financial cushion), and had no debt. I didn't know how long we could weather the lower revenue levels, especially in light of all the recent hiring, but we had at least several months to let things roll forward before making any drastic moves. The last thing we wanted was to cut any of our staff after we'd invested so much in finding and training such a great team.

Meanwhile, we'd been wondering for some time how we'd find the bandwidth to implement some key features in our product roadmap that came out of our last strategic planning session. These weren't simple nice-to-haves or incremental upgrades—they would finally take us to where we'd been wanting to be with our go-to-market approach for the last dozen years. We took some comfort in the *déjà vu* unfolding before us, as it was starting to feel a little like the sequestration experience we'd been through before, some years back. Unlike that previous product launch, though, we weren't investing our spare cycles in an experiment. In this case, upon further reflection, I could see this was a watershed moment, providing us with the perfect opportunity to finally start our "flywheel" spinning.

Our flywheel process has four steps, and for the last decade we'd been building the first three (see Jim Collins' seminal book *Good to Great*[18] or his more recent work, *Turning the Flywheel: A Monograph to Accompany Good to Great*[19]). These new initiatives finally gave us the fourth step to complete the loop, where our technology would finally mature to the point of enabling the business model we'd envisioned all along. These features were critical to our future, and suddenly our team wasn't over-booked with customer work. More importantly, we had the cash and the will to focus on developing these missing pieces, so we were starting to feel like perhaps there was a silver lining after all.

We knew, though, we'd have only one chance to build the required features. God's resources are infinite, and we were trusting He'd provide what we needed to accomplish His purposes. Our war chest, however, was distinctly finite, and until He provided or promised some supplemental manna, we knew we had to be wise stewards with what we already had. As presented in Chapter 7, "Cash is King..." we weren't going to spend money we didn't have on pursuing our roadmap. The money we were spending couldn't merely be "bench time" to cover the team as an alternative to layoffs; it was a strategic investment that had to count.

In our next monthly all-hands rhythm meeting I knew I needed to stress to our team the importance of building these features. They could see the turbulence in the customer-driven contracts, and a few were starting to wonder if we'd survive. Some of them had talked to me individually, and I had given them assurances of our corporate health, but this was one more reason I had to gather the entire team, and honestly talk through everything we were facing.

When the Enemy Punches, Punch Back!

It struck me that if Satan was trying to rob us, then I should take the battle right back to him, on the hope the Lord would make the enemy pay back more than he was trying to steal from us in the first place! (At the very least, I knew if I resisted him, he was supposed to flee.) Accordingly, I intended to expose the enemy's nonsense to the team—showing them that this was a spiritual battle we were in, not a business battle—and then use the

> *It struck me that if Satan was trying to rob us, then I should take the battle right back to him.*

opportunity to disciple the team in some Kingdom values. It was very clear, in the context of what the Lord had taught me through the circumstances of "Not in my Town," this was another one of those key opportunities to draw a line in the sand, and kick out kingdom in favor of Kingdom.

I prepared my speech, working through how I'd explain spiritual principles to our diverse corporate team in business language (this wasn't a church group, after all!). I was feeling pretty good about it, really—until the night before delivery. Then I kept hearing an internal voice saying, *That's just stupid. You can't talk to them about spiritual stuff. They're all gonna think you're crazy. And probably quit too. Or maybe just sue you instead.* It takes me a little while sometimes, so I had to wrestle with these thoughts for a while, until I finally realized where this pushback was coming from. It was pretty apparent then I should tell the enemy to shut up, and press ahead, knowing for sure I was on the right track.

Meeting day came, and honestly, I was a little nervous. I knew I was doing what I had to do, but I had no idea how the team would react. I explained right up front I was going to tell them where we were, where we were headed, and how we'd navigate from our current position to the next. I also expressed that while I could talk to them about those first two topics in business terms, I couldn't explain our navigation process the same way. Thankfully they knew I was never one to push my faith on them, but because I didn't know how to navigate our trajectory without my faith, I told them I would have to explain it in those terms, and hope they'd take it in the right spirit.

I candidly shared with them the whole picture; how every contract had blown up, and how we were rapidly turning from profitable months to unprofitable ones. I explained again how we'd built a war-chest for just this purpose, and while we could not sustain this posture forever, no one's job was in jeopardy yet. I told them we'd let things roll forward for many months, and keep them apprised of the situation in the meantime. I also encouraged them, saying I had naturally spent a lot of time praying for the company through this difficulty, and I was confident we would be fine.

Then I presented our vision for the future, explaining in general terms the "flywheel" concept described above, and how the product roadmap initiatives (with which they were familiar from earlier meetings) had finally taken us to where we'd wanted to be for a decade or more. I explained how the same market opportunity we saw back then was still in front of us, but we hadn't quite been in a position to pursue it until these customer project cuts had suddenly freed up some development bandwidth. I said we were finally on the verge of pushing into what we'd been dreaming of since all the way back to company's founding. I reminded the team we had already done some tests, using a niche derivative product we had spun out over the preceding few years, which proved the viability of our go-to-market strategy, and we were now ready to go all-in. Suddenly we were in position, with the cash and the development bandwidth, to invest in developing the missing pieces. "So this is what we are doing," I explained, "and it has to count… but if we do it right, I'm certain our best days are still ahead." I wasn't blowing smoke at them—I wholeheartedly believed everything I had just told them.

Spiritual Battles Require Spiritual Weapons

It seemed to go over well. The team was engaged and appreciative, and perhaps even a bit excited by all I had said. I felt the temptation, of course, to just leave it at that, but I knew I had to press forward. So I told them the missing piece revolved around *how* we'd navigate from the current turbulence to the glorious future I described. I explained that if this was a business battle, we'd fight it with business weapons. I gave an example, explaining that if we shipped awful software, we'd fix it and figure out how to make things right for the customers. "This, however," I continued, "is not a business battle, but rather a spiritual one, so we have to fight it with spiritual weapons."

I told them I knew some of them were probably thinking I was some hippy-dippy, spaced-out new-ager talking about a spiritual battle, but I offered to explain how I *knew* we were engaged in a spiritual battle. I reminded them that most of us had experienced other workplaces, and then brought to mind the negative emotions they had most likely felt in these commonplace work environments; things like chaos, stress, and anxiety. "Don't those things describe the experience you've each had in many other workplaces?" I asked. I saw lots of heads nodding in agreement.

I then asked what they normally felt in our workplace. I explained that they may have just grown used to it, but when customers or new visitors walked in they often remarked about the peace they felt in Yakabod's premises. I asked if they agreed our environment is usually peaceful. More heads nodded. I told them peace is a spiritual attribute which comes from God's Kingdom, whereas chaos, stress, and anxiety are also spiritual attributes—from the *wrong* kingdom. So when circumstances conspire to replace a very desirable attribute, like peace, with undesirable attributes, like the aforementioned ones, this is a good indication a spiritual battle is being waged. I told them how, when things first blew up, I could literally feel the fear and anxiety trying to gain a foothold. I reminded the team some of them had felt it too, even approaching me to discuss our standing. More heads nodded. "So," I continued, "that's how we know this is a spiritual battle, which is why we're going to fight it with spiritual weapons—and two of the most powerful ones I know in a circumstance like this are gratitude and generosity."

I had been talking to them about gratitude for the last half-year, keeping us grounded in this quality of being thankful as revenues and hiring ramped up. I told them I was still grateful as I looked around and saw our beautiful office, a great team, and considered all the great years we'd had. I truthfully admitted I'd never have dreamed, back when I started the company, or Scott either when we merged, that we'd ever have been as blessed as we had been over the years. I explained how I knew for sure these blessings had nothing to do with me being some great CEO, but rather had everything to do with a Good Father who loves his children and continually blesses them. I reminded them of how we'd been talking about gratitude for the last half-year, and we would simply continue this posture. I told them I'd love to have them join me in this but if they weren't feeling it I would understand; yet it wouldn't change our corporate posture.

Whether they were feeling gratitude or not, though, I told them they could absolutely join me in a posture of generosity. I explained the natural reaction—the one anxiety was looking to produce—is that we would hold tight, hunker down, cut expenses, and make rash decisions. I told them we resolutely weren't going to do that. Instead, we would express how grateful we were, doing the exact opposite of an anxiety-ridden reaction by responding with generosity. For our first act, we would give some of our software away.

I told them we were launching our new "Apps that Matter" program, and how we were already in the midst of giving away the first instance of our software to a new non-profit group who would use our platform to bring together the local community. At that point there were already thirty-six churches committed to not only covering our city in prayer 24/7, but also collaborating with each other in response to whatever we saw happening in our city.

I explained Scott and I had already picked this application, but once we had completed it, perhaps once per quarter, we'd allow the whole team to bring in ideas for the next app. Whether to aid a non-profit or some community need, we'd select an app to give away. We'd pay for the software and our labor, but we'd have the non-profit pay for hosting, so we knew they'd value and actually use it. In other words, our employees really would be "doing stuff that matters," not just giving away something to no effect.

A Workplace Team Embraces Kingdom Values

I wasn't sure what to expect, but I'd said my piece, and I knew I'd been faithful to what the Lord was setting me up to do, so I felt relieved. As the meeting broke, the team's energy was good and they seemed to be resonating with what I had said, but I couldn't know for sure. Soon afterwards, however, a number of the team members approached me, telling me this is what they loved about our company, and how happy they were to work at Yakabod. Then one of our more senior members pulled me aside and said, "I'm all in. I don't care if you need to cut my salary in half—whatever it takes, I'm in." A few more sent me notes on our corporate Yakabox platform.

A few days later, another guy caught me at the coffee machines—I have no idea of his spiritual background, but he's almost certainly not a Jesus follower. He said, "Hey, I was really happy to hear you say you were praying for the company. I've been thinking about that, and I reckon it's really important." A few weeks later, as I walked out to the kitchen another younger team member wandered in. Seeing he had me all alone, he told me how much he appreciated the talk at the last meeting, and how he was convinced of just how real and authentic it had been. He also told me he'd been thinking about what I had said about gratitude and generosity ever since.

During this time period I was out for a hike, again praying through the challenges we faced but feeling good about the Kingdom culture piece the Lord had set me up to deliver. I felt our team was stronger than ever but I also knew we still needed revenue. A call came through on my phone, and caller ID said it was Hal, who leads our federal group, so I took it. To my surprise, one customer had suddenly found more money, and they were going to spend it on our contract. It was about fifty percent more than we were expecting.

This increased revenue stream wouldn't quite take us back to our previous "normal," but it did help significantly. The news came just in time to share with the team at the next monthly meeting. Feeling celebratory, and also to reinforce the generosity theme, we brought in lunch and gave each of the team a bottle of our Yakawine to take home, along with the good news of our revenue increase.

The development had me feeling pretty good for a few months. I had the testimony of "Not in my Town" to draw on—I had taken a stand where there had been no logical way ahead—and God had created a way forward. Every day, I could sit in our beautiful office, enjoy a fine cup of coffee, and see how faithfully God had provided, no matter the current circumstances. In spite of the turbulence, He had also given me another opportunity to explicitly build Kingdom culture. I had taken my stand and our mixed, secular team was willingly embracing a posture of gratitude and generosity. Some revenue was flowing again, not quite all we wanted, but enough to give us that much more runway. Perhaps our next big breakthrough was just down the road!

I'd love to tell you that's a wrap on the story and we moved right into our happily ever after. Unfortunately, it turned out the story was still very much unfolding.

ARE YOU WILLING TO FIGHT FOR IT?

I'd won a little victory. The enemy was trying to sow fear and panic and the Lord set me up to punch back by mentoring our team in gratitude and generosity. Not my church group. Not my men's prayer group. Our employee team, from all sorts of spiritual backgrounds and inclinations, including atheists—now pursuing the Kingdom values of generosity and gratitude. Perhaps more openly and willingly than many church congregations! This being said, I should have known there'd be another counter-punch coming...

Here Come the Trolls
A few weeks later, we received a cryptic submission from our website. It was anonymous, from somebody claiming to be an employee but full of

sarcastic criticism. It basically said our product sucks, our management was clueless, and the company wasn't really living its core values. From the language used we were pretty sure it was someone who knew us, rather than just a troll parroting some of our website language. We couldn't think of anyone on staff who would be carrying this kind of vitriol, much less able to hide it from us on a daily basis, so we figured it was more likely a former employee.

Most staff who leave do so on great terms but there had been a few over the years we had to fire for improprieties. Even though we treated them way better than they deserved (as grace would have it), we knew there may still have been some sour grapes lingering on their part. Maybe their most recent employer had just fired them too, so they sought revenge by trolling us (unfortunately, I'd had a few girlfriends like that in my younger days). Scott looked into it, seeing if he could figure out the IP address or something else that would point to a name.

I thought about saying something to the team, and even spent a few hours working up a talk on the off chance it was a current employee. Mostly we just ignored it. If it was a *former* employee there was obviously a reason we had fired the person. I saw no reason to pay attention to that. If it was a *current* employee, however, if they didn't have the guts to talk to us in person within our Kingdom culture, then we could probably ignore that too, figuring they'd leave soon enough. So I dropped the idea of the talk, feeling sure I'd have rambled on and made it a bigger deal than it needed to be.

A few weeks later, I was having a conversation with one of our team leaders, Doug, who wanted to give recognition to one of his team members, Chris. We were implementing a new process as one of our key corporate initiatives, and Chris ran the first project to use it. Chris successfully navigated the new process and demonstrated the strategic value of it, as well as producing great results. He also showed personal growth through the course of it, so Doug wanted to do something to honor him and announce the success of the new process. We corresponded briefly on Friday, with Doug mentioning he wanted to buy a gift card for Chris, and suggested having a discussion about how this new process worked, but we ran out of time. We agreed to meet on the Monday so we could present something at the Tuesday meeting.

Eerie Timing

On Monday morning Doug and I talked. He said he felt a fifty dollar downtown gift card would be the appropriate gesture, along with some explanation. I offered to bring a bottle of Yakawine for Chris as well, since the team always seemed to enjoy that. Doug said he'd be happy to take the bottle of wine, but Chris doesn't like wine, and so the gift card was sufficient. We chuckled, and Doug walked up the hall to have some coffee. I walked next door to my desk, and not thirty seconds later, an email arrived from the "anonymous employee" again.

This time the form submission accused us of being cheap, said we didn't pay people anywhere near what they were worth—and by the way, *we could keep our gift cards and wine*, as these didn't motivate anyone. Whoever sent the submission added it was time we forked out some cash instead. I stared at the submission for five minutes before I realized the message showed Saturday's timestamp, but it had only now been forwarded to me by the web team. Still, the timing was way too suspect. Doug was still at the coffee machine, so I pulled him aside and asked him if he had told anyone else about his ideas for the Tuesday meeting. He assured me he hadn't. I told him what had happened, and while it didn't make sense to either of us, it still seemed extremely unlikely to be a current employee reacting to something they'd overheard.

My plan had been to talk to the team in more detail about the "flywheel" concept, then explain how all the new product development work they were doing on R&D dollars dovetailed into the process. The new submission made it suddenly clear I could no longer follow my plan—I *had* to talk

261

about the anonymous employee. Not about their criticisms—who cared about that? Instead I would have to discuss the cultural implications of this anonymous criticism. I wanted to be clear this was more than our leadership being annoyed—just as I had refused to allow that corporate landlord to set a negative business precedent in Frederick, it was clear I had to refuse this insidious attack from having a detrimental effect on our posture of gratitude and generosity.

Confronting the Troll's Accusations

Yet again I spent all afternoon, and a good portion of the evening, consumed with preparing the speech for the next day's meeting. The more I thought about it, the madder I got, and the more fiery my speech became. When I started thinking thoughts like, *That's just stupid. You're way overreacting. Now they're going to think you're just a big sensitive baby, or plain nuts,* it became even more apparent there was a purpose to the speech, and I had to give it. Again I resolved, if Satan was going to launch into his accusations, then we would turn them back on his head and use them as a springboard to disciple our team—a good portion of whom are not believers—in some more Kingdom values.

We reversed the order of some things in our standard meeting, so rather than opening with my speech, I'd close with it. We opened by honoring Chris and talking about a few upcoming things, and by celebrating some of the progress we'd been making on our R&D efforts. Then I told the team I had intended to—in fact I'd have loved to—spend the meeting talking in more detail about how our R&D efforts mirrored the concepts in Jim Collins' book, *Good to Great,* specifically his take on the "flywheel" and the "hedgehog concept." I also shared why I was so confident our best days were still ahead. I went on to explain we'd do all that at the next meeting, but in the meantime, I was forced to confront a cultural issue. I told them it wasn't going to be a pleasant talk but they needed to hear me out.

I launched into the background details, explaining how we'd been receiving these anonymous messages, adding it was probably someone who knew us, perhaps a former employee. I assured them it was almost certainly *not* a current employee, but there was a chance it was a parent or spouse who had heard someone grumbling every day. On the off chance it was one of us in the room, however, I *had* to address it. I shared the accusations, so everyone knew what they entailed, but made it clear the criticism wasn't the real issue. More importantly, it was vital that I address the underlying cultural issue, so everyone knew what was acceptable in our culture and what wasn't.

The room grew silent as I glanced down at my notes for the first time. The gravity of the situation dawned upon any who hadn't been paying attention. I cleared my throat and began, "I want to be very clear upfront—I'm not accusing any one of you of being this anonymous culprit." I looked around the room and everyone held my gaze, but their mood was unreadable. I couldn't be sure the person sending us the messages was *not* one of our current employees, but either way, I had to launch into my talk:

> I told them I wasn't mad about the criticism, we certainly don't think we're perfect, but I was steamed about the delivery. Most of them had never seen me mad before, so they knew I meant it. I talked about our culture being more like a family. How hiding behind a keyboard hurling insults was just another form of selfish corporate politics, which was totally unacceptable in our culture. That since we're family, we have conversations, even on tough issues, and you'll know your voice is heard and respected, even when we don't agree on everything or we follow a different approach than the one you proposed. I said if someone didn't have the guts to even talk to me or a supervisor about a potential issue they have zero credibility. I made it clear our wine was not a motivational tool, like how little did I have to think of their personal dignity to think they could be bought with a trinket like that? That the wine was simply one little demonstration of core values passion and excellence, and given out as one little thing to keep us in a posture of gratitude and generosity.

In fact, that's why I was really hot—we were pursuing a posture of gratitude and generosity, and some troll was trying to undercut that through their own entitlement and ingratitude. Essentially, I rambled on for twenty minutes or so, telling them much of what I've spent a whole book so far telling you. (You won't ever accuse me of being tight with my words!) I ended by recognizing they may well be thinking I'm over-reacting to something that we should just blow off, but that we work too hard on our culture to allow it to be compromised, and there was absolutely no way I was going to let anything that smacked of corporate politics, selfish ambition, or entitlement sneak into it, no matter how small.

Bringing the Kingdom Is a Thousand Little Decisions

I wasn't sure what to expect, but I knew I'd said what needed to be said. I knew it was critical to defend our culture, and for our younger employees, to more explicitly define it. Maybe *you* think I over-reacted on something I could have easily let pass without saying a thing. Well, I kind of thought the same thing at first. Ultimately, after the Holy Spirit nudged me a few times, I recognized that yet again, the Lord had teed a situation up for me and I was therefore *compelled* to swing at it. I'm sharing it with you for that reason: if you're partnered with God, He'll tee up some defining moments for you, and I want you to see from this story how that works.

> *This level of detail—of seeing a kingdom value try to creep in, no matter how seemingly insignificant, and being unwilling to yield ground to it—this is where the battle is won or lost.*

Honestly, I'm a little self-conscious about even including the story. I don't want you to think for a second I'm saying "Hey, look what a good leader I am." Likewise, I know this could easily feel like its way more "insider" family dynamics, and thus way more drama, than I should share or you would care about. On the other hand, I have to share it, as I want you to see *this* is what matters. This level of detail—of seeing a kingdom value

264

try to creep in, no matter how seemingly insignificant, and being unwilling to yield ground to it—that this is where the battle is won or lost.

You might understand that excellence is not one big decision, it's the commitment to make a thousand little decisions. Many of these decisions are fairly easy, some of them really hard. I'd propose it works the same way with bringing the Kingdom into your realm of influence. How do you think the wrong kingdom managed to creep into companies in the first place, even in businesses or organizations that were founded on high ideals? Probably some little erosions, some passivity, one more little step down the slippery slope, and before long the organization is in a deep, dark pit. This is why Jesus said, "Beware the yeast of the Pharisees."

Fortunately, it works the other way too. You'll restore or transform your area of influence with a thousand little decisions to stand for the Kingdom. Sometimes it's a hard decision and an obvious stand, as I had to take when looking for office space in "Not in My Town." I'd suggest it's far more often like this little story I just shared regarding the troll. Not too many years ago, I'd have let it slide. I could have easily rationalized that most other companies would have just let it slide too. Truth be told, though, ten years before, maybe even five years, the real issue was that I'd have been too passive and non-confrontational and just let the moment slip by, ignoring it on the hope the situation would simply blow over.

I may even have been too worried about what people would think or how they might react. I'm not sure if it was "fear of man" or insecurity in "who God made me to be" at the heart of my former passivity. Maybe all of the above. Perhaps you can identify with those challenges. David was just a teen when he learned to confidently confront the giant. "Who is this uncircumcised Philistine who's defying the armies of the living God?" It took me until my late 40s or early 50s to start gaining that same deep sense of confidence in who God made me to be, who He purposed the company to be, and to confront head-on this thing that was clearly standing against what God was calling us to.

This is really the culmination of the Lord mentoring me in Kingdom business for twenty years. Among other things, the confidence in who God made me to be, who He purposed the company to be, comes out in the willingness and commitment to make a thousand little decisions with intentionality. To do my best to seek Him, even partner with Him, in *all* those decisions. To pursue what Jesus did by only doing what He sees the Father doing and saying what the Father is saying. That's a hundred percent Kingdom right there. I'm still lucky to achieve this for twenty consecutive minutes (and probably because I said and did nothing for nineteen and a half of those minutes). I hope you're seeing the intentionality though. Bringing the Kingdom is in large part about intentionality, and many great Jesus-loving leaders never have that kind of impact on their area of influence. This is because they simply aren't thinking about how their Sunday matters on Tuesday, or that it's even possible for it be "at work as in Heaven."

So whether my troll story is too much drama or not, I hope you can see how these little decisions having consequence helps to explain why it's so dark in our culture at large. It's because Jesus followers have been silent, hiding in our churches, letting things in culture slide while the wrong kingdom imposes it values on more and more territory that by rights belongs to Jesus and His Kingdom. The nations are His inheritance! He has—and has already given to us—all the authority required to take back the dark places, to supplant the kingdom with Kingdom! I don't know why this little thing in our culture at Yakabod, our posture of gratitude and generosity, was such a big deal to the enemy, but our intentional stand to more clearly establish these aspects of the Kingdom was unquestionably opposed. So there must be something about taking this stand that mattered, in *more* than a generic, nebulous way!

When it was clear the Lord was setting me up to address it, unlike my earlier non-confrontational self, I just couldn't let it pass. Now I can look back and see it was another defining moment in "learning how to bring the Kingdom." Being partnered with God, asking Him about this, looking at it from a Kingdom lens, forced me to address this seemingly blow-off issue. Addressing the issue turned it into one of those defining moments that not only shaped me, but will shape our culture for years.

The Yeast of the Kingdom

To complete the story, the team actually burst out in applause, much to my surprise. We really didn't think the troll was one of our current employees, but Scott was watching their body language as well, and they had all been authentically engaged. One guy looked a little freaked out, but we learned afterwards he was afraid it might be an ex-partner of his, who had a history of such harassment. I received a few staff notes again, with people thanking me for being real and authentic with them about this situation, and saying how grateful they were to work at Yakabod. (That doesn't mean our culture is universally appealing, but the people who we want here—who resonate with our core values and our culture—were happy someone was willing to fight to preserve the very thing that initially attracted them.)

I was so fired up it took me a day or so to calm down, but the point was made and I didn't spend a lot of time personally on the "cultural reinforcement" of gratitude and generosity in the following weeks. Then some weeks later, I managed to sneak out for a four-week family road trip. (It was the first time I'd ever taken four weeks off in my life!) I came back from my trip on a Monday, the day before the monthly Tuesday all-hands meeting. In my absence, Yakabod just continued under normal operations and the team wasn't specifically trying to "not disturb Scott." We have such a great team; they're empowered, each prospering so well in their roles no one needed to call me. They had permission to call me if needed, and I did check in a few times, but still no one called me. When I returned the Monday before the monthly meeting, I had such a wonderfully uninterrupted respite, I wasn't even sure who I was or what I did with the company!

By Tuesday I was slowly getting my head back into the game, but I didn't have much to share with the team at the big meeting. I simply told them I appreciated what a great team they were and how amazing it was that I could take four weeks off, for the first time in my life, and nobody had to call me. I knew nobody was feeling too sorry for me trying to ramp back up after that, but it was just an amazing bonding time for my family, and they had enabled me to have it without encumbrance. I told them I didn't know very many companies of our size, where the guy who sits in my seat can go away for a month and never receive a call for help. I knew Scott W had also had the same experience in being able to get away as well. I suggested this said a whole lot more about them, and their stellar capabilities, than it said about me or Scott… and I let them know it was good to be back.

We always end our meetings by going around the room, with everyone saying just one word that reflects how they are personally feeling about the meeting. Their personal takeaway, if you will. (We weren't smart enough to come up with this strategy. We got the idea from someone, I can't remember who, but we've been doing it for probably fifteen years.)

To my surprise, as we went around the room, just about everyone presented either "gratitude" or "generosity" as the word expressing how they felt. As I reflected on the meeting afterwards, it struck me I had never actually used the word "gratitude" or "grateful." Much less "generosity." I was feeling all those things, of course, but *I* was the one who should be feeling grateful. There was nothing about that meeting to have triggered gratitude from any of them. (Well, on second thought, maybe they were grateful I had been gone!) It had been several months since I'd spent our meeting time explicitly reinforcing generosity and gratitude as keys for that season. Yet, unprovoked, that's exactly what was reflected and on their hearts.

So can a company look more like the Kingdom of our Lord than the kingdom of this world? Can an ecosystem of such companies help make a whole city look more like His Kingdom than the other one? I think the Lord's been giving me some clues.

As much as we've learned about how things work differently in His Kingdom, and for all the stories I've shared from our own journey, I'm sure you know that we're only just scratching the surface. There is *so* much more. That are plenty more contrasts between kingdom and Kingdom that we simply haven't unpacked in our experience yet, but which may well be perfect for that situation you're facing right now. We'll wrap up with some of those next.

Summary—Kingdom Culture
Kingdom
- Win-win transaction.

- Mutual trust.

- What's best for our whole community.

- Stand on Kingdom value—even if it "hurts" or there's no obvious solution.

  ° Make decisions with full awareness of the spiritual implications—heavenly seat.

kingdom
- We win, you lose.

- Protect our own behinds.

- What's best for us, who cares about anyone else.

- Accept some undesirable compromises in favor of expedience.

  ° Make decisions from logic and/or emotion only—worldly seat.

Key Points:
- When a kingdom value is attempting to supplant a Kingdom value (or prevent you from establishing one)—you're in a spiritual battle.

- Bringing the Kingdom doesn't happen in church—it happens in your everyday life.

  ° Not limited to believers—you can expose pre-believers to Kingdom Culture, even mentor them in it.

  ° Whichever Kingdom/kingdom you're establishing in your area of influence is the consequence of a thousand little decisions.

- God makes it rain on the righteous and unrighteous and His goodness leads to repentance.

  ○ The same pre-believers who are repulsed by religion may be highly attracted to His Kingdom.

SECTION 3.6: EPILOGUE

STILL AN ADVENTURE

I hope by this point in the book I've made it clear there's no formula to follow, no comprehensive plan that transforms your area of influence from looking more like kingdom to looking more like Kingdom. As you've seen, things just work differently in the Kingdom of Heaven, and there's an intentionality required to unwind some deeply held kingdom practices you've been subconsciously operating under. While I've shared some of our progress with you there's

> *I hope by this point I've made it clear there's no formula to follow.*

so much more to discover and understand, and we at Yakabod are really still learning.

Here are some additional contrasts to consider. I don't have big stories, concrete examples, or clearly defined business practices for these. In most cases, we're still experimenting with just what they mean to our business operations, and we know far more about the questions than the answers. Even so, I think it would be quite valuable for you to consider how each of the following apply to your situation.

Kingdom Is Faith, Not Performance

In most situations, the kingdom's highest value is based on the outcome; in other words, what was achieved by the performance. Accordingly, those who do the "most" usually receive the greatest reward.

Sowing and reaping is certainly part of the Kingdom, and with the value we at Yakabod put on excellence, we don't shy away from the hard work, accountability, and discipline required to achieve it. In fact, that's part of the beauty of the Kingdom; that you can actually reap from what you sow. (Such is not always the case in the kingdom, as we highlighted earlier.)

There is, however, a higher value in the Kingdom than simply reaping well from what you've sown well. That higher value is inheritance, and inheritance requires faith. You have to believe God is who He says He is, and what He's saying about a given situation. In fact, scripture explicitly declares that "Without faith, it is impossible to please God" (Hebrews 11:6). In the Kingdom it's not always about the outcome, but rather the faith you've exercised through the process.

> *In the Kingdom, a higher value than simply reaping well from what you've sown well is inheritance, and inheritance requires faith.*

I'd suggest this means we're allowed to carry an experimental attitude in our move toward a Kingdom mentality, meaning we ask God first to make sure He's not saying "No," but then to give it a try. Didn't work? Well, it's okay to fail and learn. The point is not the outcome, it's your willingness to exercise faith in the process. Will you allow His grace to cover your risk when you walk within the permissible realm of His will? Will you still see His goodness when things don't work out the way you hoped? How might this influence your leadership style or your business model? What effect could it have on your R&D budget or your corporate philanthropy?

Kingdom Is Excellence, Not Perfection

A posture of perfection can only judge imperfection—there's nothing to celebrate until you, or the projects you're working on, are "perfect." That's also a lot like religion—perfectly follow all these rules and don't mess up or there'll be trouble. (Maybe that's where the clichéd CYA mentality comes from!) Clearly, that's kingdom.

A posture of excellence, however, can celebrate progress. Your goal is to be better today than you were yesterday. Striving for excellence is much more like the process of sanctification, and thus far more like the Kingdom. In this atmosphere, grace allows people to be safe, vulnerable, and to learn from their mistakes. To admit they're not perfect, receive correction, and to improve, not only for their own sake, but for the organization's sake too.

How might this impact your management style, or your corporate culture? What impact might it have on your product development strategy, or your customer service?

Words Matter

In the kingdom of this world, words are often thrown around carelessly. People say and do things for expediency, to manipulate or coerce others, and sometimes just to hear themselves talk with little to no thought as to what they are saying. In short, in the kingdom, getting what you want is more important than the words it took to get there.

In the Kingdom, scripture says we're to let our "yes" mean yes, and our "no" mean no. Scripture goes even further, saying the power of life is in the tongue (Proverbs 18:21), so we are to speak life not death! Accordingly, for a Spirit-filled believer, words can release the power of the Kingdom and dispel darkness, or words can bring curses and withhold blessings. Further to this point, one of the names for Jesus is actually "the Word." Clearly, words matter in the Kingdom.

Cynicism and complaining are generally from the wrong kingdom. The complaint or cynical observation may actually be true, but it's only true because of the gap in the reality of the broken kingdom from the way things are designed to be in the superior Kingdom of Heaven. I'm sure you've seen this in some work settings, where one person's cynicism can infect the whole office. Just this morning, I woke up from a dream, in which I addressed a situation by saying, "No good deed goes unpunished." I'm sure you've heard the expression, and I'm equally sure you've felt it in many corporate settings. In light of Proverbs 18:21 above, what happens if I speak those words at my business? Perhaps not the immediate "death" referenced in the proverb, but I hope you can see that I'd be planting a little seed of cynicism? It may just bounce off one coworker and never take root, spoken around another coworker, though, who's already predisposed to cynicism, I just reinforced or amplified their cynical mindset, which is certainly not the "life" I wish to encourage in our workplace.

I'm not telling you to micromanage or overthink every little thing you say. Doing that will paralyze you, but do you see how planting little seeds of "death" rather than "life" over six months or a year can have a measurable negative impact on your team's culture and performance? What if you were aware enough to consciously speak hope instead? Better still, what is your Father saying about the situation—speak that!

Difficulty Is the Path to Blessing, Not Defeat

In the Kingdom, occasionally something dies so something new can live. There's a redemptive purpose in godly suffering. That's the story of salvation, of course; it's the symbolism behind baptism. A similar concept is reflected in the story of Naomi and Ruth: Ruth's husband dies, after which—through commitment to suffering for the sake of her mother-in-law—she meets

278

Boaz, and through their lineage the Messiah is ultimately born. I also heard one pastor explain the regenerative power of this kind of suffering through the story of Rachel naming her baby Ben-Oni, meaning "son of my sorrows," before dying in the act of childbirth. Jacob then renamed him Benjamin, which means, "son of my right hand" (son of my strength). I heard another pastor explain that sometimes you pray for a tree and God gives you an acorn—because God knows you're not ready for the tree.

I've experienced that plenty. I was so busy looking for the tree, I didn't realize God had given us an acorn. I was so busy trying to avoid the difficulty I couldn't see there was blessing rather than defeat on the other side.

In the Kingdom, with Jesus, no matter how good or bad things are right now, your best days are always ahead, never behind. How would this change the way you view that specific customer? (You know the one I'm talking about!) Or the way you navigate that market disruption? Is there a different way of seeing those challenges you're facing today? Is there a blessing visible on the other side of a market disruption that caught you by surprise? If not, is there something else you can be grateful for right now? Could this be an opportunity for you to exercise your faith, and to allow God to do the things only He can do? Is there an opportunity to trust in His grace not only for today but for a better tomorrow?

Experience Often Comes before Understanding

Given that we live in the "Age of Reason," there's a high premium in the kingdom of this world on being "right." Often, people do their best to explain, to make you understand, even to argue and reason, or try to manipulate you into seeing things their way to validate that they're "right." Plenty of pastors even do this, reasoning that if you would just understand, you'd agree with them. They *are* right after all (or at least they think so).

The Kingdom, on the other hand, is not a matter of empty talk, but of real power. It's not a matter of idle words, but of demonstrated authority. In

1 Corinthians 2:4-5 Paul proclaims: "⁴ My message and my preaching were not with wise and persuasive words, but with a demonstration of the Spirit's power, ⁵ so that your faith might not rest on human wisdom, but on God's power."

This is another of those revelations I first gained from a pastor's podcast. I'd never seen it before, but in the podcast he walked through the text in 1 Corinthians 12: 1-11 to show how the Corinthians were operating under the power of the Spirit, having received some of the described gifts, and experienced the signs, wonders, and miracles. Prior to becoming Christians, the people in the Corinthian Church were polytheists, so they didn't understand that all those gifts, as well as the signs, wonders, and miracles were coming from the same Holy Spirit, the one true triune God. Paul actually had to explain this to them *even though they were already operating under the Spirit!* Their experience came before their understanding… It was only after the experience of operating under the Spirit that they began to understand who He is.

> *It was only after the experience of operating under the Spirit that they began to understand who He is.*

You might recognize this is what happened to me in a good many of the examples throughout the book. We moved through a situation with some intuitive sense, but only later fully understood how it all aligned with Kingdom. (Shhh, don't let the editors count how many times I said "I didn't realize it at the time…") More specifically, in Chapter 18: Not in My Town, the experience of the original interactions and negotiations with the developer told me something wasn't right. I recognized I was having an experience of the wrong kingdom and needed to walk away from the deal.

Remember also that many people around me who were focused only on what they thought they understood—as opposed to living out the actual experience—were pushing me to take on the bad deal anyway.

Their "understanding" would have produced the wrong decision. My experience, rather than my understanding, led me into what was clearly the right decision, albeit in hindsight. I never understood the fullness of the why, the relationship between my decision and bringing the Kingdom to a community, until well *after* I took the stand. Clearly, I'm not suggesting you check wisdom at the door and operate from foolishness or blind instinct. I am saying, though, in the Kingdom, you sometimes experience it before you understand it!

As a believer, you might contemplate how this Kingdom reality may apply to the manner in which you witness to people. It certainly revolutionized my approach to witnessing. Perhaps Paul was onto something when he said "the goodness (or kindness) of God leads to repentance" (paraphrase of Romans 2:4b). What would happen if, instead of confronting someone or forcing Jesus awkwardly into a conversation, you chose rather to show them a good measure of His kindness? What if they need an experience of the Kingdom more than they need an understanding of it at this stage of their journey?

Similarly, how might this Kingdom reality have a bearing on your team-building efforts or your corporate culture? What about your product marketing and your sales process? How about your customer service? What if your customers or stakeholders experienced something very positive in their interactions with your team, even if they didn't fully understand it?

Christ Came to Serve, Not to Be Served

I've shared plenty of examples already so I probably don't need to convince you that in the kingdom, there's premium value on "getting what's yours." In the Kingdom however, "[11] The greatest among you will be your servant. [12] For those who exalt themselves will be humbled, and those who humble themselves will be exalted" (Matthew 23:11-12, NIV). Christ came to serve, after all, not to be served (Matthew 20:28).

Of course, you may have your carefully crafted pitch deck (or product demo, or video, or whatever) ready to go, but what if, in your next customer or prospect meeting, that was just the tool for you to learn how to bless the people you're pitching to? Not to sell them something for your benefit, but to bless them with something for their benefit? Better still, what if, before the meeting you explicitly asked God how you can be a blessing to them? Not considering primarily what the prospect can do for you, but what God wants to do for them through you?

After all, He says if you seek first His Kingdom the rest of these (the provision needed) will be provided as well. Does He mean it? Could God pull both off—blessing your prospect and providing for you—with the same deal? Does that give you the freedom to treat the prospect as a potential target of your blessing, and not as a revenue stream for you to acquire? Could He lead you into a deal where your only purpose is to show the prospect some of His goodness, and then to bring the provision from somewhere else? If He said this to you overtly, would you be obedient?

I'm just asking. Things work differently in the Kingdom…

Eternal Attributes: These Three Remain

The kingdom is temporal—but things in the Kingdom are eternal. More specifically, Paul cites three eternal Kingdom attributes: "And now these three remain: faith, hope and love. But the greatest of these is love" (1 Corinthians 13:13, NIV). The context here is "when completeness comes," meaning when the Kingdom of Heaven is fully manifest. For example, when the Kingdom of Heaven is fully manifest, there will no longer be a need for prophecy—we'll just know.

Since faith, hope, and love are eternal attributes of the Kingdom, how then might these play out in your workplace? I'm sure you understand the need for love. It might look like grace, or it might look like honor, or kindness. It may look like any number of other expressions, depending on the situation, and you can probably sort through that. Faith is simply

282

intrinsic to a believer; it's the currency of the Kingdom of Heaven. I'm not sure how to really call that out, it should just be embedded in all areas of your life if you're a Jesus follower, trying to bring the Kingdom into your area of influence.

The interesting one is hope. How might that apply? How about your annual employee performance reviews? Are they meaningless, as they are in most companies, or do they inspire hope? How about what is communicated in your corporate all-hands meeting, or the employee handbook, or your year-end letter to shareholders? Is that all meaningless fluff and uninspiring platitudes? Alternatively, does it authentically inspire hope?

There's one podcast series I listen to in which they frequently say, "The one with the most hope has the most influence." I think this is certainly true, but not for worldly hope with no anchor; that's just wishful thinking. Rick Page wrote a bestselling sales-process book some time ago called *Hope is Not a Strategy*[20]. He was spot on with this title as it relates to secular business principles, but Kingdom hope is a different thing. Kingdom hope is anchored in God's goodness and His promises. If that's where your hope is, it's a great strategy after all! How can you bring that hope into your area of influence?

Mercy Not Sacrifice

The book of Matthew shares two incidents (Matthew 9:13, 12:7) in which Jesus confronted the Pharisees, exhorting them because they didn't understand the Father's heart expressed in Hosea 6:6, "I desired mercy, not sacrifice." (Jesus must have hammered them a bunch with that scripture). In other words, the Pharisees valued the rules and principles ("we're in charge") instead of a relationship with God ("He's in charge"). Even under the old covenant, God was after the heart. His desire was for people to catch His heart, not just follow the rules. King David was actually able to pull otherwise unavailable things from the future new covenant into his present old-covenant days because he was a man after God's heart. Jesus gives an example of this in Matthew 12:3-8.

For another example, consider the widow in Luke 21:1-4, who gave a meager offering. Yet Jesus honored her, saying she gave more than the substantial gifts contributed by the wealthy. The wealthy followed the rules, the widow caught God's heart.

This is why following principles only takes you so far. Starting the process of infusing Kingdom into your area of influence by implementing basic biblical principles, however, is far better than not starting at all. It's okay to crawl before you walk because this is the way you will ultimately learn to run. Nevertheless, principles won't get you all the way there, because it's really about the heart—not just your heart, but the heart of the organization. How do you sort through that without God's help?

> *Principles won't get you all the way there, because it's really about the heart—not just your heart, but the heart of the organization.*

For example, you say you're wearing a suit to church because He's your King and you're showing respect. I say I'm wearing my flannel shirt because He's my Daddy, and I can come to Him as I am. Whose approach is right? We could surely find scripture to support both principle-based positions. Perhaps the real reason you're not wearing something more casual is because you're sure that's not as holy as a suit, and only irreverent sinners would wear flannel to church. Maybe the real reason I am wearing a flannel shirt is because I'm sure all those people wearing suits are self-righteous hypocrites, who need to pull planks out of their own eyes?

Now—who needs to repent? Again, we could surely find scriptures for both. The point is, you can't possibly sort through this stuff with rules and principles alone. In other words (at least, to my way of thinking), the answer to the question above is, "Both parties need to repent." Both were right to adhere to a godly principle, yet both need to repent for what was in their heart, that is, *judging* another person based on a principle *they* have decided is highest priority in God's eyes.

The point is, if you're serious about making your workplace look more like His Kingdom, you'll hit your ceiling pretty quickly working only on principle, because principles don't perceive the heart. By asking for God's help you'll accelerate the process, because so much depends on the state of all the hearts involved—your heart, your co-worker's heart, the organization's "heart"—all in pursuit of God's heart. Ask Him early, often, and continuously.

If then, with God's help, you were focused more on the "heart" than the "rules," how would this impact your expense reporting process, or your employee handbook, or your leave policies? Your customer retention strategy? Your sales compensation plan? If you're an individual contributor in a larger team, how would it affect your relationship with your teammates? Your meetings or project schedules? Are there things you are doing in your organization where your rules set up conflict with the values in your heart?

Just a Little Better Each Day

Even with all I've shared by this point, you understand, of course, there is just *so much more!* After twenty years, we're still largely learning how to press in and bring the Kingdom into our Tuesday. By now, perhaps you agree it's not about perfection, but more about intention. Being willing to make the thousand little decisions that come up in our work lives with a bent towards Kingdom rather than kingdom. Making it a little more so today, and then doing it again tomorrow. In that regard, our adventure continues…

By now, though, that's probably enough of our adventure. Are you ready to start your own? To see if you can bring a little of God's glorious Kingdom into your own area of influence? If so, let's move on to some practical tips to get you started on your own adventure in the next section, "*Your* Workplace as in Heaven!"

SECTION 4: YOUR WORKPLACE AS IN HEAVEN

THE CHANNELS OF KINGDOM BUSINESS INFLUENCE

Now that I've shared many stories of Yakabod's journey in learning to make our company a little more "at work as in Heaven" each day, let me endeavor to provide some assistance as you start (or continue) your own journey. First, I need to set some context which you may find useful.

I have given this significant thought and prayer time, and during this process I've come to understand there are four distinct, but interrelated channels of Kingdom influence and ministry. The four channels are defined as follows:

- Personal to People (P2P): This channel is defined by personally serving other people at some point of need, and is the channel in which most church ministries operate. In a business context, it's basically bringing "church ministry" to people who are unlikely to attend church to receive it. When a coworker is sick, you offer to pray for their healing, perhaps praying for them right on the spot. A boss is struggling with his marriage and you're able to bring biblical wisdom, counseling, encouragement, and reconciliation into his or her situation. A customer's house burnt down, so you organize a food drive. You get the idea.

Since this book addresses a business context, not a church context, your response to a given situation may be at various levels of overtness, or covertness, in expressing your faith. It will probably look different in your workplace than it does inside church, as well. The key point is, however, that you, or a group of people, are bringing ministry to other people at a point of need.

- Personal to Corporate (P2C): This channel is more like "making disciples of the nations," not just making disciples of the people in the nations. It entails bringing Kingdom influence to systems, processes, structures, and teams, so they operate more like the Kingdom of Heaven than the kingdom of this world. You work with excellence and joy, and it shifts the way your whole team works. You respectfully question business processes that manipulate your customers, then propose and implement alternative processes, bringing an improved result for employees, customers, and management alike. Perhaps while in prayer, the Holy Spirit brings you an idea for an innovation that makes your product safer and more profitable at the same time; an idea which you share with management.

Through your actions or influence, you change the way things work, and the net result is these things now work more like the Kingdom. Many of my examples in the previous section fall into this channel, like defining our approach to cash, or ensuring our business model reflects authenticity to our God-given purpose.

- Corporate to People (C2P): In this channel, the corporate entity operates in a way that brings ministry, even transformation, to the people associated with it. I know corporate entities are really just comprised of people, but what I'm saying is the processes, structures, and culture "minister" in some way to customers, stakeholders, employees or other individual people in the sphere of influence. This is what occurs in Chapter 20, where we recognized we were in a spiritual battle, not an earthly business conflict, and decided to respond corporately, with a posture of gratitude and generosity. As a result, our corporate culture influenced employees, most of whom became personally invested in carrying the same posture, not just in the workplace, but outside the office in their everyday lives as well.

Likewise, my friend Brett decided to start holding a brief, totally optional, start-of-day prayer time at 8:00 a.m. every morning at his business. The original motivation was to gather those interested to actually pray for a colleague under some crisis, or medical duress, rather than offer passing "thoughts and prayers" that may or may not ever manifest.

Now Brett leads this group in prayer most every day, and they pray for a range of things, including the business, customers, and other employees. The prayer is still brief and still optional—no one feels pressured to attend—and you'd never mistake it for the intercessors' group at your local charismatic church, and yet they are explicitly praying to Jesus, not some homogenized, politically correct non-deity.

Many who are not believers attend the morning prayer session because they appreciate the heart of the company they see in the prayer. Again, the corporation's practices have introduced some people to prayer or mentored them in the process, who would otherwise never go to a church to do so. In time, this will almost certainly open the door for Brett to do some P2P ministry in personally sharing the gospel with some or all of those pre-believers.

- Corporate to Corporate (C2C): In this channel the corporate entity's way of doing things causes other corporate entities to change their way of doing things. (I'm using the word "corporate," but of course, the same concept applies to government agencies, non-profit councils, small and family businesses, churches, and teams of any sort.) For example, Chapter 18: Not in My Town demonstrates this type of Kingdom influence, wherein we took a stand to prevent another business from shifting a cultural component of the community into something less Kingdom-oriented.

Another example of this corporate influence was demonstrated by my friend Steve when he was part of the ownership group of a Christian school. The staff introduced a culture of such excellence at this school that parents from other faiths (including Muslims, Hindus, and even atheists) sent their kids to the school too. Steve still shares many testimonies of P2P or C2P ministry miracles that happened there, like kids coming off ADHD meds, or kids having radical personal encounters with God. The school was so excellent— so markedly different in its outcomes—that numerous other schools approached them to learn and implement these best practices in their own schools.

In other words, Steve's school not only touched people personally, it was transforming other schools with varying degrees of Kingdom practices and principles. Likewise, I'm sure you've read examples where a Jesus-centered prison ministry will produce such measurably better results in the recidivism rate than a secular program that it results in the government agency reforming its practices or policies. These are all examples where one corporate entity helps transform the way things work at another corporate entity.

Now, I'm not suggesting these are the only channels, or that there are hard boundaries between them. I'm sure we could look at some of my examples in Section 3 and argue they simultaneously fit into two or more of these channels. I'm not even suggesting you study or take on my terminology. My point is there is way more to ministry than just the P2P kind, which seems to be the only channel you'll hear about in most churches.

Why Understanding Channels of Influence Matters

So why does this all matter? Well, I have this friend who's involved in ministering to poor, orphaned, and systemically oppressed children in places all over the world. Perhaps "involved" understates my friend's relationship with such a ministry. He's zealous, passionate, and totally committed. He's all in, and has given his life to it. I love his sincere and authentic commitment. If just two percent of the people in any given congregation shared his zeal for an issue like this, they would turn their city or region right-side up.

> *There is way more to ministry than just the P2P kind, which seems to be the only channel you'll hear about in most churches.*

It's between him and God of course, but if I had to guess, I'd say my friend is doing exactly what he's called to do—even created to do—because he's just so fully alive while doing it. It's beautiful and noble and necessary, and in so many ways honors Jesus. As the Church—the worldwide collection of people who love Jesus—we should honor people like my friend. Better still, we should support and/or join in with people like my friend.

My friend represents the pinnacle—the best of the best—of traditional P2P-focused church ministry. He's a real person, but at this point, I'm going to use my friend's actions and attitudes to represent a metaphorical mindset that is prevalent among believers today. The things I ascribe to my friend below are real, but represent an aggregate of many people you and I both know that focus exclusively on P2P ministry. While my friend is to be honored, I need to challenge the metaphorical mindset that carries these types of attitudes and behaviors. I know my friend is committed to excellence in his ministry but I also know others like him who are not nearly so committed or effective. My aim is to challenge the metaphorical mindset they adhere to, which is essentially a box they've all put themselves into without realizing the manner in which they fall short of an absolute Kingdom expression.

It's not entirely their fault, they've never been taught or pastored or mentored in anything beyond the box. The box, however, has to go...

The problem as I see it is, what my friend is doing is not fully Kingdom. If my friend would just pause long enough to ask, "Is this the way things work in the Kingdom?" he'd have to say "No." This is because there's no poverty, no hunger, and no oppression in the Kingdom of Heaven. My friend can, and probably has, served a million meals to thousands of impoverished kids, but it's only temporary relief for them. He'll have to do it all over again next week. The Kingdom is not based on temporary relief; the Kingdom is concerned with restoration to the way God intends things to be—to the fullness of what Jesus has already paid for.

> *The Kingdom is not based on temporary relief; it is concerned with restoration to the way God intends things to be—to the fullness of what Jesus has already paid for.*

As an example, consider the occasion when Jesus raised the widow's son after he had died, which would logically fit into our P2P category (see Luke 7:11-17). Jesus, however, wasn't just restoring a relationship to the widow, He was also restoring her *provision.* In that culture, when her son died, the widow's descent into poverty was clear and imminent. Jesus restored her financial standing—the miracle was full restoration, not just temporary relief.

I think my friend (and the metaphorical mindset he represents) vaguely recognizes the difference because he's also doing long-term, self-sustaining initiatives like digging wells or ensuring access to clean water to help with infrastructure. What he's not thinking about, though, is the bigger picture. Possibly because he's so centered on what God's called him to do, he feels if *you're* not doing the same work he's doing then you just don't get it—you're not really doing ministry.

One way this judgmental attitude manifests is when he sees a church with a big, expensive, decked-out youth ministry facility and he publicly shames them on Fakebook, saying things like, "Can you believe they spent a million dollars on this? Nobody needs this! Think how many orphans we could have fed with the money wasted on this." He expresses similar sentiments about wealthy individuals, organizations, or corporations, not just churches. My friend unfortunately only sees the P2P channel of ministry. In other words, regardless of my terminology, which isn't important here, what he's missing is that there is way more to ministry than narrow activities that he and so many in the Western Church have been focused on!

It's certainly possible the church he called out may have built the big shiny facility as a monument to someone's ego, or maybe it was just collective self-indulgence on the part of the church. That certainly happens, and if this is the case, I, along with most believers, would agree it's a poor representation of the Kingdom. On the other hand, they may have built it in obedience to God, and chose to do so with excellence. Maybe they are called to provide a taste of God's goodness to kids who normally don't experience it; to be a refuge in their city. (Anyone who's ever spent time in the mountains, like the High Sierra or the Rockies or the Alps, can surely attest to God being an extravagant architect, builder, and artist!)

Perhaps that church is called to reach the wealthy business people in the region, people who'd be more inclined to send their kids to the excellent facility.

Whatever the reason, my friend wouldn't know because he never talked to the elders or pastors to learn their heart before he publicly shamed them.

I'm not saying my friend shouldn't be doing what he's doing. The temporary relief is triage and it's absolutely necessary, but there's just so much more. If my friend understood the other three channels of Kingdom influence above, perhaps he'd understand that the reason he has to work so hard to provide temporary relief is because the people he is ministering to are under the systemic oppression of a corrupt government; a government intent on enriching or empowering a few at the expense of many. If he had influence with those in power, maybe he could change the system; perhaps he could make *that* look more like the Kingdom of Heaven, and those who are impoverished could be freed to prosper.

Loving Those in Authority

If my friend understood the other channels of Kingdom influence, he might understand that perhaps some of those "rich" people and organizations he shames have been equipped by God. Perhaps they have been given their substantial resources because there's an apostolic call on their life to transform the things around them. Maybe my friend would understand that even if he doesn't have influence with the corrupt government leaders, maybe he could partner with others who do, to transform the things he's passionate about. It may look different to sending some temporary relief again next week, but leaders with power—whether apostolic leaders of Kingdom organizations or worldly leaders in kingdom systems—would never listen to my friend. Not because they don't care, but because he's disqualified himself from the conversation.

I get that sometimes God raises up a John the Baptist with a confrontational message ("Repent or die!") and because John was explicitly anointed for this type of ministry, it actually worked. More often, however, it seems God raises up a Daniel, a Joseph, an Esther, or a Mordecai, who has a relationship with, and actually *serves* those in power. For example, Daniel had to learn new languages and new customs, but even as a boy, he knew how to carry himself around nobility, because he came from nobility himself (Daniel 1:3). More importantly, he *loved* the kings he served. He'd have had every right to stand on truth and confront each of the kings he served with a call for God's justice—at which point he'd have likely been killed. While God's justice would surely come in God's time and way, Daniel would have only been able to observe it from a distance in Heaven. Instead, Daniel *loved,* and as a result he shaped the destiny and course of nations. Even the wicked Nebuchadnezzar submitted himself before God by the end of his life, largely because of Daniel's influence.

Am I saying God can only use rich, powerful people to influence rich, powerful people? Of course not. God can use and equip anyone who is willing to be used by Him. David was a humble shepherd boy, disregarded by even his own family. Gideon, by his own admission, was the least in his family, the least family of the least clan in his tribe (Judges 6:15). God can and does use anyone willing to serve. Practically speaking, however, when it comes to marketplace ministry, having money or position provides you with some default credibility with those who only know the ways of the world (little-k kingdom). This simply provides you with a shorter path to understanding the language, manners, and ways of those who are the influencers and rulers in a company or a nation. The money or position actually has nothing to do with it.

Instead, it's the way you carry yourself and relate to those to whom you are ministering. I think it's interesting that even though God sent Moses to take a confrontational stand with Pharaoh, He first raised Moses in Pharaoh's house so he knew how to carry himself before Pharaoh's throne. Jesus, while wealthy beyond measure, arguably didn't have excessive amounts of money. (You don't really need

> *Jesus was not powerful because He had lots of money; He was powerful because He carried Himself on Earth like the King He is.*

money when you can turn a few loaves and fish into dinner for thousands of your friends, or send someone fishing to pay the tax bill!) Nevertheless, people were amazed when He spoke "as one with authority." Of course, the miracles testified to Jesus' standing as the Son of God, but even His speech announced His nobility (He is King of kings after all) in a way people clearly recognized. Jesus was not powerful because He had lots of money; He was powerful because He carried Himself on Earth like the King He is.

This is what we're talking about with the three other channels of Kingdom influence. If you're going to transform your company (or partner companies, vendors, or customer companies), you have to know how to honor, talk to, carry yourself around, and build relationships with executives. If you want to transform your city, you likewise have to know how to relate to mayors and council members.

In other words, you need to know how to *love* them, not value them only for what they can do for you. You need to be secure in the resources your Father provides, not covet the resources those in kingdom power control. Neither should you be shaming them if they're not operating in the same ministry or domain as you.

If my friend understood the existence of, much less the value of, the "more" those other three channels of Kingdom ministry represent, maybe

> *If you want to transform your city, you likewise have to know how to relate to mayors and council members.*

he'd have some influence with those in power in the places he serves. He certainly carries the credibility, authority, and experience of one who's served well in that area of need. Maybe it would give him a platform to help change the corrupt systems; to bring long-term restoration and freedom to the oppressed, rather than forever providing some fleeting temporary relief. Regrettably, he'll likely never have that voice because he doesn't love the wealthy people and organizations

298

in power. He doesn't see past their externalities and into the people God created them to be. Instead, he disdains them. Why would they give him an audience? For that matter, why would God give him favor with them?

Restoration > Relief

Sadly, I believe this is where a lot of the Church is stuck—on the P2P channel of ministry. It's good and it's necessary, and it honors Jesus, and yet, in the big picture, there is so much more. We keep fighting the same battles over and over and over. Why haven't we pushed into the *more?* In the United States—my home nation—there has been a definite movement by secular rulers to remove every hint of God from public life. Have you ever wondered why, in spite of that, the rulers in our secular culture will largely still allow or even welcome our churches to run soup kitchens, or show up for disaster response, or raise money for starving children in Africa? We're even *happy* to spend all our time on those things.

I wonder if it's because that's exactly where the spiritual powers and principalities opposed to God want us. They know we're spending all our resources and energy on these things that haven't fundamentally changed anything. We may have provided temporary relief, but never any systemic change. The broken places we're ministering in still look like the kingdom of this world, and they are still going to look like that tomorrow. People are still suffering, oppressed, broken, and living in far less than the fullness of what Jesus paid for.

Our call (a directive given by Jesus—see Matthew 28:19) is to bring the Kingdom to Earth. To make the systems, processes, companies, governments, and structures all look more like God's Kingdom than the other kingdom. The call is to make disciples of the *nations*, not just the people in the nations. This is so people can come into the purpose and destiny God has for them; to fully express that little sliver of His image He intends them to present in this world. It's ultimately guaranteed to succeed anyway: "Of the increase of his government and of peace there will be no end" (Isaiah 9:7a, ESV). Not His government and peace—the *increase* of His government and peace!

This is where these other three channels of Kingdom influence come in. I know this material has been a little abstract, so let's get more practical. How do you actually do this at work on any given Tuesday?

PARTNERING WITH GOD AT WORK (PERSONAL EDITION)

I pray the last chapter has revealed how much more there is to Kingdom ministry, firing you up to partner with God to make your area of influence look more like *His* Kingdom than the kingdom of this world. Now you're ready to add some P2P and P2C activities into your Tuesday; but how do you do that without your boss (or your team) thinking you're some weird, religious nut?

Perhaps it's simpler than you might imagine. Remember my friend Jim from way back in Chapter 2, who set his heart on cleaning toilets for the glory of Jesus?

A Broader View of Ministry

Jim's story is a great example of both P2P and P2C channels of ministry. He didn't set out to shift the culture or change the corporate entity. He didn't even set out to do ministry! Jim just decided to do his work for the glory of Jesus, and so, worshipped Him in the process of doing his every day work activities. That simple step of faith had a profound effect on many people, and created opportunities for personal ministry (P2P). It also shifted the corporate culture (P2C) in which Jim worked. Jim wasn't there long enough to see those changes "institutionalized," so we don't know if things continued to a new normal, or fell back to the old once Jim left. I don't doubt, however, that if Jim had been there longer he'd have had enough influence with the school's leadership to positively impact some of the school's policies and procedures, effecting explicit long-term change (that is, reformation) as well.

This is not your "typical" worship. There was no rock band passionately performing Hillsong favorites, no light show, and no sermon, but can we agree Jim was worshipping God?

It's not your "typical" outreach, either. There's no altar call, no "Romans Road" questions, no tracts, no "I'm dead and in hell, why didn't you warn me?" movies. There was nothing extraordinary Jim did that your missions team would typically do at their next event. I'm sure we can agree, though, Jim had a pretty effective outreach going on. So how did Jim pull this off without his boss thinking he's some weird religious nut, or getting himself kicked out of the public school system?

Again, Jim approached his work as though he was working alongside Jesus. He didn't try to make it look like church or church ministry. Doing that would have been weird to Jim's boss and coworkers. There are some things you have to navigate at work that you don't have to pay attention to in church. Likewise, there are things you do at church that just aren't

> *The modern evangelical-era Church, has been stuck in the wrong model.*

appropriate at work. The challenge is to translate your faith, your personal relationship with Jesus, to a corporate context, partnering with God to do business His way, not the world's way. The best way is to have a real relationship with Jesus, and to simply live that out.

Maybe this sounds too simple. That's probably because the Church—not any particular church—but the modern evangelical-era Church, has been stuck in the wrong model. We do this program, that event, or design some marketing plan or social media strategy in an attempt to attract people into our church, so they'll listen to our sermon and respond to our altar call. There is nothing wrong with a programs-based approach in and of itself, but at a practical level, it's not

> *Instead of trying to bring people in, our churches should be equipping saints to go out and do stuff "with God" in their everyday life on Tuesday, not just Sunday.*

working. People "in the world" aren't coming into our churches. To me, excessive reliance on the latest program trends demonstrates a *lack* of authentic relationship with God and His resulting power (1 Corinthians 4:20.) Certainly none of the people Jim influenced at that school had any interest in church before he showed up.

Instead of trying to bring people in, our churches should be equipping saints to go out. Believers should be equipped to do stuff "with God" in their everyday life on Tuesday, not just Sunday. Jim didn't have any training in this, he just intuitively decided to worship God with his work and things started happening. You can do the same.

Practical Ways to Get Started

Beyond that simple commitment of intentionally worshipping God and connecting with His presence while you work, another key to effecting this kind of P2C and P2P ministry is recognizing there are both natural and supernatural aspects involved.

In the natural aspect, you do the things you can control. For example, you start by doing your work with excellence; if the toilets were dirty Jim wouldn't have had much of a ministry. Something else you can control is demonstrating love and grace to your coworkers—that simple act was a profoundly different expression in Jim's workplace. You may have noticed these "natural" things tend to be more *principle* based. Perhaps you know the principles and the biblical verses they're drawn from, it may just be you have not applied them. Some basic examples of these principles are:

- **Work Ethic:** "Whatever your hand finds to do, do it with your might..." (Ecclesiastes 9:10a, NKJV).

- **Passion:** "[23] Whatever you do, work at it with all your heart, as working for the Lord, not for human masters, [24] since you know that you will receive an inheritance from the Lord as a reward. It is the Lord Christ you are serving" (Colossians 3:23-24, NIV).

- **Service:** "[14] You are the light of the world. A city set on a hill cannot be hidden; [15] nor does anyone light a lamp and put it under a basket, but on the lampstand, and it gives light to all who are in the house. [16] Let your light shine before men in such a way *that they may see your good works, and glorify your Father who is in heaven*" (Matthew 5:14-16, NASB—emphasis mine).

- **Excellence:** "Do you see someone skilled in their work? They will serve before kings..." (Proverbs 22:29a, NIV).

- **Kindness:** "So in everything, do to others what you would have them do to you, for this sums up the Law and the Prophets" (Matthew 7:12, NIV). This is known as the "golden rule."

- **Selflessness:** "Love your neighbor as yourself" (Mark 12:31a, Leviticus 19:18b, NIV).

You'll certainly come up with dozens more. Whole books have been written about applying biblical principles to your work. If you're still not sure where to start, the book of Proverbs is a treasure trove of this kind of wisdom. Just consistently modeling a few of these principles will make your area of influence look more like the Kingdom of Heaven than many other workplaces. It will also provide a great foundation from which to start asking God about any other elements of your workplace He'd like to transform through your influence.

When figuring out how to apply biblical principles like these to your specific work environment you may need to ask God for help or direction, but you sure don't need to ask His permission, or wonder if it's His will. Just pick one and apply it to your Tuesday. It will almost certainly make things look different in your place of work. With just simple courteousness (golden rule), Jim shifted the way people interacted at his workplace, because it was in such stark contrast to the way things had been. Likewise, if you simply loved your coworkers, how different would that look in your work situation? If you were not only concerned with how well you performed (or were rewarded) in your job, but were equally concerned your coworkers were prospering in theirs, wouldn't that be markedly different than the "cutthroat" corporate politics and "ladder climbing" so many experience in their place of work?

A Spectrum from Overt to Covert

While these are simple principles, they'll often carry profound impact just because they're so rarely demonstrated in the workplace. The beauty is, you can do these things with little risk of people thinking you're weird. Who doesn't want to be treated with kindness and respect? That shouldn't be controversial in the darkest of workplaces. Now your coworkers *will* think you're weird if they say "Man, that's excellent work," and you start quoting King James Bible verses to them instead of just saying thanks. But if you're authentic, and have a relationship with them, you can probably slip a "Praise God," or "God has blessed me" into your response with nary a raised eyebrow. Depending on your office setting, maybe you'll even find an opportunity to gracefully tell them you did excellent work because you're intent on giving it your best to honor Jesus. You likely already know your office setting well enough to know how discreet you need to be.

Maybe you need to be totally covert, and a simple "thanks" is sufficient. Your actions are far more powerful than your words anyway, so consistently following some of the principles above will still demonstrate the Kingdom, and perhaps even influence others to do the same. This, of course, means you've made things look a little more like the Kingdom of Heaven through your influence.

You may be wondering why we're this deep into the chapter, and I haven't even mentioned ethics or integrity yet. Of course effective P2P and P2C ministry includes those things, however, it's so much more than that. Ethics and integrity are just table stakes, and need to be carried graciously, not with some holier-than-thou attitude towards your co-workers. Jesus said not one letter of the Law would pass away, and He said He came to fulfill the Law, not abolish it. Likewise, when you're bringing the Kingdom, of course it's going to have a foundation of ethics and integrity, but just as in Jesus' time on Earth, even the Pharisees can claim ethics or integrity as their focus, and yet totally miss a relationship with the King and the effective propagation of His Kingdom.

A Higher View

While applying certain biblical principles can provide a great, non-controversial place to start carrying your faith from Sunday into Tuesday, that's just part of it. Like the Pharisees, you may grasp the *principles,* but still miss the *Kingdom.* Jesus told us to pray it would be "on Earth as it is in Heaven," and this requires some focus on the *Heaven* part of the statement, not just the Earth part. Which brings us to the supernatural component of bringing the Kingdom to your area of influence.

The "supernatural" is accessible to every follower of Jesus, because every such believer has the Holy Spirit living inside of them. Some believers get stuck on this word, so let me simplify it. The natural aspects of workplace ministry involve the stuff you can do by following principles. The supernatural aspects involve the things that only God can do or facilitate. As believers, we often think of Holy Spirit

> *The supernatural aspects involve the things that only God can do or facilitate.*

activities in a church setting, things that happen in our "spiritual" times through prayer, worship, and reading scripture. This may manifest into outward things like prophecy or even miracles, but the same supernatural aspects are available in a business context. From a posture of worship, for example, the Lord may inspire you with ideas, solutions, and innovations in the next engineering team meeting that you'd never have produced on your own. Someone may even be supernaturally healed, as I shared in Kim's amazing story in Chapter 17.

So how do you operate within the supernatural realm in your office? It's not like, if you're an evangelical, you're going to crank up the Hillsong or Jesus Culture video, close your eyes, sing from deep within your core and throw your arms up for the touchdown. Or, if you're charismatic, do all the above while waving your flags or praying in tongues. That'll definitely get the office thinking you're weird.

Maybe someone reading this *is* called to be a John the Baptist type. You can be that weird guy because you're not supposed to be in the office anyway. In a business setting you'd be perceived as being so "spiritual," and heavenly-minded that you're no earthly good. You're supposed to be out in the desert wilderness, and if you're anointed for that, you'll see people saved all over in spite of the fact they think you're weird. For most of us, though, we're more like the twelve and the seventy Jesus sent out to demonstrate and proclaim His Kingdom. We're fisherman, trades folk, tax collectors (IRS workers), etc. We need to navigate the real world.

As I said earlier, the key to this is partnering with God. To be "doing what I see my Father doing, saying what I hear my Father saying." In other words, if I'm doing what I see Him doing, then I'm bringing His Kingdom into my setting, making it "on Earth as it is in Heaven," and *that* implies a prayerful connection and ongoing conversational intimacy with God. That is, of course, available anywhere. The Holy Spirit indwells believers, so He goes where you go. Including the office or workplace. The challenge is just listening to Him there, and not constraining Him to your church activities.

Assuming you believe God speaks to you through the Holy Spirit, it just might happen a little differently at work. When you're in church, you may need the band playing to get you into worship mode. That's not going to happen at work, though you could possibly wear headphones during your day. Likewise, it's typically not viable for everyone to pray out loud, whether at your desk or by gathering a quick prayer circle. Company policy may allow you to use a conference room or empty office to duck in for prayer, though, either by yourself or with a fellow Jesus follower.

Of course, you can always pray quietly or silently at your desk, as I often do. As the one meme says, "As long as they keep giving tests, they'll never take prayer out of schools." There's plenty of truth in that for your office too: no matter what the organizational chart says, as a son or daughter of Christ you have authority, and your prayers for your office carry authority. I'm not saying disrespect natural authority, but I am saying don't underestimate your own spiritual authority either. If none of the above work, or it's just too noisy to focus on quiet internal prayer, take a restroom break. Seriously.

What we're ultimately after here is not only a deliberate, demarcated time of prayer, but rather an ongoing conversational intimacy with God. You can literally ask God if He has some input on any given situation that pops up, and you should. Do it often, throughout your day, because by consciously connecting with our Father in that way we gain access to the supernatural. We can trust God to give us ideas, approaches, discoveries, knowledge, and insights—discernment that can only come from Him.

To show you how simple this is, how it's just a matter of intentionality more than anything, next time you see someone walking down the hall, ask God if He has something for them. He might surprise you. I don't do this as much as I should, but when I do, He'll sometimes give me a simple word of encouragement for that person that lights up their day. If you just got an email and you're not sure how to respond, ask God if He has some insight for you. Especially if your first reaction is heated! The Lord has saved me from sending more than a few emails that would have turned into train wrecks if they left the station. If you're struggling with a technical issue, ask God. If Jesus can heal people— even raise the dead—He certainly knows how to fix that bug in your software.

> *What we're ultimately after is not only a deliberate, demarcated time of prayer, but rather an ongoing conversational intimacy with God.*

If you don't have some experience in listening to the voice of God there are plenty of excellent books already written on that topic. (One of my favorites that really got me thinking about all this as I moved from servant to friend, as in Chapter 5, is Frank Laubach's book, *The Game with Minutes*.[21] It's more case study than how-to, but it sure will open your eyes to what's possible!) It's not my goal to replicate those books. If you're stuck there and your prayers are only in one direction, you need to start with *that* spiritual foundation more than you need to worry about making your workplace look more like His Kingdom just yet.

Assuming you have some experience in prayerful conversation with God in general, and you're still having trouble hearing from Him in your workplace context then perhaps there are some roadblocks you need to overcome. We'll explore this more in the next chapter…

PARTNERING WITH GOD AT WORK (PERSONAL EDITION)–OVERCOMING ROADBLOCKS

As we said in the previous chapter, partnering with God to make your area of influence look more like His Kingdom requires an ongoing conversational intimacy with God. While not all believers practice this, it's not because it's unavailable. Jesus accomplished everything necessary for every one of His followers to enjoy such a connection. Not just in church, but at work too. What if you're trying and it's just not happening?

Does God Talk Shop?

First, of course, you need to believe God wants to talk to you, expect He'll provide an answer, and take the time to listen for it. If you don't believe this, I'd challenge you to consider why you are praying in the first place. Maybe you need to move beyond just giving Him your list of requests, and start listening for His response instead.

Perhaps it's the work context you're struggling with. Does God actually speak to us about business? Yes, of course He does. What good father doesn't talk to his children about their interests and activities? Different people converse with God in different means—some are more visual, some more aural; some receive visions and dreams, others get impressions; some hear in conversational language, others largely in scriptural quotes. For me it's some combination of the above.

> *Does God actually speak to us about business? Yes, of course He does.*

Often, when I've sought God's guidance on corporate strategy, He'll respond with a description of the season we're in, which is, I guess, a good P2C example. In Chapter 18, I shared some insight into our move to a new office, but one of the triggers for that season was Isaiah 54:1-3, in which we knew from much prayer that the Lord was telling us to "enlarge the place of our tent… and not hold back." (Verse 2 wording in the NLT captures this sentiment even better: "Enlarge your house; build an addition. Spread out your home, and spare no expense.") Sure enough, that's the season both my company and my family entered into!

While in prayer, some time before that, it was clear He was saying it was a "year of cleansing"—a description of the season we're in. Sure enough, in that period, we separated from a board member, a bad contract, two key (and we assumed critical) employees, as well as a few key consultants. At home, our family separated from some toxic relationships, and even moved on from our church. Whether at

> *You need to believe God wants to talk to you, expect He'll provide an answer, and take the time to listen for it.*

home or work, I'd never have envisioned so much change in such a short period, and in fact, left to our own devices at the company, we might have considered all the changes to be our downfall. Instead, the Lord gave us a grid to navigate each circumstance, kept us encouraged, and showed us the "blessing in disguise" we'd find on the other side of each upheaval during the "year of cleansing."

As that season came to a close, it became apparent just how much stronger we were as a company from a series of changes we'd have never undertaken of our own volition. In another example, the Lord revealed to us some fraudulent things an employee was doing in secret that were really hurting our business. Of course, there are many other examples embedded throughout Section 3, but the bottom line is, yes, we expect God to speak to us about the business. And He does.

Pastoring a Company?

We're certainly not unique in this regard. My friend Steve called me excitedly some months back to share the amazing things God revealed to Him in prayer. If you're an evangelical, you'd recognize Steve is very sensitive to God's voice. If you're a charismatic, you'd say Steve is prophetic. Well, Steve has been in a men's group with a number of business guys; one in particular, whom Steve considers a friend, would be considered the "most unholy one" by religious-minded folk, because he curses like a sailor and drinks like a fish. (If any of those same religious folk worked for the guy, they'd most likely be praying for God to get them out of that job and into some "real ministry.") Steve doesn't care, he just treats the guy with respect and appreciates him for who he is.

One day Steve was out for a walk, and felt like God was giving him a download about his friend, so he called him and asked very respectfully, "I was praying for you, and I just felt like I heard some things, are you okay if I share those with you?" The guy said yes, and Steve gave him a solution to a problem he didn't know he had, and which Steve couldn't have known about without hearing from God. The guy was blown away, so wanting to learn more he invited Steve to dinner. As Steve arrived, he realized it was a setup; his friend had invited the whole executive management team to join them. None of the other executives were believers, but after hearing Steve repeat "the download" the Lord had given him for their company, they decided they wanted Steve to pray for them too.

Further, they insisted on engaging Steve via a consulting contract so they could continue meeting with him on a monthly basis. Do you see what happened? By giving Steve some words to share that only He could have provided, God opened a door. Nobody gave Steve the title of Pastor, but I hope you can see this is exactly the service Steve is providing. By mentoring its executives, Steve is effectively and lovingly pastoring the whole organization, and by the time Steve is done it will look a little (or a lot) more like the Kingdom of Heaven than it did before. This is the power of partnering with God, in this case, to bring P2C ministry.

I know this chapter is about your role as an employee, but I added this example with Steve as an outsider so can you see what's possible. If God will use someone like Steve in that way, who doesn't even work for the company, can He use you to "pastor" your team, your manager, or even the whole company? It won't look like what your pastor at church does, but the people Steve is pastoring have no interest in going to church. Yet Steve is connecting them with the Kingdom, and ultimately—in fact very likely—the King.

All of this may be a revelation for some of you. You've been giving God your list in prayer, but you haven't been listening for a reply, or you don't believe He wants to talk to you about your work. I hope you can see from my examples God *does* speak to people about their work. In other words, there's nothing special about me or Yakabod or Steve in this regard. Give it a try.

Intentionally Shift into Gratitude

Assuming you're past the stumbling block of doubting whether God speaks to people about their work, and you already have some experience with talking to God, but you're still not hearing from Him regarding a particular work situation, then another practical suggestion mentors have taught me is to practice gratitude. If you're not already there, shift your posture into one of thankfulness. Look for goodness in your current circumstances or environment, and thank your Father for it. There's certainly something to be grateful for, no matter how awful your workplace may be.

That conscious posture of gratitude and time spent thanking God in response, will help get you back into your "heavenly seat" where you can see the ways of the Kingdom more clearly. If you're complaining, angry, or bitter, you're more disposed to listen to your own voice or the voice of the enemy. You're more inclined, like the ten spies, to see the giants in the land. Gratitude is one tool that will help position you, like Joshua and Caleb, to see the milk and honey instead, and to trust God will render the giants an afterthought for you as well.

> *The conscious posture of gratitude and time spent thanking God will help get you back to where you can see the ways of the Kingdom more clearly.*

You might let this act of looking for the good by carrying a posture of gratitude move beyond your internal thought patterns and into your broader workplace environment. Some church cultures call this "treasure hunting." Instead of calling out the negative or the problems or the brokenness around you (anyone can see those things), look for the good, and then call that out in your coworkers or your company. Offer hope and encouragement.

Embrace His Presence

Referring back to something I learned from *The Game with Minutes*,[22] if you're having trouble hearing God, remember the aphorism, "As a man thinks, so is he" (paraphrase of Proverbs 23:7, NASB or KJV). Therefore, set your mind on God. Imagine performing the task in front of you *with* Him. Invite Him into it! The more you think of Him, the more you'll express that unique aspect of His glory in a given situation. This doesn't take elaborate prayer, just a quick, even silent, "Lord, I'd love for You to join me in this." This will start you down the path of simply being conscious of His presence, and will allow you to engage with Him in a more focused way. It may be a simple truth, but it's exceptionally profound. Honestly, if you could do this even for twenty minutes a day—just being aware of His presence while you're typing that email or painting that wall, or performing whatever task is in front of you—how different would things look? What if you did it for an hour a day?

Once you're focused on His presence, you're then in position to ask your Father for His input in a given situation. What does He say about the situation and what does He want to do through it? The practice far too common in our lives is to just plow ahead on our own and not even ask God. It's really just a bad habit, and I'm as guilty as anyone of this, but as with any habit, the more you are conscious of embracing God's presence with you in your activities, the more it will be become habit to bring Him into your decisions, and even become second nature.

Does It Sound like God?

There is a potential roadblock I occasionally struggle with, and maybe some of you do too: I know I'm hearing something, but I'm not sure it's actually from God. Maybe it's just my own crazy idea? Maybe it's coming from the wrong kingdom? Some of you may find your workplace so miserable you have to wonder if it's demon-possessed and you're hearing from the wrong team! If this is the case, here are a few key tips various mentors have shared with me, which I have found quite useful in discerning God's voice at work.

I'm sure you know God won't contradict scripture, or His nature, while speaking with you. On the other hand, He has no problem contradicting

316

your religious baggage. (I've heard at least one famous pastor say this a few times, so don't give me any credit for this nugget, but take it to heart, because it's so true!)

It's also true He's a God of grace, and He's a great Father, so another key is to evaluate what you think you are hearing from that perspective. Fathers lovingly teach and raise their children; He doesn't expect you to be a master when you're getting started. When your own toddler first crawls, then walks, you celebrate. You don't yell at the child or

> *Fathers lovingly teach and raise their children. How more is this so with our loving Father in Heaven?*

consider her a failure because she's not yet running. How much more is this so with our loving Father?

Further to this, what's the fruit of what you're hearing; that is, what is the potential outcome? Is it good? Is it redemptive? Is it restorative? Those things all *sound* like God, especially if it's aligned with scripture and carries the heart of a good Father.

What's the Risk?

I'm certainly no expert at hearing God, so if I'm still questioning what I think I'm hearing is actually from Him, in light of His Fatherly grace, I'll ask myself, "What's the risk?" Maybe I get the impression I should give an encouraging word to a coworker and I'm not sure it's coming from the Lord. It could be, but I'm not sure. What's the risk? Would it do any harm to give that coworker an encouraging word? Is there something inconsistent with the Kingdom by doing that? No, if the words are true, then there's no risk really, it seems there's only an upside. On the other hand, if it was God and I ignore it, at best I missed an opportunity, and at worst, I'm being disobedient. So why not just go ahead and give that encouraging word?

Maybe it's a bigger step, like whether I should agree to take a certain meeting or pursue a specific opportunity. If I'm not sure I'm hearing the Lord on the matter, I'll use my best judgment and take a step. Probably a small step. What's the risk in taking the meeting? Well, I might waste an hour of my time, or a few people's time, but in most cases, there's not a lot of risk so I take the meeting and see if there are any of God's fingerprints on it. Is a door opening that I couldn't open on my own? Does it provide some benefit to our company, our employees, or our customers? Maybe it's not for us, but for them. Can we somehow be a blessing to them? Maybe it was just an opportunity for them to come into our space where they'd feel the presence of God. All these may provide an indication if a bigger step is warranted.

Please understand, though, when I talk about asking "What's the risk?" it's in the context of discerning whether I'm hearing God's voice properly. Sometimes, when I've heard Him properly, obedience to His words may feel like it carries plenty of risk! It's helpful to remember then, that our Father will often confirm His instructions through others, particularly a spouse, though also through coworkers, friends, and trusted associates, especially if it's a bigger step of faith carrying more risk. In fact, this is another key to avoiding the "weird religious nut" label—if it's a bigger step, or if it will seem weird or awkward in your workplace, just talk with Him.

All you need to say is, "Lord, I'm not sure I'm hearing You correctly. I'm willing to take that step if it's You, but if it's not it'll do some damage, so will you please confirm Your word so I'm sure it's You?" If He does confirm you can move ahead in confidence. If not, keep praying about it until you're at peace one way or the other. Have you noticed how Jesus did stuff that was totally counter to the religious leaders' actions and instructions, who in turn accused Him of all sorts of things? Yet the common people, the ones without an agenda, marveled at how He "spoke with authority." If you have confirmation from God, it will carry authority, and won't be nearly as "weird" as you might have imagined.

Just a Little Mustard Seed

Let me give you a real example of how this plays out in practice, on what seemed like just a little nudge to me from the Lord. One of our employees is embedded in one of our customer locations so he's often under the stress of their atmosphere, not the peace of our office. For some reason, on one particular Friday afternoon, I just felt a nudge to check in with him. I could have easily let it slide by. I'm glad I didn't. I discovered he'd been on edge because a lot of "fake news" had been circulating through that office; just negative office politics really. He was fearful our contract would be cancelled, and then presumably he'd be without a job.

In our internal Yakabox exchange, I encouraged him to disregard the fake news, and that through plenty of prayer I was at peace over the situation. I assured him we'd be fine, and even if the contract was cancelled—which I told him seemed extremely unlikely—there'd still be plenty of work for him. I encouraged him to have a relaxing weekend with his family and not to think about the customer's office politics. He gave me a quick thanks and we said goodbye.

After the weekend he responded with more feedback, saying it was the best sleep he'd had in a while. He hadn't realized just what stress he'd allowed himself to come under, and how he was convinced God had given me the nudge to reach out to him exactly when he needed it. Now that may seem trivial, but when you consider the cumulative effect of relentless stress over time, you realize the negative impact it was having on his family life. A few encouraging words had the power to actually shift his atmosphere, both at work and at home. Those few words brought him out of a state of anxiety, and into an atmosphere of peace.

Please note it had nothing to do with any careful deliberation, or crafting of just the right set of words to say to him. My words were encouraging and honest, but certainly not sophisticated or eloquent. Honestly, I didn't even think about the words beyond the general awareness that they'd be encouraging, not discouraging. The employee himself recognized it wasn't my doing at all. The Lord gave me a nudge, and I wasn't even sure the thought was coming from Him. I just took a chance, and wrote our employee a simple note, just in case it *was* a nudge from Him. In retrospect, it clearly was the Lord! He took my simple words, and through the exchange that followed, multiplied their impact far beyond anything I could have planned. In essence, they brought life to our employee's situation, rather than death. (This is also a good example of having the freedom to experiment within the permissible will of God.)

It's not complicated, it simply required awareness and intentionality for my little mustard seed step of faith to yield something tree-like from our employee's perspective. Which causes me to wonder how many times I've missed other opportunities like this because I just let them slide by as insignificant?

Keep It Real

There is one more key in my experience to avoiding the "weird" label at your office. Not that you should be beholden to "the fear of man," or worrying about what people think, but at the same time, if they think you're really weird you have no influence or ministry. The key is, as you practice this and God gives you insights, wisdom, and guidance, you need to communicate in language the office speaks. Don't default to quoting scripture, and certainly not in the language of the King James Bible, because your coworkers don't place the authority on it you do, much less speak that way. Instead, once you've prayed through a situation with God, and you feel you know how to proceed, communicate it in the language of the office, minus the office swear-words preferably!

Move from Asking to Declaring

Let me emphasize again, bringing the Kingdom starts from a foundation of prayer, but I hope you can see this goes beyond just asking God for stuff. We're instead pursuing conversational intimacy and we're expecting to hear back from Him during our Tuesday. Sometimes that means the King will bring the Kingdom by doing things only He can do.

Sometimes, though, you get the privilege of participating with Him doing the things only He can do. Because you've set your heart on "doing what you see Him doing," sometimes you discern through that prayerful, conversational intimacy with Him, that He is ready to do something. So in faith, you then declare it. You didn't make it happen, of course, you just partnered with Him to state a reality He showed you from Heaven, and you declared it on Earth. The power of His Word makes it happen.

> *Sometimes, though, you get the privilege of participating with Him doing the things only He can do.*

Again, I'll point back to the example of Kim, the woman who provides and maintains the plants in our office, whom the Lord miraculously healed from late stage cancer. I got to participate in that miracle in some small way by following His lead to declare that she was healed, rather than continuing to ask that she be healed. Of course, God can intervene with signs, miracles, and wonders like this wherever He wants to, and He surely didn't *need* me to participate, but it seems He's more apt to show up and do them where His Kingdom is being established and proclaimed.

Another tip in this regard is to keep your eyes open to see the things God does that you didn't anticipate, and which He didn't reveal in advance; where He does some good thing only He can do. That new contract showed up just in time, or the new hire with skills that were going to be impossible to find just sent their resume in. We have that kind of stuff happen a lot. It may or may not be "miraculous" but it was obvious He intervened to work things together for the good of us who love Him and are called according to His purpose. So if you have "eyes to see and ears to hear," you'll see some things like that where you know it *had* to be Him. Make sure to thank Him! Let your gratitude keep your eyes open to the Kingdom, and then let that strengthen your faith for what else He may want to do. And let it strengthen your faith to declare things with His authority when He shows you those things in advance.

I know, if you've never taken this perspective on your daily work before, it might feel complicated or overwhelming. It's not really. Turns out it's actually simple. If, like Jim, you just make it a point to intentionally worship your Lord with your work, everything else will fall into place in time, under His guidance. Now that you're personally equipped to bring some P2P and P2C ministry into your workplace without your boss thinking you're weird, let's explore the two corporate channels of ministry.

PARTNERING WITH GOD AT WORK (CORPORATE EDITION)

In the previous two chapters, we explored some examples of how you can personally bring your Sunday into your Tuesday. Specifically, we called these Personal to People (P2P) and Personal to Corporate (P2C) channels of ministry, meaning your actions demonstrate and actuate the Kingdom of Heaven for another individual, or for the corporate entity in which you serve, respectively. Many of you are in leadership positions within your organization, so you act, not only on behalf of yourself, but on behalf of the organization. Let's explore how the information we covered in the previous chapter translates into your specific role as a leader in your organization.

Basic C2P—Corporate Giving

Allow me to start with some examples demonstrating the possibilities. I know of one company that takes a set portion of their profits and invests it into a third-party non-profit Christian ministry which operates a 500-bed facility, to disciple heroin and opioid addicts through recovery and restoration. I'm sure you know other examples like this, where Jesus-loving founders or owners express their personal faith through corporate giving to Christian causes. Perhaps the company is even more proactive and doesn't just give cash, but also provides volunteer labor to the local homeless shelter or food bank. These are all examples of the Corporate to People (C2P) channel ministry, in which the corporation is sowing a portion of their resources into third-party non-profit ministries that directly care for people.

The company can likely do so from an overt posture, stating the owner's Christian heritage as the reason for supporting these ministries. As long as those ministries are aimed at crisis response for people who are hurting (as opposed to political issues), this support is generally not objectionable to an employee base who are mixed in their religious convictions. I'm not suggesting a few objections should stop you, I'm just saying a focus on helping people will cause most employees, at least the ones you'd want to hire, to appreciate your corporate philanthropy in this regard. This type of C2P activity is good and proper, and honors God.

Can you see there's so much more opportunity here, though? On a personal level, it's good and proper for you to give tithes and offerings and time to your local church and other non-profits, but that's just a small expression of the bigger purpose for which the Lord created you, not the entirety of it. Likewise then, the same is true for the corporate entity.

Better Still—Engaging the Team

In this regard, Corporate giving is probably one of the earliest examples on our journey with Yakabod, where we started to expand beyond P2C ministry and into broader C2P ministry. From the beginning, my business partner Scott and I agreed we'd devote a portion of our corporate profits to the support of various non-profits. Some are local, some are regional.

Some are boots-on-the-ground services to those in need, like our local Rescue Mission, while others have a more national focus. These could be teaching ministries like Ransomed Heart, or The Institute for Faith, Work & Economics, while others are secular organizations that simply focus on the prosperity of our community, like the Downtown Frederick Partnership.

Our list is much bigger, but I'm only using these as examples to show the variety of organizations we'll support. You'll never see pictures of us posing with an oversized check on Fakebook; that's just not us. We aren't giving for any marketing or advertising purpose; we prefer to work quietly behind the scenes supporting a number of organizations that either directly advance the Kingdom or simply support our community. This is one small aspect of C2P channel ministry. You may do something similar, or maybe you choose to focus all your giving in one place. We've been doing this from the beginning, and we continue to do it today.

Maybe twelve or so years back, after some prayer, Scott W and I decided to bring all our employees into the process. This was, in part, to help inspire a spirit of generosity in them if it wasn't already on their radar, but more so to give them the dignity of participating in the process, and to make them part of something of which they could be proud. We carved out a portion of the overall corporate giving, maybe twenty or thirty percent of it, and split that into an allocation for each employee. This amount typically works out to around $500 to $1,000 per employee, depending on the year, how many people we've added to the team, and various other factors. Each employee is then allowed to designate the non-profit who should receive their allocation. To gain approval for their selected allocation they have to post an internal blog entry stating why they have chosen that specific non-profit organization.

The blog entry, which the whole team can see, must also highlight the recipient organization's mission and specify how it aligns with our core values. It has to be focused on helping people, and we won't approve political causes. Naturally they choose a range of causes Scott and I would never think to support, but as long as these don't run counter to our core values, we're fine with supporting them. We provide a rich and comprehensive benefits package, but employees consistently tell us this is their favorite one. (We tell them we're just priming the pump on their giving, and that hopefully they are personally supporting causes they are passionate about.) I've also been surprised at the impact of this initiative in the community.

There are several organizations to whom we've provided these modest contributions who are not just grateful, but genuinely moved, which is always another pleasant surprise to me. I've realized it's not because of the money, which candidly, when split among so many employees to allocate, ends up being a rather modest contribution. Instead, they're moved because someone outside their normal circles noticed what they were doing,

> *Organizations are moved because someone outside their normal circles noticed what they were doing, and believed in it enough to contribute.*

and believed in it enough to contribute. In this way, we've turned a C2P channel activity that blesses our community, into one that also mentors our team and in turn blesses a broader community. In other words, we're not just doing C2P through third parties to people in our community, we're also ministering to our own employees.

Even so, while this is a step in the right direction, at least for us, there's still much more to corporate ministry than giving.

Corporate Ministry Goes Way beyond Giving

Let's further explore this "much more," both in terms of the possibilities and the responsibilities you carry as a leader in your organization. I'll assume you're already doing some of the P2P and P2C channel activities we described in the previous two chapters, or at least, that's probably where you should start. Then you do the same things on behalf of your company, bearing in mind the actions you take in your leadership role will be interpreted as not just representing you, but also representing the company.

Consider again my friend Jim, the janitor for Jesus, who in a personal capacity shifted the atmosphere of his workplace to one in which personal relationships could be reconciled, respect re-established, and collaboration fostered. If you were the principal at Jim's school, you may have been able to actually institutionalize that shift. You'd honor Jim at some staff function, reinforcing his model as the kind of workplace behavior the culture most desires and will reward. Maybe you'd send out a weekly staff email in which you recognized and honored other examples from your team that fit the model. Perhaps you'd reevaluate your school's policies, procedures, and practices to root out any that were unjust or ill informed. You would also replace staff members who were found to catalyze or amplify poor employee morale and behavior in the first place. You could then possibly fix those things so the shift Jim initiated could be sustained.

Initially you'd be doing a P2C channel activity in personally transforming the actions of the corporate entity. This, however, would soon turn into a Corporate to People (C2P) channel as well, in which the transformed corporate practices would then minister to other staff. Once the staff in other schools heard of the remarkable turnaround at your school, you may then be doing some Corporate to Corporate (C2C) channel ministry. These activities could help transform the processes, policies, and practices in another corporate entity, making that second organization a little more aligned with the Kingdom as well.

This is the potential progression of impact from this Kingdom mindset in ministry. You can simply start from the P2P activities you'd normally do, but since you're a leader, your scope is bigger than just you in your personal capacity. You're not just praying for *your* issues, you're praying for *your whole team*, whether seeking His purpose for the team, some concern they've identified, or just proactively asking the Lord how He'd like to bless each one of them. You can do the same for the corporate entity by prayerfully asking, "Is this the way things work in the Kingdom?" and responding to what God shows you. These P2P and P2C channel activities then have the potential to turn into C2P and C2C activities, especially if you're actively and prayerfully engaged in pursuing these outcomes.

Many of the examples I shared in Section 3 follow a similar progression. For example, in Chapter 7: Cash Is King (but Not Necessarily Kingdom),

> *You're not just praying for your issues, you're praying for your whole team.*

when we resolved to use cash as a tool to honor employees and vendors rather than using it to manipulate them, this now in turn mentors our team in the same practice. In other words, neither Scott nor I have given the team a big whiteboard talk on any of this—the practices themselves have mentored the team. Daily, the team is experiencing a more Kingdom-like approach and many see the obvious contrast with the more worldly ways they experienced at some prior employers.

Don't Be Creepy

This is powerful stuff, and I'm certain it's a type of ministry into which God is calling our generation of believers. Note, though, that the expanded scope and impact of C2P and C2C channels of ministry also render discretion a more complicated matter. As a leader, you're not just responsible for yourself but rather for a whole collection of people, as well as other people's experience of the corporate entity. If poor discretion in your P2P and P2C channel ministry can leave your boss thinking you're some weird religious nut, the risks are greater in C2P and C2C channel activities. You won't just be viewed as weird, but creepy. So how do you partner with God to bring His Kingdom into your workplace without those you manage feeling harassed?

The first thing I'd counsel is to take the pressure off yourself. As a leader, you're probably a bit type A anyway; the kind of person that "gets stuff done." Well, you don't have to sell people on the Kingdom. The Kingdom is attractive, even to those from different faith traditions. Discretion may cause you to operate at various levels of overtness or covertness in your particular organization, but honestly, if you took a simple step like implementing the "golden rule" in your team meetings, who would protest the increased level of respect at work? No reasonable person would feel harassed or think you're creepy, because

> *You don't have to sell people on the Kingdom. The Kingdom is attractive, even to those from different faith traditions.*

that attribute of the Kingdom is inherently attractive! It makes sense, right?

Sure, some people might protest if you make a big fuss of it being a biblical principle, but if you just mentor the team in the practice of treating each other with mutual respect and kindness, and someone gets all offended by that, do you really want them on your team? (I guarantee the rest of the team will thank you after you get rid of that person.) You don't need to preach or thump your team over the head with your Bible. Just give your team a taste of the superior Kingdom. It's the Holy Spirit's job to lead them to repentance and belief from there, which may or may not involve some specific words from you.

You're Mentoring a Team, Not Pastoring a Church

Now if the Lord tells you to share the gospel of salvation with someone, likely because your C2P and C2C activities softened their heart to it, then definitely be obedient and do so. He knows when it's time, but it's still not your job to make them believe, so take the pressure off yourself and them. Just remember, the company is not paying you to be your team's pastor; they are paying you to be a leader in some aspect of achieving the corporation's objectives. If you do the latter correctly, God may covertly (or even overtly) set you up to do the former.

This leads to the second piece of advice I'd offer, which is only going to make sense to Jesus followers reading this. I understand there's a whole range of environments in various churches, from those walking in ultra-grace to those who are hyper-holy. What you do in your church you'll have to work out with your pastor and elders. At work, though, as a leader, it's not your job to "manage the sins" of your team. You have to resist that temptation, otherwise your team will think you're creepy, and feel harassed. I'm not talking about ethics or integrity—if someone is cheating on their timecard or sexually harassing a teammate, or stealing from customers, well of course you discipline them (or outright fire them). Those are clear offenses *against the company,* and you have authority and responsibility to deal with such infringements.

You are not responsible, however, for the personal holiness—or lack thereof—of the people you manage. If they are doing things you think are sinful, then those are offenses against God, and you can leave that up to Him to deal with as He sees fit. (He might see it differently to you anyway!) For example, if you know Joe's cheating on his wife, it's not your corporate responsibility to make him stop. Now as Joe's friend, you know there will be a whole lot of pain for a whole lot of people coming into the mix somewhere along that terrible train ride. Maybe you have the relationship with Joe that enables you to engage in P2P ministry; a friend helping a friend. Experience suggests this will probably occur after Joe's crash, since Joe most likely won't want your help before then. (That doesn't mean you can't offer him help if you have that relationship, but you can't force him to take it.) Likewise, in your leadership role, maybe Joe's situation triggers a C2P type response, where you explore resources the company could offer to all employees. Offers like access to counseling services in the event Joe would choose to pursue that opportunity.

> *You are not responsible for the personal holiness—or lack thereof—of the people you manage.*

Nevertheless, any corporate action you take towards Joe should be in the context of his work responsibilities and performance. If his dalliances cause his performance to fall short of expectations, you have the responsibility to hold him accountable for that. When his situation blows up, and he doesn't show up to work for a week, well, that situation is yours to deal with, too. This doesn't mean you are condoning Joe's behavior, it simply means you are working within the limitations of your role and authority. You have authority over Joe's work performance—you don't have authority over his personal journey with God. Don't worry about things you can't change; just give Joe a taste of the Kingdom, like Jesus did!

As I noted, this is really aimed at Jesus followers, because unfortunately a lot of church cultures preach "grace" from the pulpit, but pursue "sin management" in practice. In fact, it's so steeped in some church cultures that congregants may even feel a unique guilt for working in a normal secular work environment because of all the "ungodly" people they experience there. They haven't learned to be "in the world, but not of it." If this is your Sunday, you should not bring that part to your leadership approach on Tuesday.

We've been discussing things you shouldn't do so your team doesn't think you're creepy. Let's shift our attention to some things you *should* do.

PARTNERING WITH GOD AT WORK (CORPORATE EDITION) PART II

In the previous chapter we explored some things you shouldn't do as a Kingdom-minded leader so people don't think you're creepy. Likewise, we took the pressure off you to get anyone saved or sanctified in the workplace, since you are leading a corporate team not pastoring a church. Your goal is to make the business look more like the Kingdom, not like a church.

Now let's explore some things you *should* do to make the business look more like the Kingdom. In general, one key role of a leader is keeping the team aligned with the corporate mission. The question is, how do you do that from a Kingdom mindset?

More Basic C2P: Establishing Kingdom Principles

To get started, just as in Chapter 25: Partnering with God at Work (Personal Edition)—Overcoming Roadblocks, you can simply begin with some biblical principles.

For example, as a Jesus-following leader you are to "Let your 'Yes' be yes, and your 'No' be no" (James 5:12, NRSV). In other words, you (and your team) do what you say you're going to do. You also understand from Matthew 20:25-28 that you should lead people with a servant's heart, not "lord over them like the Gentiles do" (paraphrased). You also understand each of your team members is "fearfully and wonderfully made" for a purpose by God, and your job is to put them together as "one body, many parts," so they are working together as *we*, not me. Now as a believer, you may argue that 1 Corinthians 12:14-26 describes "the body of Christ," which is, "the Church," and so it doesn't apply to your team at work, but that *is* the point. "One body, many parts" describes the way things work in the Kingdom of Heaven. It's every bit as aspirational for your local congregation as it is for your team at work. Jesus didn't tell us to pray it would be "in church as it is in Heaven," but rather He prayed His Kingdom come "on Earth as it is in Heaven."

None of this should sound like groundbreaking material. I know you could remove the biblical language and read the same principles in just about any well-respected business or leadership book, perhaps under the label of "Servant Leadership." I'm not seeking to reinvent these concepts. The reason basic servant leadership belongs in this book is to explore the mindset of actively partnering with God to view your practices through a Kingdom lens. The above set of principles is nowhere near comprehensive, and you probably have three more examples in your mind right now that I could have included above. That's great. I'm not trying to give you a formula for C2P and C2C channel ministry activities, I'm just showing how you make a conscious practice of bringing the things you learn on Sunday into your Tuesday.

It all sounds so simple, and in theory, it is. Religion is hard—it takes ever more advanced levels of learning and sophistication to work it all out. Faith is simple. Child-like even. I've said many times, the challenge in "at work as in Heaven" is not the complexity of the actions you take, but rather the intentionality and focus of your actions. The intentional practice of doing simple things like the list of scriptural phrases embedded in the above paragraph (James 5:12; Matthew 20:25-28; 1 Corinthians 12:14-26) will make your workplace starkly different to most places of work. If you don't believe me, just consider your real life experience with that same short list of sample phrases.

Doing What You Said You Would Do

Let's start with "Yes means yes." Is this your experience with most companies you interact with? Have you ever dealt with the cable or phone company? (Remember last time, they told you they'd "be there between 8:00 and 10:00 a.m." and at 4:00 p.m., after you've burned a whole day of vacation, they still haven't shown up or even bothered to call?)

Have you had any home improvement projects lately? We've worked with some great contractors recently, but I can't help but think of one contractor my wife and I engaged several years back, to remodel our guest bathroom. He jumped right on the destruction part of the project (enough to collect the deposit check), with the promise he'd complete the construction part within a few weeks. He'd show up for an hour here, an hour there, and a month later, with no end in sight, he finally scheduled some full workdays. Yet each time, after my wife had completely rearranged her schedule to accommodate him, he failed to show up.

My wife would text him, trying to figure out if he was still coming, and he'd apologize saying his back was hurt, then reschedule, and repeat the no-show. We figured it must be bad, we were really praying for his back. A few weeks later, the project *still* not completed, and months overdue, my wife saw him in the grocery store. "How's your back?" she asked.

335

He gave her a puzzled look and replied, "What are you talking about? There's nothing wrong with my back." I'd like to think that in response to our earnest prayers Jesus miraculously healed the guy. He does that kind of thing, after all, but I think you know what really happened in this case.

I could go on giving examples, but I'm sure you have plenty of your own experiences, not just with schedules, but with payment terms, or product quality, or any number of things where reality didn't match the promise. What I'm saying is you'd probably agree that "let your yes be yes" is a rare practice in the corporate world. Now I get it, sometimes a project delay is unintentional. Things happen, but the examples above, like many you've experienced, are just plain lies. Lying has just become an accepted, institutionalized business practice in each of those organizations.

Somewhere along the line it became normal, even expedient, in that corporate culture to just tell customers what they think customers want to hear, or what they need to tell customers to achieve their desired outcome. Call it what you want to, it's still lying. That comes from the wrong kingdom. There's no lying in the Kingdom of Heaven. God's Kingdom is built on truth. Can you see how simply standing on this one scriptural principle—letting your "yes be yes"—makes your team or your company look radically different? (And this is just a simple principle, we're not even talking about supernatural stuff yet!)

> *Simply standing on this one scriptural principle—letting your "yes be yes"—makes your team or your company look radically different.*

Leading, Not Lording

Another simple yet effective principle from the list above is "Leading, not lording." Again, if you haven't had a self-centered manager, you haven't had very many jobs. If you've spent any time in a workplace, you've almost certainly had a boss (or coworker) who took credit for your work.

In fact, you've probably experienced some cultures, like I have, where it was explicitly understood that your job was to make your boss look good. Not to accomplish the mission of the organization, mind you, but rather to make the boss look good. (The theory being that as he climbs the ladder, you climb the ladder with him.) There's no focus on *we*, but rather it's on *me* in those kinds of workplaces. Following the boss's modeled behavior, the team is typically a collection of *me's* competing with each other. They are usually more worried about personal promotion, rather than working together to fulfill the team's role in achieving the corporate mission.

This is because, in the worldly kingdom, I have to get what's mine, I have to look out for me, and that leads to lording instead of leading. Using shame, guilt, or other forms of manipulation to get the team to do what I want for *my* gain. Even making them look bad so I look good to be promoted before they are. In contrast, as a leader in the Kingdom of Heaven, I can focus on the whole body, not just my part, because I know God is looking out for me. I can "seek first His Kingdom" and trust He'll provide everything else I need (Matthew 6:33). I can take the "lower seat at the table," rather than seeking my own promotion (Luke 14:7-11).

We could continue our study in contrasts, with "one body, many parts" from the list above, of course, but I think you get the point by now. Just implementing a simple biblical principle consistently across your realm of leadership will make things look markedly different than many (or even most) businesses.

C2P through Authenticity

If one key role of leadership is alignment, then another aspect, in some circumstances, is establishing culture. As we've said, Kingdom looks different than kingdom, so bringing a bit of it to your organization will provide employees and customers with an experience different to what they typically encounter. As the scope of your leadership grows, so does your ability to accomplish this process. All levels of leadership have the responsibility of keeping the team aligned with the organization's purpose, as well as accomplishing *their* piece in achieving the organizational mission. In the process, a leader of any level can shift the culture, as my friend Jim demonstrated. Senior levels of leadership, however, can institutionalize and sustain such a shift, or even define the organizational culture at the start. As we explored in Section 3, this all begins with core values. Culture should be an expression of the organization's core values, and if done correctly, actually implements C2P and C2C ministry.

Expanding further on responsibilities: if you're an executive level leader at your organization, another key role you play is in actually defining the purpose of the organization. When Yakabod

> *Another key role of an executive level leader is actually defining the purpose of the organization.*

started, there were really only two choices for a tech company: we could be a high-growth firm focused on scaling to sell (you'd call it a "unicorn" now, but that wasn't in the lexicon back then), or we could be a lifestyle company. Notice that both categories were defined solely by the way in which the owners were enriched.

Recently, however, there is a growing trend of companies formed along a third model—a community impact company. The company may provide well for its owners—and I'm not suggesting it shouldn't—but it also measures success based on the good it does, or the transformative impact it has on some community, whether its own community or another.

I'd suggest this third model is more in line with Kingdom, and as an executive, you have influence in determining the greater purpose for the organization beyond simply enriching the owners. In other words, moving beyond a me-centric culture ("I'm in it for me"), and even beyond a we-centric culture ("we're all in this together"), rather into a they-centric culture ("we're doing some greater good benefiting them too"). As a Jesus follower you aren't limited to your own ideas; you can and should seek God's counsel with regard to your purpose. It will likely include some C2P activities, where corporate resources yield a blessing to people outside your organization, and C2C activities, where corporate resources help transform other organizations and entities.

As a side note in this regard, I don't think you set out to do C2C ministry, at least not initially—"Hey, we're here to transform your company." Since you're an outsider to that other organization, it would feel like "posturing" to them. Kind of the way pre-believers feel at a personal level when you try to take responsibility for their personal holiness or "manage their sins." No, your personal impact on others around you starts from your relationship, from them inviting you in because there's something about you they respect. I think it's the same way with C2C ministry. When you do the C2P stuff well, other organizations notice something very attractive about your organization and then invite you in "to share best practices," because they want that attractive thing for their organization. I guess you could come up with examples where one organization led the charge to catalyze and transform their industry, but I don't see that as the norm.

In either event, in effecting C2P and C2C Kingdom influence, the real challenge, as in Partnering with God at Work (Personal Edition), is your intentionality in the process. It's the willingness and discipline to look at every situation with the clarifying question ("Is this the way things work in the Kingdom of Heaven?"), and the resolve to consistently make the thousand little decisions you are required to make in your role accordingly.

How Leaky Is Too Leaky?

There is another topic we should address when it comes to partnering with God at work. It's a matter I hinted at above, as well as in the earlier chapters pertaining to the "Personal Edition." There's more at stake in this regard, however, here in the "Corporate Edition." The subject we need to address is how overt or covert you need to be in bringing the Kingdom of Heaven into your workplace. Or if you prefer, how "leaky" you are with your faith? Mostly, you're going to have to work this out with God. I trust He'll guide you through the specific nuances you have to deal with in your company, because there's no universal formula, but let me share some examples of where we've landed after much prayer. My examples revolve around the topic of prayer, but you can use this to extrapolate to other activities and aspects of your faith.

In a personal capacity, I'm praying in my head, at my desk, or under my breath as much as I think to, which isn't often enough, of course, but is also far more than zero. Likewise, my business partner, Scott, and I pray for the company every morning we're in the office together. We have two other executives who have shared their position of faith with us recently, and we'll now occasionally invite them to pray with us as well. We're praying in a corner office we call "The Founder's Lounge." In our old office, it had a solid door and was set back from the main hallway. In our new office, it's out of the way in the far corner, but it's on the main hallway, and has a glass door. While we're certainly not praying like the Pharisees to put on a show for our people (Matthew 6:5), it's no secret to our team that we're praying. As far as we know, it doesn't bother anybody, but if it did, they'd have to get over it, because Scott and I are certainly not pushing our prayer activity on anybody, or making it a required corporate practice.

So how do I do pray more "publicly" in my corporate capacity? Well, if we do an all-employee off-site event, like our post-holiday party, I'll typically take a moment to "say grace," and thank the Lord for His provision as evidenced by the hospitality attendant with the celebratory event. If it's our event, it's almost certainly a feast and I need to thank Him. When I do, I'll always give the team an out. I preface my prayer with something like, "I'm going to say a word of thanks to my Father in Heaven because I know Who takes care of us, but if you aren't comfortable with that, you're welcome to ignore me or duck out of the room for a moment. I won't even know you've left because I'll have my eyes closed." We have employees from many faith traditions, and a few will openly tell you they are atheist.

Even though I explicitly pray "in Jesus' name," no one has ever had any issue with this kind of prayer because they've never felt I've forced it on them. As I shared much earlier in Chapter 5: No Longer Servant but Friend, I don't feel any need to force prayer on our team because our actions over time, and His presence in our workplace, are a far more effective witness than anything I might pray in front of them!

Meanwhile, we've hosted some community events in our space that were explicitly Christian, faith-based events. One of these events was convening Jesus-following leaders from across our community in government, education, business, church, non-profit, healthcare, and other sectors, for a Kingdom response to the opioid crisis in our community. (The call to action: there's no addiction in Heaven, so why do we have addiction in our community? Let's come together to pray it would be "in Frederick as in Heaven.") Of course, there was a lot of prayer in that meeting, and with sixty people attending, we couldn't tuck them away into the far corner.

No, the event was front and center in our big main conference room, the one with the glass walls. It was very obvious to our employee team that the big meeting brought some serious prayer into the house, but no one felt any pressure, because no one was forced to participate. Just like my "saying grace" prayer, no matter their personal spiritual position, many team members expressed their pride in our company afterwards, because they resonated with us playing our small part in the overarching purpose of convening community leaders to respond to the local opioid crisis.

In another example, I had a small group of charismatic Kingdom-minded business leaders visiting in our corner office at the old place one day—the one with the solid door. After some discussion, we were inspired to pray together for our community. The one guy got pretty worked up—which was awesome—except he was also pretty loud. About the time we were wrapping up the prayer session, one of our employees knocked on the door so I slipped out. He was quite concerned. "Everything okay in there?" he asked. He had heard the commotion, thought we were fighting, and was ready to step in to my defense. I told him, with a lighthearted smile, that the only thing we were fighting were the spiritual forces of darkness. We had a good chuckle, and left it at that. Interestingly enough, later that day another coworker who overheard that conversation pulled me aside, said he knew we were praying, and that he had a history with God, but had drifted away recently and felt God tugging on his heart. He then asked me to pray with him regarding some personal circumstances!

I'm not saying these are the things you have to do, and I have friends who approach it differently. I mentioned Brett in Chapter 23—he has one person open the office in prayer at 8:00 a.m. sharp every day, at the front desk. Attendance is optional, but highly visible. Brett has had many pre-believers join in the prayer, not because they're forced to, but because they love their company and feel that praying for it is a good thing.

I have another friend who did something similar in their small company. Initially, they were all Jesus followers, so they would gather around their desks to open the day in a prayer circle, far more extensive than what Brett does. Recently, though, as the company has grown, they've hired a few pre-believers. While the prayer circle was optional, it wasn't all that private due to the small space and it started feeling awkward with the mixed team. I'm sure as they seek the Lord's guidance they'll find a way to adapt and make it work in their environment, and it may well turn into a more private thing.

I've focused on prayer as an example but the point is, there is no prescribed place on the spectrum from overt to covert in which you need to operate. You don't need to feel any shame, nor is it any less valid a ministry if it's more toward the covert end of the spectrum. You just need to seek the Lord's wisdom for your particular situation. Trust He'll guide you into the process when it's time to be overt with your words or your stance, and when it's better to be covert.

Being Equally "Yoked"

One final consideration I should address. If you're trying to bring your Sunday into Tuesday as a business owner and not just a leader, you have some additional complexities. As an example, before I ever joined forces with my business partner Scott, I had to know we were on the same page spiritually. I knew I couldn't push into building a company for God's glory (the very name of the company) if I was "unequally yoked" with someone who didn't share that purpose. Being "yoked" together like oxen pulling a plow doesn't work when one pulls in the opposite direction.

In that respect, I got things right. We were also careful to ensure we didn't put ourselves in a compromised position by bringing on investors. I'm not saying pursuing Kingdom business and taking on equity investors is mutually exclusive. Not at all. It just adds another level of complexity you'll have to work through, which fortunately, we never had to do. The one area I messed up, however, was in assembling our Board... well, to be fair, I excelled with two choices and learned an important lesson with my third selection.

Emma is a rock-star senior executive, and ultimately an executive coach and mentor who provides our strategic perspective. Bob is a pastor, counselor-turned-author, and an organization builder who affords the "heart" perspective. Both are strong, open believers.

The third outside director we appointed was in the middle of successfully leading startups himself, and he provided a tactical viewpoint for our business. He's a great guy with strong experience, who sometimes attends church, but whatever his standing with Jesus is, he keeps it there—in church. He tolerated our opening prayers at board meetings, but he was very uncomfortable with conversation around deeper spiritual matters. He just didn't really think Sunday had any part in Tuesday, or that God had much to do with business, and he'd tell us that in some of our meetings. As you can imagine, this severely constrained our meetings, making certain discussions awkward, and leaving us dancing around some topics we should have been openly talking about.

I take responsibility for that error; I had placed us in an "unequally yoked" situation which forced me to call Bob and Emma separately if I wanted to discuss the business from a spiritual or Kingdom standpoint. That third outside director was on our Board for many years, I'm grateful for the practical, actionable business advice he often provided, and I certainly don't want to dishonor his helpful and generous contributions to our growth. Once we eventually parted by mutual agreement, however, Board meetings have become much more explicitly and openly focused on the Kingdom aspect of our business. This is now the cake in our meetings, not the icing, and we're far better for it.

In spite of having spent 27 chapters talking about it, honestly, I—as perhaps you—still have more questions on this Kingdom business thing than I have answers. I suspect it will be that way until I go home to see my Lord, where I'll still keep learning of His amazing ways. In the meantime, as a business person, you're probably goal and achievement oriented. One final question we should look at then, is how do you measure success in Kingdom business?

DEFINING SUCCESS

In the previous chapters in this section I've shared some strategies and tactics for partnering with God in your area of influence, from more overt to more covert activities, in both your personal and corporate capacities. As you grapple with how to apply some of these to your own unique workplace setting, it may be helpful to explore what success would look like from a Kingdom perspective.

Making your Sunday matter on Tuesday—bringing your faith into your workplace—can be (or can start out) really simple. Not necessarily easy, but simple. So how do you know it's working?

Defining Success in the Worldly Kingdom

There's a way the world defines success that I'm sure you've experienced. It typically involves money, revenue, possessions, power, or other transient things. As an example, I was invited to speak at a "fireside chat" event for a startup-focused organization, meaning the audience consisted of a roomful of early-stage and aspiring entrepreneurs. In the Q&A portion, someone asked me, "What would success look like for Yakabod?"

The questioner asked it innocently enough, but the clear implication was that we *hadn't* achieved the elusive goal yet—our success was something we still hoped for in the future. Maybe this inference was made because I wasn't cashed out and driving a Ferrari, or featured in Fast Company. Yakabod is certainly well known in and around our community, but the attendees who came in from Washington DC and Baltimore most likely hadn't heard of us. The featured speaker was just plain old me, not Zuckerberg or Elon Musk or even some local luminary they would ordinarily associate with their definition of success.

We've explored plenty of examples in the previous chapters on the way this narrow, worldly definition of success manifests in a corporate culture. At a personal level that may mean turf battles, people acting in self-interest, ladder climbing, and more. In other words, in terms of success, it's all about "me." Or at a corporate level, especially if a leader derives identity from the corporate success, it may be about "us" but still in a dysfunctional way, putting our group's interests well above others.

In a roomful of entrepreneurs and founders, that same spirit often manifests as pursuit of the "unicorn." That next Facebook or Uber or whatever, which generates billions of dollars for you and the investors. I'm not saying it's wrong to build a high-growth, world-changing company. I'm saying I knew what the questioner was really asking: at what level of personal enrichment (or recognition or whatever) would I consider Yakabod a success? In other words, the dysfunction wasn't in his innocent question, but rather the assumptions and worldview behind the question.

The Church Has Its Own Struggle with Defining Success
Before we jump to the conclusion that such dysfunction is just a symptom

of corporate behavior in a fallen world, I'd like to point out the Church has plenty of its own difficulties when it comes to defining success. In fact, remember my friend Jim from Chapter 2, who set his heart on cleaning toilets for the glory of Jesus? I've told his story in evangelical circles many times, and often someone will ask, "Well, did anyone get saved?" Honestly, we don't know if anyone was saved. Sadly, this causes some to wonder, then, if Jim's story is actually valid ministry.

Here's the even crazier thing—before I started retelling Jim's story, many years ago, once I properly understood the significance of it in a Kingdom context, I verified the story with Jim to make sure I had the details right. Jim was initially hesitant, almost ashamed even, to think I might share the story. Not ashamed of his actions in the story; after all, Jim had shared it with our little group in real-time, as it unfolded. We had also prayed with him through it and praised God for the way He was working through Jim's simple act of faith. No, Jim was worried someone might think he thought his story was worthy of retelling as a case study beyond our little group. "Well, we aren't sure if anyone got saved," Jim noted. His hesitation to have his story shared was because Jim was in a church culture where his amazingly powerful testimony didn't count—it simply wasn't valued because the only metric that mattered to certain key influencers was a salvation "transaction."

Of course, this is the same dysfunctional view on success found in the corporate setting. In both cases, participants are counting transactions to indicate success. The same symptoms of pursuing this type of success manifest in church organizations as much as corporations: turf battles, ladder-climbing, self-promotion. Unfortunately, in addition to all the normal, worldly corporate measures of success, the Church sometimes brings its own unique dysfunctional metrics, such as attempting to measure (and judge others based on) personal holiness. In other words, it's all about how you *appear* on Sunday, not what you actually do on Tuesday. Fortunately, God cured me of that disease a long time ago, as I confessed back in Chapter 3.

347

Reformation > Revival

I sure hope it's obvious by now, but the point of this book is not to inspire revival. I'm not suggesting revival wouldn't be good. It's just not our measure of success. Instead, this book is focused on stirring up something greater amongst my business network, namely *reformation.*

Renowned Bethel Church pastor, Kris Vallotton, describes in his book, *Heavy Rain*[23], how he tasked his intern staff to research which American cities had the most evangelical churches. After reviewing the statistics compiled by the study, he referenced this fact: cities that have the greatest Christian churchgoing population density also have some of the worst social statistics! This means the most-churched cities also had the highest crime, abortion, divorce, and poverty rates per capita. How can this be? Pastor Kris suggests it is because *a pastorate is ineffective at cultural transformation.* He points out that apostleship is way more effective, due to the principles upon which it is based: an apostleship trains, equips, and deploys the saints to *transform society.* Or in more simple terms, often the churches in the "most-churched' places have spent disproportionate effort on trying to get people into the church, rather than equipping their members to go out and bring the Kingdom to their community.

The point is, many Christians have been praying for and desiring to see "revival" and employing techniques that fit with that goal. What I'm describing in this book, however, related to your everyday work life, is not revival, but rather reformation. *Reformation* is more expansive than revival, and is in fact the environment that produces *lasting* revival. Churches generally disciple those who are already believers, but Kingdom-minded businesses mentor both pre-believers and believers. This means some of the methods we're used to employing in a church environment or a "revival culture" aren't productive or even relevant in a business context. The way to reformation, then, is more

> *What I'm describing in this book is not revival, but rather reformation.*

348

about living out our faith in our normal everyday life, including Tuesday. This means seeing His Kingdom come, and His will being done in our own area of influence, as it is in Heaven. It helps create an environment where people can see the goodness of God, which scripture tell us is designed to lead to repentance. In other words, reformation, in making things look more like the Kingdom of Heaven, actually creates an environment for revival.

As we explored throughout this book, there are two aspects of bringing Heaven to Earth in your area of influence: a natural aspect, and a supernatural aspect. As a Jesus follower, you are equipped to operate in both, and both will come into play as you make it "at work as in Heaven."

This, however, is where reformation gets interesting. You might think it's exclusively the work of believers to bring the Kingdom, but God can use anything and anybody to accomplish His purposes. Including pre-believers. If His Spirit can speak through a donkey (Numbers 22:28) or a pagan soldier (Judges 7:14), He can certainly move through your boss or coworker or the cranky businessman down the street.

Ultimately, my Jesus-following friends might notice this whole focus on reformation tracks well with Jeremiah 29:7, where God commands His chosen people living in an enemy Babylon that they should prosper right there, in Babylon, so it would go well with them.

What Then Is Kingdom Success?

Quite simply, Kingdom success means you've made your area of influence look more like the Kingdom of Heaven than the other one. This may be through your personal level of influence. It may be through your corporate capacity. Your efforts may be overt. They may be entirely covert. The bottom line is that things work differently in the Kingdom of Heaven. Success is bringing some sliver of that reality into your current situation. And then doing more of it tomorrow.

Since Kingdom success looks different than the way the world or a lot of churches define it, it's ultimately going to look a whole lot more like reformation in your realm of influence than wealth accumulated through a series of successful transactions (whether measured in souls or money saved). Reformation and wealth accumulation are not mutually exclusive outcomes ("seek first His Kingdom, and the rest of these..." after all). I firmly believe, however, Kingdom success lies in the former.

> *Things work differently in the Kingdom of Heaven. Success is bringing some sliver of that reality into your current situation. And then doing more of it tomorrow.*

Back to that fireside chat, where I addressed the roomful of aspiring entrepreneurs. I hadn't thought through all of the above in advance, but I had been reflecting on Yakabod's adventure in that period, so here's what I *did* tell them:

> Back in the early go-go dot-com days when we started, I was caught in the trap of thinking we weren't successful if we hadn't grown to a $10 million revenue overnight (or raised this capital from investors). Real life got me over that foolishness pretty quickly. Reflecting on the journey now, however, I think we were successful by one measure even back when we first turned a sustainable profit. We'd started from nothing, and actually had a real, viable business that was providing for our families and delivering value to customers. Measured by this metric it seems like success. The company wasn't just enriching the owners, it was blessing our small band of employees and our modest collection of customers.
>
> Of course, there were long periods of slow growth, but I'd consider those successful too. We further developed our products on our own nickel (no outside investment). More importantly, we were providing an increasing number of families with a solid wage and a great work environment. When I look at how much this enabled our employees to spend in the community, supporting other businesses, and how much we've plowed back into the community through charitable

giving, that looks like success too, even though we were growing slower than we wanted to. This doesn't mean we've settled for what we have; we are certainly pushing to scale up, and in fact, growth has accelerated recently. How big we get, however, has nothing to do with how successful we are.

Ultimately, my encouragement to the young entrepreneurs was that they didn't have to be "unicorns" to be successful. In truth, they could be a unicorn and *not* be successful according to many measures, so I said perhaps they'd do well to consider their definition of success and broaden it if necessary.

In the scope of this book, looking at the question through a Kingdom lens and with some time to think it through, I know there's no poverty, no lack of work, no lack of purpose in Heaven. Accordingly, I know if we can contribute to or create these Kingdom aspects to the same effect within our community, then we've made it look a little more like the Kingdom, and we've had some success. Those were some of the things I intuitively pointed to in my off-the-cuff answer.

I couldn't use this Kingdom language or explore any of the nuance in that setting, of course. The audience wouldn't likely resonate with the word "reformation," either. I hope you can see, though, that's exactly what I called them to.

How about Your Tuesday?

Let me wrap up by going back to Jim one more time. If you can't tell, it's one of my favorite stories from the realm of Kingdom business. I've been on a twenty-year adventure (and counting) to understand not just the "what" of Kingdom business, but the "how," that is, the practical reality of actually doing it every day. Over the years, my understanding of Kingdom business has deepened and broadened through ever more layers of nuance and ever larger questions.

Even so, I may never know a more powerful illustration of the power of bringing your Sunday into your Tuesday than Jim's simple act of resolving to clean toilets for the glory of Jesus. Of course, since Jim is a follower of Jesus he carries the Holy Spirit, which means Jim was actually cleaning toilets with Jesus, whether he was conscious of that or not. Since Jim invested some intentional effort into worshipping Him while working, Jim became a bit more aware of God's presence with him as he worked.

Whether intentionally or not on Jim's part, that Presence "leaked out" into Jim's work environment. In turn, his workplace came to look a little more like the Kingdom of Heaven than the kingdom of this world. Neither Jim nor I had language to describe any of this back then. We're not sure if anyone got saved, at least immediately or directly, but the tangible effect of Jim's simple act was that several people had explicit encounters with God, some learned biblical approaches to their current challenges, and many more who would never set foot in a church had their hearts opened to Jesus.

> *I may never know a more powerful illustration of the power of bringing your Sunday into your Tuesday than Jim's simple act of resolving to clean toilets for the glory of Jesus.*

So, did Jim's contribution matter? What do you think? I dare say it did! Does God think it matters? I'm willing to bet He's more than proud of His son, Jim. Maybe you'd agree with me when I tell you I know plenty of high-powered CEOs and executives who are nowhere near as successful as Jim when viewed from the Kingdom of Heaven.

Maybe it's not your job to clean the toilets, but if Jim can do that for the glory of God, you can certainly do the stuff you need to do on Tuesday for His glory as well. Things like marketing, sales, engineering, physical labor, project management, whatever it is that you do. If you get nothing from the previous twenty seven chapters except the simple resolve to make your

Sunday matter on Tuesday, and you simply take on your tasks with Jesus, then, my friend, you will be well on your way to being successful. Over time, your workplace will look more like His Kingdom.

Of the increase of His government and His peace there will be no end. You can't stop it. Are you going to be part of it?

Endnotes

1   Matthew 6:10

2   A Big Hairy Audacious Goal (BHAG) is an idea conceptualized in the book, "Built to Last: Successful Habits of Visionary Companies" by James Collins and Jerry Porras. A BHAG is a long-term goal that changes the very nature of a business' existence, and is meant to shift how business is done, the way the business is perceived in the industry and possibly even the industry itself. BHAGs are described on a corporate level as nearly impossible to achieve without consistently working outside of a comfort zone and displaying a high degree of corporate commitment and confidence. BHAGs are bigger, bolder, and more powerful than regular long and short-term goals. They typically take a ten to thirty-year commitment, but they are exciting, tangible and something everyone understands without further explanation.
Collins, James, Porras, Jerry. *Built to Last: Successful Habits of Visionary Companies* (Good to Great Book 2). New York City: Harper Business, 1994.

3   Honnold, Alex. Free Solo. DVD. Directed by Elizabeth Chai Vasarhelyi and Jimmy Chin. Washington, DC: National Geographic Documentary Films, 2018.

4   Mayberry is an Americanism for a utopia-type setting—a blissful small-town locale in rural America.

5   Paraphrase of Strongs word number 3519 definition.

6   Or, as in Strong's word 350, "(there is) no glory".

7   Gibney, Alex. The Smartest Guys in the Room. DVD. Directed by Alex Gibney. New York City: Magnolia Pictures, 2005.

8   Miller, Michael. "Enron's ethics code reads like fiction." The Business Journals, Columbus Business First Website. https://www.bizjournals.com/columbus/stories/2002/04/01/editorial3.html (accessed 9 November 2019.)

9   This is where some believers break out the persecution complex, and while I understand the realities of suffering for one's faith, please also remember the other side of that coin—Jesus is the desire of the nations! (Haggai 2:7)

10   Johnson, Bill. When Heaven Invades Earth. Destiny Image Publish-

ers, 2005.

11   U2. The Joshua Tree. Island Records. 1987. Vinyl.

12   Ries, Eric. The Lean Startup. New York City: Crown Publishers, 2011.

13   Pine, Joseph B., Gilmore, James H. The Experience Economy: Work Is Theater & Every Business a Stage Hardcover – Illustrated. Harvard Business School Press; 1st edition, April 1, 1999.

14   MacLellan, Lila. "The surprising fragility of a powerful perk: company culture." Quartz at Work. https://qz.com/work/1417538/the-surprising-fragility-of-a-powerful-perk-company-culture/ (accessed January 13, 2020).

15   Harnish, Verne. Mastering the Rockefeller Habits: What You Must Do to Increase the Value of Your Growing Firm. New York: SelectBooks, Inc., 2006

16   Some Christians may use the persecution complex to argue against this concept. I don't dispute that the children of God can or will be persecuted for their faith, but you also can't argue against facts: Jesus is the desire of the nations, and God's kindness leads to repentance. There is certainly something attractive when people experience the person God made you to be.

17   Davids, Richard C. The Man Who Moved a Mountain. Minneapolis: Fortress Press, 1972.

18   Collins, Jim. Good to Great: Why Some Companies Make the Leap and Others Don't. (Harper Business, 1st edition, 2001)

19   Collins, Jim. Turning the Flywheel: A Monograph to Accompany Good to Great. (Harper Business, February 26, 2019)

20   Page, Rick. Hope Is Not a Strategy: The 6 Keys to Winning the Complex Sale. New York City: McGraw-Hill Education. 2003.

21   Laubach, Frank Charles. The Game with Minutes. Eastford, CT: Martino Fine Books, 2012 reprint of 1956 American Edition.

22   Ibid

23   Valloton, Kris. Heavy Rain: How to Flood Your World with God's Transforming Power. South Bloomington MN: Chosen Books, 2010.